# WOMEN OF DARKNESS
## II

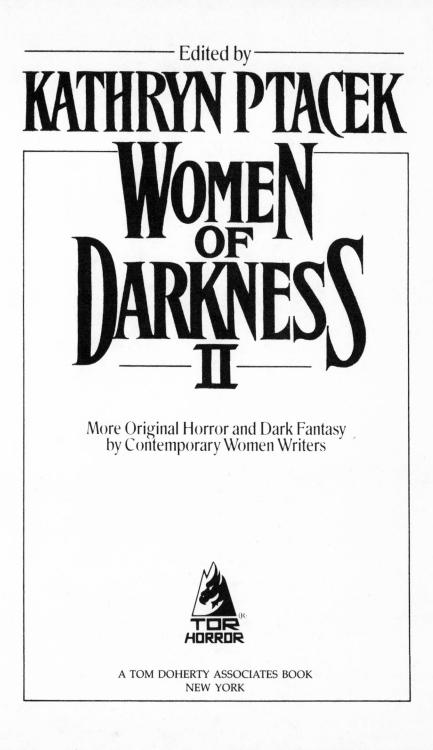

Edited by

# KATHRYN PTACEK

# WOMEN OF DARKNESS II

More Original Horror and Dark Fantasy
by Contemporary Women Writers

A TOM DOHERTY ASSOCIATES BOOK
NEW YORK

Library of Congress Cataloging-in-Publication Data

Women of darkness II / edited by Kathryn Ptacek.
p. cm.
ISBN 0-312-85027-1
1. Horror tales, American—Women authors. 2. Fantastic fiction, Amercian—Women authors. 3. Women and literature—United States. I. Ptacek, Kathryn.
PS648.H6W63 1990
813'.08738089287—dc20 90-38184
CIP

# Acknowledgments

"The Drought," copyright © 1990 by Lois Tilton. By permission of the author.

"The Nightmare's Tale," copyright © 1990 by Tanith Lee. By permission of the author.

"He Whistles Far and Wee," copyright © 1990 by Kiel Stuart. By permission of the author.

"Dirty Pain," copyright © 1990 by Lisa Swallow. By permission of the author.

"Last Echoes," copyright © 1990 by Janet Lorimer. By permission of the author.

"Daddy's Coming Home," copyright © 1990 by Lynn S. Hightower. By permission of the author.

"A Touch of the Old Lilith," copyright © 1990 by Nina Kiriki Hoffman. By permission of the author.

"Footprints in the Water," copyright © 1990 by Poppy Z. Brite. By permission of the author.

# Contents

# Introduction

Welcome to the second volume of *Women of Darkness*.

Once again this anthology represents a unique showcase of original short stories by contemporary women horror and dark fantasy writers. Some of the writers here have published dozens of stories; for others this is their first sale. Some are just starting out in their careers; a handful have been writers for a decade or more. But whatever the status of the author, you won't be disappointed by what she has to say.

While I was reading for this second anthology and as well for the first, I noticed a fairly common thread in the submissions—over seven hundred—that I received; that pattern appeared, too, in the stories I finally selected.

Strangely enough, I realized as I read story after story, horror short fiction was not following the popular perception. Given most people's definition of the genre today (it begins and ends with freshly spilled blood, mostly splattered by the bucketful on the walls and the protagonists, not to mention the camera lens) and given the old-time definition (devils and witches and Unspeakable Things From Beyond), you would expect noisy, bloody, spook-filled flesh-creeping tales. I read few stories like that. Frankly, it wasn't what I expected; perversely, I was pleased.

And so you won't find splatter here, nor will you encounter much supernatural. No, rather, these stories are far more quiet—they murmur rather than shriek. These stories are deeper, much more personal, much more devastating.

Visceral, not evisceration.

Disquieting . . . like the turn of a knife in your soul.

Personal, yes. Very. Many of the stories explore relationships: mothers and their children, a man and his dog, a little girl and her family, a man and his lover, husband and wife, a mother and her son, a young man and his father. . . .

Personal . . . intimate . . . secret.

Unblinking, often stark, these are not comfortable tales. These are not stories of ghosts in filmy gowns haunting middle-aged men in ancient English manors, nor of noble werewolves roaming the murky woods of Eastern Europe, nor even of crazed men-caricatures in hockey masks with axes or chainsaws or butcher knives held aloft.

You won't find Satan here: here dwell only the devils of our own making. What you will read in these eighteen stories is the stuff of our nightmares. Sexual and emotional abuse. Desertion and betrayal. Hate and apprehension. Fear. Death. Love.

Dark tales . . . sometimes unpleasant, always unsettling . . . but then isn't life a little more than frightening at times?

Dark tales to be read, alone, as you wait for your husband, your wife, child, parent to return home.

Waiting.

Alone.

With darkness approaching.

Tales of the soul and heart and mind. Tales of the night in each one of us.

Cheers.

Kathryn Ptacek
Newton, New Jersey
April 1989

# THE CO-OP

## by Melanie Tem

Melanie Tem, a social worker, has worked with abused and neglected children in foster and adoptive homes, and with disabled adults. She has published in *Fantasy Tales, Whispers, Skin of the Soul, Women of the West, Final Shadows, Women of Darkness* I, and in collaboration with her husband, Steve Rasnic Tem, has appeared in *Isaac Asimov's Science Fiction Magazine, Post Mortem,* and *SF International.* Novels just completed are a dark fantasy, a mystery—first of a planned series featuring an elderly and disabled sleuth. A novel-in-progress is a realistic/magical realistic/heroic fantasy/dark fantasy about grief and a hero's journey. She's also finished a novel written with Steve and has published numerous articles in professional journals. A native of rural Pennsylvania, she lives in a nineteenth-century Victorian house in old North Denver with her husband, children, two dogs, and two cats.

This story, Melanie told me, grew out of a conversation we and other women writers had at the World Fantasy Convention in Nashville a few years ago.

♦ ♦ ♦

The din of the children in the basement rec room had been a white noise in the middle ground all afternoon, with occasional thunderous white-water surges like this one. Somebody was wailing, and two or three other piercing little voices were threatening to *tell.*

Outside was real water, rain in the streets, and more voices like water. A crowd was filling Cascadilla Street and, Julie supposed, the other streets of Ithaca, and flood waters were rising.

Steadying the baby against her body, where even in sleep she nuzzled for the breast, Julie started to get up to investigate the commotion in the basement. It was her house, and she'd noticed that up to a point everyone in the co-op parented everyone else's children. She liked that sense of community; it was one of the things, along with a need to be with other mothers who knew what she was going through, that had made her join the babysitting co-op the minute there'd been an opening.

But Diane, swearing, beat her to the basement door. Diane was tall, broad-shouldered, and obese, yet somehow she seemed emaciated; the many cracks and crevices in her flesh looked deep and gray, and there was always a sour odor about her. Three of the kids downstairs were Diane's, Julie thought, or four; unsuccessfully, she tried to remember their names or even which ones they were. Diane's voice carried even when she was engaged in ordinary conversation, and just now she was shrieking at the kids, competing with their noise but not noticeably diminishing it.

Julie frowned. She didn't like the way Diane talked to children, her own or anyone else's. That wasn't the way mothers should be. Mothers should be like Julie's mother: loving their children, loving motherhood, tired and cranky only once in a while. That was the kind of mother Julie wanted desperately to be, but it wasn't easy, in the middle of the night, when Megan wouldn't stop crying no matter what Julie did, or when she bit her breast, Julie was sure on purpose.

Her mother had never felt about her the way she often felt about Megan. Her mother had never said awful things to her, or wanted to hurt her, or wished she had never been born. Julie would never be as good a mother as her own mother had been.

But when she looked around her, no one else was, either, and this town fairly teemed with mothers and children. Everywhere she went, especially since Megan had been born, she saw them, was pulled into the milling crowds they formed. On the streets, in the stores, in the wet green parks of this town, mothers screamed mindlessly at their children or mindlessly ignored them, and the children howled and played and scratched at windows. Julie and her sisters had never acted like that.

Linda was talking to her. "Well, all I can say is, you better enjoy her while you can."

She'd said that before. Julie smiled somewhat vaguely and put a spoonful of Diane's orange Jell-o into her mouth. She was startled to discover something gooey in the middle and for a moment was afraid to know what it was. But then she knew, and it was only cream cheese.

Cautiously, she let the Jell-o dissolve inside her mouth. It left a thick film of cream cheese on her palette, like skin. Suddenly she was imagining that the cream cheese was fleshlike, and then it was hard to swallow.

Outside it was still raining; she was constantly aware of the rain. It rained a lot in central New York State, which might be why all the mothers she knew here had such pale and wet-looking skin. Julie glanced sadly at the fading watch-band stripe around her own wrist; since the baby had been born she hadn't been able to catch even what few hours of sunshine there were.

This house they'd moved into on Cascadilla Street was long and narrow, like a coffin. From where she sat, Julie could sight along the pinkish-brown living room wall, which had tiny dots in it like pores; along the kitchen wall with its bulbous cream-colored flowers; and out the high windows that overlooked the street. The streets and the sidewalks were slimy with rainwater; the crowds were without umbrellas, because they were used to this weather. The green of the trees was nearly black, and they dripped with coagulated precipitation; leaves curled like lips, exposing their pale undersides. There were rivers and lakes and streams and gulches everywhere around here, like exposed veins or hungry stretched mouths. It hadn't surprised Julie, though it had made her shudder, to learn that Cornell had one of the highest suicide rates of any campus in the country, particularly in the spring when the beckoning gulches were layered with heart-red and tongue-pink rhododendron.

Linda was still talking. "Like my mother always said, and of course I wouldn't listen to her, it only gets worse as they get older."

"I can hardly wait." The intended sarcasm was undercut by a real excitement, a real eagerness to see her daughter grow up, which made Julie feel terribly vulnerable. She managed to swallow the last of the orange-flavored cream cheese, though it left a gummy patina on her tongue and on the backs of her teeth. Gelatin, she suddenly remembered, was made from cows' and horses' hooves; she wondered whether that was still true or whether nowadays it was chemically constructed, and didn't know which she would prefer.

"This is great potato salad," Linda said. The whitish chunks of boiled potato and egg in her mouth looked like broken teeth. "Who made it this time?"

"I did," Julie admitted, almost shyly. She didn't know any of the co-op mothers very well yet, but they'd all been nice to her, and Linda especially had taken her under her wing.

"*Great* potato salad."

"Thanks."

"Nobody ever listens to their mamas about kids," Yolanda declared. Three-bean-salad juice dribbled from the corner of her mouth, looking like brown blood across her white lipstick and oddly colorless dark brown skin. When she wiped it off with a crumpled white napkin, it left a stain among other stains, and Julie looked away. "My mama had eight kids before she was thirty," Yolanda was saying. "She *knew* what she was talking about. But did I listen? Did any of us listen? I got six kids myself, and my oldest sister's got *twelve*!"

"Twelve children!" Julie whispered to her baby. "Twelve little monsters like you!"

In her lap, Megan was asleep, tiny fists balled at her ears and tiny jagged mouth wide open. Julie slid her index finger gently into the infant's mouth. She could just feel the minuscule ridges along the gum line where before long teeth would erupt. She'd heard that some babies were born with teeth.

Softly she rubbed at her daughter's nascent teeth, as though to push them back down. The baby opened her eyes, focused them directly on her, and clamped her mouth shut around her mother's finger. Though there were no teeth yet for biting or tearing her flesh, the baby's sucking was so strong that it hurt, and when she took her finger back it didn't come easily. Julie felt a little thrill of maternal horror.

In a sudden panic, she yanked her hand away. Too hard: her daughter's head twisted to one side, and she howled. Julie bent guiltily to kiss her, tasted the salt tears and the sweet-sour baby flesh. Fear that she had hurt her child, remorse that she had wanted to, clouded her thoughts like the fatigue that had been with her since the baby's birth. She was, she thought suddenly and clearly, being eaten alive.

"My mama died when I was seventeen of acute anemia. Like us kids sucked the blood right out of her. Like we just ate her right up."

Linda nodded. "That's how it is when you have kids. It's a matter of survival. Them or you."

"My mama did not know how to protect herself," Yolanda said sadly. "The doctors told her to eat raw liver, but she couldn't do it."

A small fair-haired woman named Kathy or Katie wrinkled her nose and made a delicate gagging sound. Kathy's skin was so fair that it seemed barely to cover her flesh, and the makeup around her nose and mouth was grainy. She had an odd, halting way of speaking, as if she could hardly remember one word after the next. Her blonde hair was firmly sprayed, but it still straggled around her face and neck so that it looked as if it were falling out, and her chipping nails had been painted with thick variegated polish, as if to hold them together. Her entire face and body looked rebuilt, reconstituted for viewing. "Probably," she said in her breathy voice to Yolanda, "it was"—she paused for a long time before she could collect her thoughts—"stress that killed her. Stress and fatigue and"—she stopped, ground her teeth across her lower lip—"and not knowing where she stopped and her children began."

"Occupational hazards of motherhood," Annette observed, and a glob of coleslaw slid out of her mouth onto the front of her gray business suit. Apparently she didn't notice, since she made no move to clean it off. She had announced at the beginning of the co-op meeting that she'd have to leave early for a lunch appointment; Julie tried to imagine her making corporate decisions with coleslaw and baby spittle patterning her vest. "It's certainly done us all in," Annette said.

"Not all yet," Linda said. "Julie still looks alive." She patted Julie's knee.

"I love my child," Julie said automatically. Megan was crying again, but half-heartedly now, and there were no tears, only noise.

"We all do," Linda said.

"You know all—those things you swore you'd never—say to your kids?" Kathy passed a hand over her face, jagged fingertips massaging at her own flesh as though she had a headache. She was sitting in the pale blue bar of light cast by the fluorescent fixture over the sink, and her teeth looked fluorescent themselves, and sharp. "I can't—help it. All that—stuff just flows out of my—mouth like milk flows out of your—breast when your—when your baby's born. I—can't help it."

"She's forgetting the words," Linda explained to Julie, quietly but with no real attempt not to be overheard. "We all do that sometimes, but Kathy's been at it longer than the rest of us. She's one of the organizers of the co-op. Her children are all grown. Her mind is going."

"Sometimes I have fantasies about these awful things I'd like to do to my kids," Annette said conversationally. "So far I haven't done anything really awful, but only because they'd take my broker's license if I did."

"I swore I'd never"—Kathy closed her eyes and allowed

a long painful pause before she finally managed—"Spank. Or—eat. I swore I'd never do—what my mother did to me. But I do."

Yolanda nodded. "I swore none of that would ever happen to me."

"Well," someone said, "at least *you* didn't die of acute anemia, did you?"

"Close. Even though I did eat raw meat. Still do, right?"

There were some knowing chuckles around the room. Julie's stomach churned, and indignantly she demanded, "Why'd you all have kids if you don't like raising them?"

Megan was regarding her with a murky blue gaze. Julie often wondered what she saw. Part of the baby's self, probably. An extension of her own mouth and her own bowel and her own lungs. A gigantic umbilical cord attaching the world to Megan.

Julie wondered if Megan would always see her like that. She thought of her own mother, emptied now by Alzheimer's, but still able sometimes to make fried chicken and chocolate chip cookies better than anybody.

Suddenly she realized that the lanky and very pregnant young woman on the sofa next to Yolanda, with even darker skin and an underlying pallor thick as chalk, must be Yolanda's daughter. Embarrassed by what she'd said about Yolanda and the others not wanting children, Julie added feebly, "I mean, six kids are a *lot*, no matter how much you love them."

"Actually," Yolanda said, "I had seven. One died."

Julie caught her breath. "I'm so sorry."

"Yeah, well, that's the only reason I'm here to tell about it. One more would've done me in for sure. There'd have been nothing left of me for the others. So the baby died for a good cause. 'She gave her life that others might live.' Right, Regina?"

She reached to pat the tall girl's hand, then her huge belly. Regina's coppery gaze, flat as the pennies on the eyes of a corpse, followed her mother's hand, and her lips pulled back from her teeth a little as if she couldn't control the muscles of her face. She said nothing.

Distant thunder shook the house in a regular beat like a pulse, and rain bled against the windows. Carefully cradling Megan against her own impulse to drop her, Julie got awkwardly to her feet and walked through the line of rooms to the windows. Cascadilla Street was filling up with water and with people; she could see that the crowd was entirely made up of mothers and children, some few of them garbed against the weather but most of them bare-headed, bare-faced, hair streaming, clothes adhering to the contours of their bodies which seemed to dissolve into the rain.

In the odd play of light between gray sky and shiny rising floodwaters, some of the mothers and children seemed to be gnawing at each other, tearing at each other's flesh or at each other's reflections. Through the thin cold glass, which was wet even on the inside when she put her free hand against it, Julie could hear them and she was sure Megan could, too, wordlessly shrieking at each other in the wind, moving closer. She shuddered and fumbled for the curtain cord, drew the heavy curtains, turned away from the windows.

She looked at the other mothers one by one, trying to decide whether they'd all known about Yolanda's sacrificed child. Probably they had, since she understood that the co-op had been going for some time, and since no one seemed surprised.

No one said anything, in fact. Yolanda's little confession lay in the room with them like the unburied corpse of her child. The mothers were eating. In the brief, companionable silence, Julie was surrounded by the wet sounds of the mothers chewing and swallowing, by the busy gurgling of Linda's digestive system so close beside her that it could have been her own, and by the blending white noises of the rain and the gathering crowd and the kids downstairs.

"It would be terrible to lose a child," Julie said aloud. Her cupped palm hovered just above her daughter's tiny head, where she could feel the hole that opened like a halo onto her brain.

"Sometimes," Kathy said, "it's either lose a child or lose—yourself. I mean, I—love my kids, but they were killing me."

"I don't think I could stand it," Julie said.

Linda looked at her, and Julie felt a chill pass through her even before Linda said, "We've all had a child die. Every one of us in this room has lost a child."

"And all our mothers did as well," Annette added.

"And all our daughters will, too," Yolanda finished. She put her arm around Regina, who tried feebly to pull away, then gave up and snuggled her enormous bulging body as best she could against her mother's scrawny one. "Guess you could say it runs in the family."

"It's one of the reasons this group formed," Linda said. "It's one of the things we have in common. It helps to be with other mothers who understand."

"How—how do you live through it?"

A look passed among the co-op members, a sisterly smile. It was Linda who said, "We don't, Julie. We didn't."

Julie laughed a little, experimentally, waiting for Linda and the others to join in, to explain the grisly joke to her. No one did. Finally she managed to say, "I feel that way sometimes myself. Raising kids is hard."

Kathy nodded. "When the baby cries all—night and you don't know what's wrong and you—know you're a terrible mother."

"When you just gave her a bath," Yolanda suggested, "and she shits all over herself again, and you're trying to get ready to go someplace."

"When she's two and you have to keep an eye on her every minute so she doesn't hurt herself or destroy your house," Linda said. "When she's six and the bully in the third grade keeps beating her up, or she's in the third grade and she bullies the six-year-olds."

"When she's twelve and failing seventh grade algebra

and you have to go talk to the teacher again about her attitude." Annette shook her head appreciatively.

"When she's eighteen," Yolanda said pointedly, "and pregnant."

"I didn't like being pregnant in the first place," Julie said, her own resentment suddenly rising to meet theirs. She looked at the baby in her lap and tried to think of it as a stranger, an alien, an intruder. But the baby was part of her. As strong as the resentment was a huge hot love. "And labor was a bitch. They say you forget the pain, but you don't." She saw Regina's frightened look and was immediately sorry, but could think of no way to soften what she'd said. "I don't know why any of us have kids," she said.

"Oh," Kathy said airily. "I do. I—love my kids. You just have to—learn to cope, that's all."

"I don't know how." Julie's eyes were so full of tears she was afraid she'd drop the baby. She laid her down on the couch. Megan did not protest.

Yolanda had started talking again. Yolanda's voice was rough, as though her throat hurt. It was painful to listen to her, and she did talk a lot. "I was already way pregnant when my mama died, and after that she didn't have much to say to me, even though she did talk all the time. I wasn't a bit older than Regina is now when I had her. Barely eighteen. Now here she is, look at her, following right in her mama's footsteps but not listening to her mama at all. Look at her. Tired all the time. Sick all the time. The baby's eating her alive."

Julie did look at Regina, and was struck by how much Yolanda and Regina looked alike, mother and daughter, how closely they both must resemble the mother and grandmother who had died at the mouths of her children and who had not died.

Diane trudged loudly up the basement steps and slammed the door behind her. The latch didn't hold, and the door swung open again; Diane leaned back against it with all her considerable weight. Almost at once, the cacophony from the basement rose again. Julie thought uneasily of penned animals, of water in a cooking pot coming to a hard boil.

Kathy got up and, stumbling a little, made her way across the rooms to open the curtains again. Julie didn't say anything or try to stop her, though it was her house. The crowd outside was at the foot of the steps now, where the hill that the house sat on met the sidewalk. Julie held Megan up to the window so she could see, but the baby, of course, didn't look. She was screwing up her red little face and grunting vehemently. Julie felt a warm stickiness on the inside of her forearm and knew that the diaper was leaking, but didn't do anything about it. It wasn't important. It made no difference. She could clean the baby and herself, change the diaper, wash the clothes, clean the carpet, wash the windows, turn the co-op mothers out of her house, chase the crowd away from the steps, and the baby would just mess again.

Still leaning against the basement door, which gapped along the top, Diane sighed heavily. "How many times do you suppose I've done that over the years? For all the good it does."

"It would be worse if we didn't," Annette said serenely, glancing down at her folded hands as though she were consulting notes. "They'll thank us when they grow up."

"I don't know about that," Yolanda said. "My girl doesn't understand yet all the sacrifices I make for her, and here she is about to be a mama her own self."

Diane crossed to the littered table and filled a second plate. The paper of the plate got soggy almost immediately and bent around the edges; Julie watched a clot of cottage cheese fall to the floor, watched Diane step in it and smear it across the yellow and pink linoleum.

While the other mothers chatted around them, Linda said quietly to Julie, "I'm glad you decided to join the co-op. I think you have a lot to add, and I think you're ready for us."

Regina gasped and arched her back, gripped the arms of

her chair, spread her legs and braced her feet against the floor. All eyes turned to her, even Megan's, and her mother said her name. "Regina? Honey? Is it time?"

"We need to get her to a hospital," Julie said, but she could see out the windows that Cascadilla Street was completely flooded and impassable now. Water was up over the curbs and the sidewalks, rain still falling so hard that it looked like viscous sheets, all of a piece. Mothers and children were so crowded and faceless that she couldn't tell one from another. Except that she saw Kathy join them, the stiff blonde hair getting stiffer in the rain, the thin skin parting to expose pale flesh, and Kathy's pale blond grown son beside her, nearly indistinguishable from her.

Regina cried out. Yolanda was standing over her, saying her name. The other mothers gathered around, murmuring, and the children began to come up from the basement.

Regina's baby was born on the kitchen floor, among the stains of food and the accumulating footprints of the mothers and their children. Julie watched, clutching her own baby, not knowing what to do. Labor was long and hard. There was a good deal of blood. Rain kept falling, and voices gathered. Children and mothers milled at the windows, inside and out, scratching at the glass and at each other, making wordless mewling sounds. Julie's daughter cried and cried in her arms.

When Regina's baby was born, it tore out part of her body with it, and left part of its new body inside hers. Julie saw the tissue and the blood. Regina screamed. Yolanda said her name. Julie slid her own daughter's tiny clawing hand into her mouth and bit down hard.

# FRUITS OF LOVE

## by Chelsea Quinn Yarbro

Chelsea Quinn Yarbro is a two-term president of the Horror Writers of America. She lives in Berkeley, California, and has a horse named Magick and two cats. Her short stories have appeared in *Shadows, Whispers,* and many other well-known anthologies. She has written a number of mysteries, one of which was nominated for an Edgar, and a historical YA, but she is best known for her historical horror novels and the creation of one of the most intriguing characters—the vampire St. Germaine. She has just sold her fortieth book, a historical horror novel, *Out of the House of Life,* published this year by Tor.

This is the second of only two historical stories in the anthology, and shows Quinn's great skill in evoking the mood of a terrible time.

♦ ♦ ♦

As soon as he had slammed the door in the lackeys' faces, the Baron was on her, fumbling greedily at Désirée's stays, his big, lean hands dry as reptiles as he dragged her breasts out of her corsage.

She had feared it would be bad with him, but nothing had prepared her for his rapacity, and she retreated, her voice high and shaking. "You are too eager, *mon Baron.*" She struggled to break away from him, her delicate fingers closing to fists which she did not dare to use.

Le Baron Clotaire Odon Jules Valince Pieux de Saint Sebastien laughed unpleasantly, contemptuously, as he reached for the ties of her panniers. "How can I not be eager when you are so charming?" he taunted her in a travesty of the grand manner he had learned as a young man. He was the last of a bad lot: dissipated, corrupt, some said blasphemous, and long since out of favor at court. He was also very rich and, in certain circles, powerful. Now he watched while Désirée struggled with her trailing skirts and undone corset, no sympathy in his hooded green eyes. "What is this, *ma belle*? Why do you hesitate? Surely you are not going to pretend virgin shyness?"

Désirée smiled desperately. "No," she said, more wistfully than she knew. "But perhaps . . . first . . . something."

"Courtship?" He sneered. "But to what purpose? Why should I court you when I own you?"

Her body went cold at his implacable words. "Perhaps we could talk?"

He regarded her narrowly. "Are you going to be tiresome? What prattle of yours could possible interest me? You have one use for me, and if that is denied me, then I have made a poor bargain and I will have to recoup my losses however I may." His stare grew harder and more calculating. "There is a brothel I know; the madame takes girls like you, she prefers them, in fact, so that they can be chastised."

Désirée would not let herself scream, though she felt the sound and outrage building in her. "Tell me of yourself, then? Your lackeys said nothing in the coach. I . . . I have seen you only once before." She was inching away from him as she tried to gather enough of her bodice and corset to cover herself. While his hands had been on her she had been contaminated, debased; even his cynical gaze had a filth about it. "I know little of you, *mon Baron*."

"Have you considered I might prefer that?" He was almost certain that her silly young lover, de Vandonne, had told her tales, undoubtedly going back to his grandfather, who had been part of de Montespan's set. "What do you need to know but that I want you and will keep you so long as you please me?" He strolled over to the trestle table and started to pinch out the candles of the nearer candelabrum.

She was still retreating from him. "But I know so little . . . I have had just one lover, and he . . . he—"

"Was a foolish, handsome young man and you think you

love him, and that he adores you," Saint Sebastien finished for her. "You will come to learn otherwise."

"There has only been Michon," she pleaded, wishing that Michon were here to save her, to see what his stupid, reckless, unforgivable wager had wrought.

"I assure you, *ma belle,* I am experienced enough for both of us." There was no humor in his voice. "I pay well for my pleasures, do not doubt." He paused. "And do not doubt *you* will pay dearly for my disappointment, Désirée."

Her panic was rising, but she fought it down. She had to get out of this salon, she had to find the servants and enlist their help, or run away. If only she knew where she was, what estate this was. "I do not want to disappoint you, *mon Baron,* but . . . but I have not learned much . . ."

Saint Sebastien was tiring of their game. "I do not wish to have to hurt you, child. But I am not a patient man and your loveliness and your reluctance may drive me to it." He had taken off his heavy silk coat with the wide whale-boned skirts, and was starting to unfasten the thirty pearl buttons that closed his gold-brocaded waistcoat.

Now the door was only a few steps behind her. Once through it, Désirée thought desperately, and she would have a chance to save herself. She pretended to trip on her ripped petticoat, and flung out an arm to break her fall, her fingers closing on the scroll-handled latch. She put her weight against it, but to no avail.

"Ah, yes," said Saint Sebastien as he snuffed out three more candles. "It is locked, I am sorry to say. And I have the key. Though if you did get out of the room, the lackeys would bring you back." He tossed his waistcoat aside. "Little as you may like it, I won you in fair play, Désirée." He recalled the shock in Michon de Vandonne's turquoise-colored eyes when he realized he had gambled away his mistress, and lost her to Clotaire de Saint Sebastien, of all men. "You are mine now. I won you and have the deed to prove it. Accept that. You are mine, to do with as I wish. I could have you deported to the American colonies, with a load of whores. I could give you to my servants to use. I could blind you and leave you somewhere on the high road. I have done these things before to others, and I may do them again. So be grateful that for the moment I desire you for myself." He looked dreamily into the fire, and his expression was not a good one. "I do not want to continue your game: do not make me go to the trouble of fetching you."

The last of the candles was out; the salon was ruddy in the glow from the hearth. To Désirée, it was a vision of Hell. She stared, her courage deserting her, as Saint Sebastien dropped into a leather chair and began to unfasten his jabot.

Désirée leaned on the locked door and wept silently. She was just seventeen years old, and for one happy year she had been the mistress of Michon de Vandonne. For the second daughter of an Anjou carriage-maker, she had done well, and though her family did not wholly approve, they did not object—for they were realistic enough to know that de Vandonne could offer her more than any suitor they might secure for her—or they would not object until now. Now she knew they could cast her off. She had to force herself to look at the man who waited for her on the other side of the room. Her body was clay-cold and as awkward as a puppet with tangled strings; it seemed to her that her fine violet silk dress—quite ruined—was a shroud.

As the clock on the mantel chimed the hour, Saint Sebastien rose with a sigh and walked to the door. There was deliberation in the sound of his high-heeled shoes. "I asked you not to make me come to you." His mouth smiled, but his eyes never lost their stoniness; when she winced at his touch his lips stretched wider.

"Ah, no, *mon Baron*," she whispered as he took her chin in his hand, pressing hard.

He pulled the last of the silk out of her hands and away from her body. He flung her panniers aside. The laces of her corset were already torn and it came away quickly; in his haste, he left bruises as testament to his anger. When at last she was naked and weeping with dread, he pinned her to the floor and fastened on the secret places of her body.

♦ ♦ ♦

When Désirée tried to escape the first time, he beat her into unconsciousness and let it go at that: his estate was an isolated one, and he was aware she had no real chance to get free. Had the game been more equal, he might have let her continue the farce, but it did not amuse him enough for that. It had taken his gamekeepers less than two hours to find her and to drag her back to his chateau. His thoughts, too, had been on other matters; there was news from Austria of the new Empress, and Saint Sebastien wanted an ear in Maria Theresa's court. He had other arrangements that demanded his attention and he did not want to lose precious time disciplining his reluctant mistress.

But the second time she ran away was another matter.

"Well?" he demanded when his warden finally brought her back to him, more than a day after she had fled. A night in the open had taken its toll: her clothes were disheveled, her shoes muddied, one of them lacking a heel. Her face and arms were scratched and smirched, and she limped painfully on a swollen ankle. Her jaw was raised and her eyes hard and bright. As he surveyed her, Saint Sebastien took snuff from a gold-and-enamel box and dusted his satin coat with a lace handkerchief. From his brocaded shoes and silk stockings to his pigeon's-wing bagwig, he was the picture of the perfect gentleman. Only the lines scored into his face marred him. "I am waiting for your answer."

"I don't have one." Hatred burned at the back of her eyes, hatred for Baron Clotaire de Saint Sebastien, who had brought her to this, and for Michon de Vandonne, who had lost her with the same concern he had lost a *rouleau* of *ange d'or*. What had she meant to him, if he could let her go so easily, for nothing more than the turn of a card?

Saint Sebastien regarded her evenly, his hooded green eyes unfathomable. "I thought you understood, Désirée. I thought I had made matters clear to you. But I see I will have to demonstrate once again, this time more forcefully."

He smoothed the broad cuff of his salmon-colored silk coat, a frown puckering his brow.

This was a familiar expression to Désirée and though it frightened her, she was not overwhelmed by her fear. "You will beat me, I suppose."

The defiance in her words made him look up. "So. You are growing strong in your anger." The polite bow he favored her with terrified her. "I see I will have to use other tactics. It would not do for you to learn to resist me. It would not be acceptable." He rose, taking his silver-and-ebony cane from beside his chair. He paused, then said at his most urbane, "Oh, you need not fear I will use this on you. I would do that only if I intended to kill you."

She loathed herself for revealing her terror, but she could not make herself keep silent. "Then what will you do to me?"

He pursed his lips, taking time to relish her fright. "I assumed I had made that clear, *ma belle*. I am going to make sure you learn your lesson this time." He picked up a silver bell and rang it, pleased to see her bewilderment. "I have decided to delegate my punishment to another."

She stood as if impaled. "Who?"

"You remember Tite?" It was an unnecessary question, for she had never disguised her dislike for Saint Sebastien's large, saturnine manservant who was virtually her jailer. "He was distressed when you disappeared, and requested that when you came back he might have the schooling of you." He tapped his cane lightly on the marble floor. "He is a strange man, Tite, a very strange man. Tite lusts the most where he is most angry. Your foolish rebellion has infuriated him, and therefore he is enflamed as well. He has no regard for affection, I ought to mention; he finds his greatest satisfaction in resistance and the submission of his . . . victim."

"And I am his victim?" she asked in spite of her resolution to be silent.

"Why, of course. You have shown that my chastisement means nothing, so you must have a more obdurate tutor."

His glance raked over her, taking in all the dirt and tatters. He flicked his handkerchief toward her, suddenly fastidious. "Certainly you are more fitting for him, or a stablehand, or a pig farmer, than for me in your present state."

The trembling that seized her almost made Désirée fall. She steadied herself against his writing table. Her mouth was too dry for speech. Dumbly she shook her head, her body filled with protest. She wanted to take the standish and throw it at him, hoping the ink would mar his beautiful clothes and reveal him for what he was. Her hand would not move.

Saint Sebastien enjoyed her distress as he went on smoothly, "You should be grateful, *ma belle*. You have made it plain enough that my embraces disgust you, that you would prefer another; I am offering you the variety you crave."

At that she blurted out one name: "Michon!" though Saint Sebastien did not understand it for the curse it was.

"Oh, no, I am afraid there is no hope for you from that quarter, not now. That puppy de Vandonne would not take you back now, Désirée; he is too nice for that. He would never touch what I have had. Ah." He looked up as the door opened.

Tall, raw-boned, more a bodyguard than a valet, Tite came forward, his eyes on Désirée. He bowed.

Saint Sebastien looked directly at Désirée as he spoke to his servant. "I promised her to you, didn't I?"

"Yes, master," said Tite, his face avid.

"Then, naturally, she is yours." He gave Désirée a slight, contemptuous nod before he left her alone with Tite.

♦ ♦ ♦

After the agony and humiliation, Désirée shut most of herself away, to be infected with her shame, her fear, and to fester. Outwardly she was no more than a sleepwalker, seemingly immune to Saint Sebastien's cruel amusements and taunts. Even when she discovered the profane altar in the cellar, she did nothing more than shrug, as if the inverted crucifix with its aroused Christ was little more than another tasteless decoration. She spoke rarely and, when she did, the words were gentle, emotionless, as her eyes were strangely vacant and unresponsive.

At first Saint Sebastien was pleased with this change in her, and invented new torments to provoke her into another burst of rebellion. Only occasionally was he able to abuse her enough for her to resist or object, and eventually he grew bored. Only her pregnancy kept him from turning her out.

"I do not know why I continue with you," he said to her one evening as they sat alone in the cavernous dining room. The food on her plate was largely untasted. "There are others who can conceive."

"Nor do I know," muttered Désirée. She pushed a dollop of veal around her plate with her fork.

"I do want your babe," he said, with extravagant unconcern. "I have a use for a newborn, if not for you."

She swallowed hard, but said nothing, keeping her eyes on the smear of sauce at the rim of her plate. In four more months she would deliver, and then God alone—or perhaps only the Devil—knew what would become of her. Désirée had reached a state where she was not able to imagine any life other than this one. She would not permit herself to imagine what awaited her child when it came.

"He will be offered on the altar, before I return to Paris." He wiped his mouth with his lace-edged napkin. "Would you like to participate? It helps to have a woman on the altar, to use as a woman, and to hold the basin for the blood."

She kept silent.

"Well, in four months you may make up your mind." He patted her arm in a deceptively avuncular way. "In the meantime, Tite and I will find new ways to amuse you. As long as Tite continues to be so inventive, my interest will not slacken. Once it does, I will need to find other sport."

♦ ♦ ♦

Three weeks later, Désirée miscarried. She lay in her room, her teeth clamped shut so that she would not scream, would not gratify her captors with her suffering. When it was over, when the blood had dried and she had come to her senses again, Tite found her.

"You brought this on! Out of spite!" he thundered at her.

"I didn't have to, not with what you have done to me," she said, weary and desolate.

Tite suddenly laughed. "It might be worth the entertainment we had, but it's a pity we lost the sacrifice." His nose wrinkled at the coppery scent of blood. "You've ruined the bed."

"Do you care the baby was yours?" she asked harshly. She looked at the incomplete lump, no larger than a clenched fist, with little of humanity to identify it. It was Tite's, and that made it despicable. But also it was hers, she realized. It had lived in her, and now it was dead, because of the man who fathered it. Like everything else in her life, it had been contaminated by Clotaire de Saint Sebastien. As she fought down her sudden rush of tears, she promised herself and her dead child vengeance.

♦ ♦ ♦

That night the herb woman came to treat Désirée and to take away the thing she had lost, promising that she would find a way to bury it in sacred ground. "For it wasn't its fault that it had no proper birth," she said. Marta was not as old as she looked: an ugly facial birthmark and prematurely gray hair made her appear ancient, but her walk and the firm tone of her skin betrayed her youth. Traces of native Italy clung to her in her accented French and her lambent dark eyes. She realized Désirée's predicament before the desperate young woman could speak. "There," she said reassuringly when she had finished bathing Désirée and assured herself that there was no infection from the miscarriage. "The men know nothing, not the worst or the best of them. You do not need to tell me how it was."

"I could not," whispered Désirée, all her anguish wakened afresh at her loss.

"Do not worry; the infant is out of reach of that satin-clothed pig. The child is gone to Heaven where Mére Marie will treasure it until you come."

"I, come to Heaven?" she started to laugh, but that gave way to weeping she could not stop. She attempted to apologize, to stem the tide of her sorrow, but for once she was not able to control her emotions, or to disguise them.

"A mother's tears are holy. There is nothing disgraceful in shedding them." Marta put her hands over Désirée's as if to reinforce her prayers. "God knows what beasts like this Saint Sebastien do, and He will judge them. It will be the worse for Saint Sebastien, I think, because he came by his title through the Church; Saint Sebastian is a benefice and a Vidamie. His grandfather was made a Baron, or so they say, but the estate came from the Church, for service to God."

"How do you come to know this?" Désirée was able to ask the question as if it had nothing to do with her or anyone she knew.

Marta had been searching her bag for the herbs that would lessen the bleeding and ease the hurt. "I know because I live here, for everyone near this place knows about the Baron."

"This has happened before?" Désirée told herself that she was not shocked, but new pain wrenched inside her.

"Let us say that there have been women here before, sometimes more than one, and what has happened to them has not often been good." She pulled out a cloth bag of tansy. "*Le Baron* prefers it if we all pretend not to notice."

"And you?" Désirée asked, turning even more pale. "Oh, God, what will happen to me?"

"No, no, little one. You are not to be afraid. I will stay with you," she said as she sorted out her supplies, "until you no longer need me."

e." Her hands were strong and sure as she lifted the ng woman and bathed her in water of motherwort and mary. She did not let her outrage enter into the tone of voice, which remained low and soothing. "You will ve vengeance for your pains, for that is the way of jus- e."

Once Désirée called for Michon, and when he did not ome, fell to weeping and cursing. "No, no. You do not ome. You let me go for a card, a card. It is because the Baron has me. I am lost for a card. The Baron . . . I am not for you, Michon. You would not know me now. You would not know me. Or want me. I am lost. How could you gamble me away? You let me go. I could kill you. Both of you; both of you."

"Hush, poor one," Marta whispered. "Hush. There is justice in Heaven and we will have justice on earth."

The sound of Marta's voice at last pulled Désirée awake, and she opened clear, intelligent eyes. "Yes," she said faintly, but with purpose, "there is justice. I will avenge my dishonor and the death of my babe. You will help me, oh promise me your help."

"I will help you," Marta vowed as she lifted Désirée back into her bed and pulled the sheets around her. Then she took up her position on the pallet as if guarding Désirée while she slept.

♦ ♦ ♦

Three days later Désirée had improved and Saint Sebastien stopped in her room to see her.

"Not dead yet, *ma belle*?" he asked, pinching her cheek enough to leave a red mark where his fingers had been. He was elegant and languorous in saffron satin with gold-and-topaz buttons and gold lacing. "Somehow that disappoints me."

"I am sorry to have done so, Baron," she replied with extreme courtesy, her breathing rapid. "I did all that I could to oblige you, but it was not to be."

"And yet, I would not want to raise a brat of Tite's get.

It had been so long since Désirée ha that she had no response to offer Mart "Why would you do that?"

"For love of God, and to shame the Dev

"Thank you," Désirée murmured, beginn the first time since she arrived at Saint Seba that she had an ally, and some comfort in her

Marta was building up the fire in the grate. "Y back and pray for the soul of your lost little one. will send peace to your heart." She was heating wa and the steam from the pot smelled of winter sav tansy.

Désirée doubted that was possible, but did as sh told. Her body ached as it never had from a beating, was dizzy when she moved. "My head is sore," she s wondering why she should notice that, with so many oth hurts clamoring for attention.

"I know. It will pass. I am here. We will deal with everything." Crooning other words, she lulled Désirée into a light sleep. As she looked down at her, Marta knew what it was that Saint Sebastien wanted in the girl—she was lovely, even now when her face was haggard with suffering and she was thin from her ordeal. What a pity that she should be the prey of such a man as Saint Sebastien. Marta shook her head in resignation. She had not been brought here to mend the morals of Clotaire de Saint Sebastien, but to heal his mistress. She uttered a prayer and a curse as she set to work.

♦ ♦ ♦

Sometime that night, while her body struggled to throw off the last effects of her miscarriage, Désirée cried out, tossing in delirium and pain. From pieces of what she mumbled, Marta pieced together her story; Marta's heart grew bitter as she listened.

"There, there," she said as she wiped the sweat from Désirée's brow. "Marta is here now. Marta will not fail you. You will have your revenge. I will help you gain your re-

Perhaps the next one will be mine. Or my groom's." He twirled his quizzing glass at the end of a long silk ribbon. "You are getting too thin; that does not please me," he observed critically. "When you leave your bed, see that you put on flesh before you come to me again. I do not want to be poked with hips and ribs."

Désirée turned her head away on the pillow, which made Saint Sebastien laugh.

"She is tired, Baron," Marta said as she brewed another special tea from a pot on the hob.

"Women are always tired, or so they claim. It is usually an escape so that they will not have to lie with men. Fatigue is supposed to explain their lacks. When she has come to my bed, she has been worse than a doll, lying without moving or making a sound. She has no passion."

Désirée began to weep again. She thought she would never stop, and she was disgusted with herself for showing such weakness to her enemy.

Marta was about to dismiss the remark when a thought occurred to her. She put the kettle near the ashes and said, "I venture to guess, Baron, that she longs for a more stalwart lover." Marta knew that such bold words could mean a beating and her dismissal without pay. She waited while Saint Sebastien considered what she had said.

"Go on," he said, a strange light in his narrowed eyes.

"There is a remedy, perhaps; one that I have learned. I know of a plant that can be mixed with meat, red meat . . ." She hesitated as if embarrassed to continue. "It is a remedy for the weakening of the virile parts. If I could supply you with this plant—the fruit is eaten, not the leaves—in a few months it might answer your needs. By that time your mistress should be anxious for your touch." Looking toward the bed he saw the horror and betrayal in Désirée's face, undisguised and open. "It renders the man like Priapus."

"You interest me," Saint Sebastien said with a nod as he looked toward Désirée. "In a few months, then, *ma belle,* we shall try again. If you please me, perhaps I will not give you to Tite for some time." He minced toward the bed. "Your breasts are larger now. That is satisfactory." He said over his shoulder to Marta, "In July, then, I will want that fruit. If you do not have it for me, perhaps I will give you to Tite for amusement because you have not fulfilled your pledge." He gave the two women the tiniest of bows and left.

When he was safely out of earshot, Désirée let her wrath pour down on Marta's head. "How could you betray me! How could you promise your help and then do this! Is there a place in Hell for those who destroy the trust of those who are in need?"

Marta came to Désirée's side. "No, no, do not say this, my little dove. Hush," she said softly, "do not fear. No, do not. Marta would not give you again to that monster. Never would I do that. Before God, I would die before I would do that. Listen to me, *poverina*."

"For more lies," Désirée said, averting her face.

"You must listen to me," Marta insisted, and in a moment, Désirée sighed and looked at her. "There have been lies told here, but not to you—to him. I would rather open my veins than lie to you, and I sing with the angels when I lie to him. This fruit I told him of, it is real, but it is not for the virile parts. It is the deadliest poison." She saw the beginning of hope in Désirée's eyes. "Now, hear me out, for you will have your vengeance. This fruit will give you vengeance."

"What fruit is it?" Désirée asked, not quite curious but anxious to know what Marta could offer her.

"Some have called this the fruit of love, for the shape is like the fruits of men, the sacks that are so precious to them. The shape is something like a pear. There are fools who will eat it because they have heard that the shape lends passion and lust to their parts, and for this vanity they die hideously."

Now Désirée's face was bright and her smile held an echo of the ferocity of Saint Sebastien's smile. "Tell me, Marta. I want to know about this fruit."

Marta nodded, bending closer to Désirée in case someone

at the door might be listening. "The fruit is mashed—it is not so firm as an apple but not so soft as a ripe melon—and mixed with meat for a pie, so that the poison will penetrate all that the man eats. It has a taste that is not unpleasant, or so they say, but that is part of the deception of the plant. Like the love of madmen, the fruit does its work. Because of how it looks it is named for love, but it gives death."

"He will not eat it. He will suspect," said Désirée, her fear returning with full power.

"He will suspect nothing," said Marta, tossing her head to show her disdain. "He wishes to believe that he will be as potent as a young goat, and he would eat a hedgehog if he thought it would add to his lust."

A second doubt came over Désirée. "This is murder. You and I will kill him, and it will be on our souls."

"It will not, not for the death of Baron Clotaire de Saint Sebastien." She considered the problem. "He has degraded you and killed your child before it was born. Those are his sins, not yours, and you are not held accountable in Heaven. Therefore you must seek the aid of Holy Church. You must confess. Can you write?"

"A little. Enough," said Désirée, listening with real attention.

"Good. Then you will write a confession to the priest at Sainte Genevieve's, and say that you were maddened by the death of your child and the indifference and humiliations of your protector. Beg that Holy Church receive you as a penitent. Say that the loss of your babe so preyed on your mind that you wanted death for yourself and for Saint Sebastien. Say that you resign yourself to prayer and the Mercy of God, and that you seek peace not in this world but the next. No magistrate can strike that down if the priest has it before the crime is revealed. We must prepare the confession before I bring the fruits, so that it will be in the hands of the priest as soon as Saint Sebastien is dead. That way no one here can hurt you, for you will be in the care of the Church on the strength of your confession. After a time you will be able to leave your penitent's cell, and you and your child will be avenged. I will carry your confession myself, and see that it is placed in the hands of the priest."

Désirée lay back, assessing what Marta has said to her. At last she let her breath out slowly and nodded. "It is good. I will need paper and ink." Once again that disquieting smile settled on her face.

◆ ◆ ◆

It was a warm afternoon when Marta brought the poison, showing the red and yellow fruits to Saint Sebastien before taking them to Désirée and receiving her written confession.

"Now you must have care," Marta said as she prepared to leave for Sainte Genevieve's. "Mash the fruits well and see that they are thoroughly mixed with the meat for the pies. I will be back by the time you are ready to serve him, and I will help you then, you have my word on it."

Désirée followed the simple instructions, mashing the fruit so that skin and pulp and seeds were little more than a paste in the bottom of a big crockery bowl. She was elated at Marta's plan, at her foresight in arranging for the confession to be in the hands of the priest before any magistrate or courtier could attempt to detain her for questioning and torture. With her confession in the hands of the Church there was not a court in the land that would be able to hold her. She knew she could endure the seven years of penance that would be required of her for the joy of killing Clotaire de Saint Sebastien.

At supper that night Désirée found she was almost happy as she watched Saint Sebastien eating his pie with such gusto.

"The taste is not bad," he said. "I was afraid that you would want to make it horrible, because of how little you want to come to my bed again." He sipped a little of the white wine he favored. "I might come to like these fruits in my food; do you think you would enjoy me then, with my lust enhanced?"

"How can I know?" It was not difficult to answer him, realizing how soon it would be over. She waited for him to die, and wondered how long it would take. It could not possibly be long, she knew: for in 1741 everyone in the world knew that love apples—sometimes called tomatoes—were virulent poison.

# SARA AND THE SLIME CREATURE

## by Resa Nelson

Resa Nelson was born in 1956 and has been writing fiction since she was nine. She earned degrees in sociology and physical education at the University of Kansas, where she lettered as the student manager of the men's varsity baseball team, the second woman in the university's history to hold this position. She also holds a master's degree in sport management from the University of Massachusetts. She attended the Clarion Science Fiction Writers Workshop in 1985, and belongs to the Cambridge SF Workshop and the Space Crafts SF Workshop. Her short stories have appeared in *Aboriginal SF* and *2040 AD*. Living in the Boston area, where she works as a technical writer, she swims, plays classical piano, and loves baseball, ballet, and wind-up toys. Her novel-in-progress, *All of Us Were Sophie*, is about a woman who makes four exact copies of herself before she is murdered.

When I first saw the title of this story, I thought it was science fiction and almost rejected it without reading on. Then I decided I should give it a chance—I'm glad I did, because it's overpowering dark fantasy.

◆ ◆ ◆

Once there was a little girl named Sara who was held captive by a slime creature that had no name. No one else knew about the slime creature or how he held Sara captive. It was kind of like a secret.

Sara was very young, so young that instead of getting a letter grade in school, she had a grade card with boxes reading Fair, Average, Good, and Very Good for the teacher to mark. Sometimes Sara was Good (especially in Current Events), but most of the time she was Very Good. Whenever she brought a grade card home, her mama hugged Sara. Not because of all of the Very Goods, but because

Mama knew that Sara always did her best and that's all that mattered.

Mama had always asked Sara to do her very best to get used to living with Paul and his fifteen-year-old son Calvin. It was hard to watch Paul put his arms around Mama and pinch her bottom. At times like that, Sara wished her daddy would come back (but she knew he never would) and knock Paul's block off and kiss Mama the way he used to and kneel down and open his arms and say, Come here, Sara Bear.

It was hard to live with strangers in her home, but Sara did her best.

It was hard at night when everyone had gone to bed and Paul's snoring rumbled down the hallway, when ghosts walked through the living room and kitchen and up the stairs to where the bedrooms were even though Mama said all the creaking was just the house settling. That's when the slime creature came into Sara's room.

At first she thought it was Calvin because it kind of looked like him (but it was dark and she wasn't a baby and had stopped using a nightlight last year) but couldn't really *tell* who it looked like in the dark. It even talked like Calvin. It couldn't have been Calvin, though, because he hardly ever talked to Sara in the daytime. Besides, the slime creature was slimy and smelly like a monster, not like a person. And he could read her mind.

The first time the slime creature came, Sara woke up scared 'cause she felt smothered. It had clamped its clammy hand over her mouth and was sitting on her, squeezing all the air out of her chest. It whispered in Sara's ear, telling her Not To Make A Sound. It raised itself a bit so Sara could breathe and that's when she felt its chest against hers. Sara frowned. Her nightgown had been pushed way up so it was bunched up under her chin. The creature's skin was hot and slimy and it rubbed against Sara, leaving its slime on her.

It did other stuff, too. Stuff that was just so weird and

dumb that Sara squirmed underneath him. When Sara started to say something, the creature told her to be quiet.

The slime creature told her not to tell anybody. It told her a lot of other things and Sara obeyed because she thought it was Calvin. Mama had told Sara to do whatever Calvin said because it was like he was Sara's big brother now. Sara did whatever Calvin said because Mama wanted Sara to do her best. And Sara didn't want to be Fair or Average or even Good. She wanted to be Very Good.

♦ ♦ ♦

It was like she was a princess in one of those fairy tales that Mrs. Hargrave read to them at school or that was on TV sometimes. The princesses were kept prisoner when they had done nothing wrong at all. There was one who was locked high up in a tower. She had blonde hair like Sara's and let it grow for years and years until she could braid it and cast it from the tower window like a rope. Then a prince climbed up her hair.

Ouch. Sara winced when she heard that part. Sure must've hurt. But it would've been worth it, 'cause then the handsome prince would slay the wicked witch

(the slime creature)

and they'd live happily ever after.

From what Sara could tell, the princesses weren't any nicer than any other girls in their neighborhoods (except for the obviously wicked stepsisters). In fact, sometimes they weren't even princesses at all but ordinary girls. But they always got what all the other girls wanted—the prince's true love. But the other girls in the neighborhood never had to spend years locked up in a tower with nothing to eat but bread and water. They never did anything to earn a prince's true love. Like being held captive by the slime creature.

Or having their minds read. Or being Responsible for other people's lives.

The second time the slime creature came, Sara told him she didn't want him to do any of that dumb stuff again. The last time he'd left slime all over her *and* her bed and it was gross. Sara was scared to talk to the slime creature like that, but it was *her* room and *her* bed and she didn't have any other place to sleep. Besides, she thought to herself, I'll tell.

That's when he read her mind. "If you tell," he breathed in his slimy voice. "I'll make you step on a crack."

Step on a crack, break your mother's back.

Suddenly the whole house seemed too quiet. "Just like I did to Linda Noller."

Sara blinked hard and tried not to shake. Linda's mother was real old and Mama said just yesterday that she had fallen and broken her hip. Paul had laughed (it was like a smirk, really) and said that's not how it happens. The bones in someone her age get real weak and can't support the weight, so the bone breaks. *Then* she falls.

Well, that didn't make much sense at all. Everyone knew old people (like Linda's mother) were always falling down and breaking things. But *now* what Paul said made sense. It made a whole lotta sense.

If the slime creature made Sara step on a crack, snap would go Mama's bones and down she'd go. She might even die.

But Sara wouldn't let Mama die because Sara was Very Good at being Responsible. She dried the dishes (well, most of the time) and kept her room clean (except for the closet and under the bed), but she would have to *always* do whatever the slime creature said and never tell.

So Sara concentrated on other things when the slime creature came to her room. Sometimes she thought about school. Too boring. Sometimes she thought about playing with her friends but somehow that made her feel sad. Pretending made Sara feel better. Especially when she was a captured princess.

♦ ♦ ♦

Sara pretended she was a princess who lived as a peasant girl because the king had disappeared and an evil magician had kidnapped the queen.

The magician had mixed awful-smelling powders and a

bottle of muck and other things too disgusting to mention. He mixed it in mid-air, the potion spinning and swirling at his command, taking shape and form, pulsing a pale green light from within. Then lightning crackled across its surface and the potion exploded. And what was left behind was rough-skinned, greenish-gray, and the size and shape of a boy, dripping with endless slime.

Sometimes Sara pretended she was locked high in a tower. The tower room was small and cramped and there was sawdust all over the floor, but there was a window that overlooked the entire kingdom: fields and valleys and thatched-roof cottages and the castle in the distance. Twice a day, a dove would fly to the high tower window, carrying food wrapped in a white handkerchief.

Sara's favorite pretend was the maze. She pretended she was kept in the creature's garden. It was as beautiful as the creature was repulsive, filled with flowering trees and peacocks and shrubs shaped like animals and *real* animals like deer and kangaroos. The garden was surrounded by a maze made of old dead thorny vines, twice as tall as Sara. She would play with the animals, biding her time. She didn't know where the slime creature was, but she *felt* him watching, always watching. All at once she'd make a break and run into the maze, hitching her long skirt up in her arms so she wouldn't trip over it.

She'd hear the creature cry out in anger. And she knew he'd followed her into the maze.

Sara ran well and ran fast, dodging around corners, digging her heels in, taking chances. The thorns reached out and tried to grab her, but they caught only at her sleeves, ripping them and scratching her arms bloody.

The creature pounded behind her, heavy footsteps, heavy breathing. The thorns cowered back, out of his way.

Sometimes Sara fell down so hard it knocked the wind out of her and made her chest ache. She scrambled to her feet as fast as she could and ran harder. Always, near the end of the maze, the path narrowed and Sara drew her arms up to protect her face as the thorns struck angrily at it.

Sometimes she had to leap across a widening fissure, sometimes she fell down an embankment. Once she curled up in a ball and rolled through a wall of fire.

She always made it through the maze. And at the end was a prince astride his horse or a knight standing in shining armor ready to battle the slime creature as it followed Sara out of the maze.

Always, Sara faced the knight, beaming. Her dress torn, her face and arms smeared with blood and dirt, her hair in tangles, (or singed)—she stood, panting, hearing the creature behind her, panting. Always, she felt brave and strong and beautiful.

♦ ♦ ♦

Many years later, Paul and Calvin moved away. As Sara grew up, she made herself forget about the slime creature and went on with her life. Except when things got real bad.

Walker was the best thing to happen to Sara at the worst time of her life. In a year she had lost her job, her mother, and her self-confidence.

Walker made her laugh and he wouldn't let her be alone. He knew that when she was alone, Sara sat in her apartment, sometimes with the TV off, sometimes in the dark. He took her out to movies and parties and *anywhere* away from her apartment so she could be with people. After a while, Sara began to feel good. Walker never made her feel Very Good, but Good was a lot better than what Sara had felt in a long time. And at least she was able to feel again.

Walker wanted to start his own consulting business and asked Sara to loan him the money she had inherited from her mother. When Sara agreed, Walker told her he loved her and they began to live together.

Sara had been a tour director until she was laid off. She had given tours of the company to student and marketing groups. Sara was very

(Responsible and)

good at her job. She was cheerful and funny and

(Very Good and)

a wealth of information and she was a fine liaison. When she was laid off, someone with more seniority took over her job. The only job Sara could get was as a secretary at a different company: she went from being a department head to being the bottom rung of a ladder for someone else to climb. She acted as a liaison between her boss and the photocopier. Sara hated the sound of her alarm clock in the morning.

Walker rescued her. He needed a partner in his consulting business, someone to help him get set up—and he asked Sara to work with him. They turned their apartment into an office. Walker asked Sara to do all the secretarial work until they could afford to hire a part-timer. But business was slow and they never did. Sara became the liaison between Walker and the photocopier. And the phones. And the files.

One day when he snapped at her, she said, "Walker, stop treating me like dirt—I'm not your secretary."

He sat at his desk, she stood in front of it, holding a stack of files. He gave her a long, hard look. "You didn't get the mail out yesterday."

Sara turned away and began to leave Walker's office (what used to be the den) for the kitchen table that now served as her desk. "I didn't have time."

"Well, *make* time," Walker said loudly. "The mail *has* to go out. Today. Every day."

Sara turned around. "Stop acting like a jerk."

Walker kept his gaze fixed on her, stroking his beard, beginning to show flecks of gray. "Sara, I need your help. I depend on you. I'm not trying to be a jerk, it's just the pressure. If this thing is going to fly, it will take a lot of hard work but will be worth it. Once we get on a roll, money'll come pouring in and we'll be golden."

Sara's expression softened. "You can count on me," she said, and turned to leave.

"Good," Walker said. "Just be sure you get the mail out."

♦ ♦ ♦

Sara went to bed early that night. She was almost asleep when Walker came to bed. He drew himself to her.

"Please don't," she said.

"Why not?" He reached under her nightgown.

"I'm tired. I was almost asleep." She tried to turn on her stomach but Walker held on to her. "Walker, stop it!"

"But you like this," he whispered, touching her.

Sara couldn't move. His skin was getting hot and sweaty and smelly

(and slimy)

"Stop it!" Sara pushed against him but she wasn't strong enough to push him off. He wouldn't stop.

It wasn't Sara's fault about the slime creature, it wasn't her fault that he came to her room for a long time

(for years, off and on)

and then stopped coming all of a sudden. It was just that Sara had begun to grow and change and just when the slime creature had stopped coming she had just begun

(to like it)

to imagine it was really the knight, the one who was always there waiting at the end of the maze ready to slay the slime creature, who came to Sara's room at night. Sometimes it seemed so *real:* she could hear the knight walking into her room. Clank, clank. And he'd take off his armor, shining in the moonlight, and set it down gently on the floor. He seemed so real . . . but Sara was Very Good at pretending. When Sara pretended it was the knight, the stuff the slime creature did wasn't as weird and dumb. It was kind of romantic and nice.

But then the slime creature stopped coming. One day when Calvin came to Sara's room to tell her to come to dinner, she asked him to come to her room that night.

"Why?" Calvin said.

Sara looked down at her hands. "You know. When everybody's asleep."

Calvin said nothing, so Sara looked up at him. The color had drained from his face. He licked his lips. "Why?" he said.

"You know."

"No," he said. "I don't. Dinner's ready."

Sara's eyes widened. Calvin was acting the way he did when Mama and Paul found out Calvin had been skipping school. He was acting like he'd made a Big Mistake but Sara had made a Big Mistake, too, because

(she liked it)

she had asked Calvin to come to her room so if she told on him he'd tell on her and Sara had a feeling it was

(Very Bad)

a lot worse than skipping school. And Mama would probably hate Sara for it when all Sara wanted to do was protect Mama from the slime creature's breaking her bones and save her life. But no one would ever understand how Sara had believed in the slime creature, they'd think she was a baby and maybe some of it *was* her fault, anyway.

"Walker—stop it!"

So she had never told anyone.

She tried to get out from under him; she wriggled and squirmed but he held her still. "I mean it, Walker," she cried. "Get off of me!"

"You want it," he said. "You know you do."

There was a lamp on the nightstand. Sara turned her face toward it. She couldn't see even an outline of it in the dark but she could probably reach it if she tried. But if she turned it on, she might see that it really *was* a slime creature because it couldn't be Walker, he'd never do this to her. Sara didn't want to look at the slime creature's face.

Sara was still, looking in the dark at the lamp.

After a while, when Sara had said nothing, done nothing, been nothing, Walker stopped. "Screw this," he muttered and left the room. When he opened the bedroom door, there was enough light from the hallway so that Sara could see the lamp on the nightstand, briefly, then Walker slammed the door shut.

Sara wished she could have made her arm move. She wished she could have grabbed the lamp and hit Walker over the head with it.

She stayed awake in the dark a long time, knowing she couldn't leave because

(she was afraid of losing him, not because he was Walker, but because he was someone to keep her from feeling lonely)
she had no other place to go.

So Sara stayed and they both acted as if it had never happened.

♦ ♦ ♦

"I need you here," Walker said.

"Not twenty-four hours a day. It seems like I never see anyone but you. I can't live like this."

"Why not?" He frowned. How Can You Hurt Me Like This was all over his face. "At least, keep working for me—*with* me—not some corporation. If you have to get out of the house, take a night class."

♦ ♦ ♦

He sat next to her in Modern Poetry. He was short, gray-eyed, and blond. When he smiled, Sara thought he looked like someone who cherished his friends. His name was Daniel.

It began when he saw Sara reading the sports page before class, and he asked if she had seen last night's game. They heatedly analyzed the playoffs and the upcoming World Series. They talked until class started, then whispered during the lecture. Afterward they crossed campus to a coffee shop. "Let's sit in Siberia," Daniel said. Laughing at Sara's puzzled look, he led her to a secluded corner. "The air conditioning's always on full-blast, but it's quiet."

They talked about everything: poetry, sports, the state of the world, their work, their lives. Their dreams.

They went to Siberia after every class, and Sara found herself caring less about poetry and more about Daniel.

He sipped his coffee, leaned back in his chair, and looked at Sara seriously. "What do you want from life?"

Sara searched his face for a moment, unsure. She laughed. "What do I want from life? What do you mean?"

Daniel smiled. "I mean, what do you want from life? What's important to you?"

Sara paused. She placed her hands gently around her coffee cup, concentrating on the cup instead of Daniel. "Once I was in an accident—a car accident. It was a long time before an ambulance came." She steadied her hands against the cup. "I was losing so much blood that I thought I was going to die. All I could think of was that I had nothing to leave behind me. I hadn't left my mark on the world."

"Children?"

She kept her gaze fixed on the coffee. "Not necessarily. I just want to leave something that has my imprint on it. I want to create something special so people will know I was here."

He reached out and touched the back of her hand lightly.

Sara looked up and found Daniel staring at her with the greatest intensity she had ever seen in a man's eyes. She realized that she had poured herself as if he'd cupped his hands and not spilled a drop. Walker never let her talk like this. He'd change the subject to something *he* wanted to talk about. Or say yeah yeah yeah, never hearing or trying not to. Or gaze outside or read the paper or do *anything* but try to listen to Sara.

It struck her so powerfully and so immediately that it must have shown on her face. Walker would have missed or ignored it. Daniel saw it right away. "What's wrong, Sara?"

Automatic: she smiled brightly. It was a façade she had polished to perfection; it worked on everyone. "Nothing's wrong. It's getting late, though. I should go home."

As she made her move to leave,

(the prince)

Daniel stared at her. Sara repressed a shiver, feeling as if he were

(about to sweep her into his arms to rescue her from the slime creature)

staring past her eyes and straight into her soul.

"Cut the crap," he said quietly. "What's the matter, Sara?"

There was nothing else she could do, so she told him.

She told him about Walker and how unhappy she had become and to a small extent she told him why. But she didn't tell Daniel about the slime creature and how it had consumed Walker and made him less than human. It was too soon. And besides, a small part of Sara told the rest of her, we don't *really* know about Daniel, now do we?

Daniel listened completely to Sara, hearing and digesting each word, each phrase, each thought. His gaze, steadfast and strong, never unlocked itself from hers. At times he sighed and shook his head. Once or twice he said, "Oh God, Sara," and touched her arm gently.

Finally, she paused, afraid she had said too much. After a brief silence, Daniel said, "He doesn't even know you."

Sara was stunned. What Daniel had just said was precisely the problem. Walker had never made an attempt, a *real* attempt, to know Sara. Instead, he spent his time and effort on shaping her into the someone he wanted her to be.

But someone like Daniel . . . someone like *him* would sit back and watch her evolve into who *she* wanted to be.

Daniel took her hand in his and squeezed it.

Sara knew about Pam, Daniel's girlfriend. Fiancée, actually. Daniel had made it clear from the beginning that he was taken. Off-limits. "Look," she said, suddenly feeling flustered. "I'm sorry to dump this on you. I shouldn't have."

Daniel's face remained solemn. "That's what real friends are for."

Sara trembled, wanting to run away and curl up in a ball and cry until her body ached. Because Daniel's concern was for such a little, insignificant thing. She could only wonder what his understanding would be like if she could work up the courage to tell him about

(the slime creature)

the really important things.

Someone like Daniel, she thought as she smiled and applied a little pressure to his hand. I have to hold out for someone like Daniel.

♦ ♦ ♦

Walker smiled at her as if she were a four-year-old asking if she could keep a pony in the backyard. "Sure, Sara."

She stared at him incredulously. He thought she was making empty threats. Quietly, she said, "I'm serious, Walker. I'm moving out. We're through."

"Sleep on it," he said. "You'll feel different in the morning."

She began to pack, starting with the kitchen. An hour later, Walker leaned in the kitchen doorway. "You're just making a lot of work for yourself."

"How so?"

"You'll unpack it all tomorrow. Why don't you come to bed?"

"I'll sleep on the sofa. I'll call the movers tomorrow." She turned to face him. "I don't love you anymore. I told you a long time ago to stop wiping your feet on me."

She knew then that Walker understood she would leave. And he did what she expected least: he sat down at the kitchen table and began to cry.

As sorrow welled within her, Sara steeled herself. He doesn't love *you,* she told herself. He's in love with what he thinks you ought to be. What he was trying to shape you into.

Walker cried all night and into the next day, stopping once to ask, "Was I really that bad to you?"

When she found she wanted to put her arms around him and say she'd make everything all right again, that she'd stay and be

(Very good)

good to him and he'd be good to her, Sara made herself think of the slime creature. Walker had been different once, before the slime creature had tainted his soul by convincing Walker that his own needs were far more important and immediate than anything Sara could need or want or even be.

When Walker stopped crying, he watched the movers take Sara's sofa and chairs and kitchen things. He stood, arms crossed, as if carved from ice.

"Are you all right?" Sara said.

Walker smiled. "You'll be back. You've forgotten how hard it is for you to support yourself—you had trouble doing that before you met me, remember? You've forgotten what it's like to be alone. You can leave—I know you'll come crawling back."

♦ ♦ ♦

Sara got a job and an apartment and went to Siberia with Daniel and he told her how much he had always been attracted to her.

Sara told herself, Go slow. It's too good to be true. "What?" she asked him carefully.

"Always," he said, excitedly. "Ever since the World Series." They gave each other a knowing look and burst out in simultaneous laughter.

Be careful, Sara. Don't get your hopes up.

He told her everything he liked about her, endlessly.

In mid-sentence she calmly interrupted him. "What about your fiancée?" Sara knew the woman's name but couldn't bear to say it, as if it would bring bad luck. "I mean, you *are* going to get married, aren't you?"

Daniel hesitated and looked away. "I don't know. I've told you about Pam, about our problems. It would never work with her. The only thing to do is break it off."

All hope broke loose, and it was all Sara could do to contain it within herself.

Daniel glanced at his watch. "Might as well get it over with. If I don't do it now, I never will." He kissed Sara's forehead. "I'll call you tomorrow."

Sara sat alone in the booth, overcome. Feeling that, at last, her hair had grown long enough to braid and cast from the window, no matter how high the tower.

♦ ♦ ♦

Daniel never called. He didn't show up in class for two weeks. When he came, he sat on the opposite side of the room from Sara.

"Hi," she said to him after class. "Are you game for Siberia?"

Daniel hesitated. "Yeah, sure, Sara. But I'll have to leave early tonight."

They crossed campus in silence. Sara made a few awkward attempts at conversation. Finally, Daniel said, "Look . . . I don't think it's such a good idea for us to talk after class anymore."

"Why not?"

He sighed. "I come to class straight after work—by the time I get home after talking to you, Pam's already asleep."

"You live with her?" Sara said.

"Well, yeah," Daniel said. "I moved in so we could see more of each other."

"I thought you were going to have a talk with her," Sara said, quietly.

Daniel cleared his throat, looking straight ahead. "I thought I told you already."

Sara fought to keep the shock out of her voice—and the panic. "No. You haven't told me anything." What if she had imagined his attraction to her. Maybe he had just been trying to tell her how much her friendship meant to him and she had misunderstood. That's it. She had misunderstood and made a fool of herself. And now she was putting Daniel on the spot.

Silence. Oh God, how long had there been silence? Nothing but the sound of their steps on the sidewalk.

Daniel cleared his throat again.

Damn him. Sara stumbled upon a fragment of memory: he had said he could talk to few people the way he could talk to Sara.

Friendship. Damn it, friendship.

He had said he loved talking to Sara for hours on end. Friendshp again.

Daniel. Sara stared straight ahead, the night seeming unreal, unfocused.

He had said he fantasized about her—*Sara*, not Pam!—living with her, about washing dishes together, making chocolate chip cookies and eating the batter raw, and waking up with her in his arms.

She hadn't imagined anything. Goddamn you, Daniel. She bit down on her lip until it made her wince.

He spoke, finally. "I tried to break it off with Pam. We talked for about a day and a half, straight through the night." He sighed, his breath clouding in the cool night air. "We didn't go to work, we didn't eat, didn't sleep—we just talked. Talked, screamed—she cried, I cried. We're going to try to work things out. I mean, we've known each other for years. She's . . ."

Safe, Sara thought. That's exactly what she is.

(an ordinary girl from the neighborhood who never did anything to earn a prince's true love—like being held captive by the slime creature)

Sara looked at Daniel, tears in her eyes. You've only known me for a couple of months, she thought. And I feel as if I've known you all my life.

◆ ◆ ◆

Sara dreamed that night. She dreamed of her adult self in her apartment visiting with her mother, no longer dead, and her father, no longer absent. Her parents laughed and looked happy together.

Sara went to the kitchen to pour some tea but noticed the pantry door ease open. A stranger emerged, a man with a large hunting knife. Sara's eyes widened, but she couldn't move. "Mama!" she yelled. "Mama Mama Mama Mama Mama!"

The stranger, a heavy-set man with a crew-cut, laughed softly and walked toward Sara. The knife blade gleamed in the kitchen light.

"Daddy!" Sara cried out, panic rushing through her. "Daddy! Help me!"

Her parents stood in the doorway between the kitchen and the living room, their eyes vacant. Sara didn't know whether they were frozen in fear or if they just couldn't see the man with the knife. They did not move.

As the stranger raised the edge of the knife to Sara's throat, she screamed, "Sara Bear!"

Sara bolted upright in bed in the dark, gasping for breath.

She raised a hand to her throat and, finding it uncut, pressed both hands against it.

Her clock glowed red numbers in the dark, 3:56. Sara sat perfectly still until it read 4:10, concentrating on breathing slowly, evenly, and listening for footsteps in the hall.

Someone pounded on her front door.

Mama Mama Mama.

Sara reached for the phone but stopped when she heard a girl's voice cry out. She ran to the front door in the dark. She wanted to fling it open, but she thought of the man in her dream. This wasn't a dream—it was too real. She rested her fingertips against the door and jumped as the pounding came again, reverberating in her hand. Her throat clutched.

"Help me!" the little girl screamed.

Sara opened the front door.

The little girl scrambled inside and shut the door, panting. She wore a beautiful gown, torn and bloody. Her blonde hair was singed. "Lock the door," she said.

Sara shook her head. She closed her eyes and rubbed them. When she looked again, the little girl was still there. "Lock the door *now*!" she said, urgently.

Sara rubbed a hand through her hair and headed back to her bedroom. "This isn't real," she muttered.

"How real," the girl said quietly, "does it have to get?"

Sara stopped suddenly, unsure of what mistake she'd be making if she kept walking.

(how real does it have to get?)

Sara remembered the feel of the slime left on her skin by the creature, sticky and sweaty and smelly. She remembered the scratch of the thorns against her skin, real enough to draw blood.

She remembered how it was to feel brave and strong and beautiful.

Footsteps behind. A small hand touched her. "I need you to help me," the child said seriously. "We have to kill the slime creature."

"Why?" Sara said.

The child cocked her head, squinting, as if trying to decide whether it was a trick question or a real one. She decided on the latter. "How can we make new friends if we're afraid they're going to hurt us? How else will we know the good people from the slime creatures?"

"What's the use?" Sara cried. "Don't you understand? There *are* no princes, no knights in shining armor. There *aren't* any good people—only slime creatures and mazes with no way out."

The little girl put her hands on her hips and held her head up proudly. "I *told* you. We've got to be able to tell the slime creatures from the good people. Slime creatures *pretend* to be princes sometimes."

In the distance, something cried out in anger.

Sara's voice trembled. "Will it follow you here?"

"I think so. I don't know for sure. We need a knife. A big one."

Tears welled in Sara's eyes. Mama Mama Mama. "Why?"

The little girl spoke matter-of-factly. "We have to chop its head off. That's the way it's done."

"Oh, God." Sara backed away.

The little girl crossed her arms, looking at Sara steadily. "I don't think I can do it by myself, but I will if I have to." Solemnly, she embraced Sara. "I love you," she whispered.

Stunned, Sara stroked the little girl's blonde hair. "I love you, Sara Bear."

And so they sat by the front door, waiting. With large knives from the cutlery drawer at their feet.

There was a wet, squishy sound of footsteps in the hallway. In the crack under the front door, there was a faint green glow.

They sat, holding hands, waiting for the slime creature to come into the room.

# JUST IDLE CHATTER

## by Jean Paiva

Jean Paiva, born and educated in New York City, yearned to be free of cement. Her first story was published in her school yearbook when she was eleven, but the murder mystery so shocked her mother that, for a while, Jean put down the writing pen and picked up the drawing pencil. She worked in New York, Alabama, London, and Argentina at a variety of jobs including typesetter, graphic artist, horror-film producer, music reviewer, columnist, paperback copy editor, marketing manager, and director of corporate communications. She was also interested in weaving and scuba diving. Her first horror-thriller novel, *The Lilith Factor,* was published in 1988 by New American Library under their Onyx imprint. In mid-1989 she turned in her second novel, *The Fortean Gamble.*

On a sad note, Jean died of cancer in the fall of 1989, long before she could see her story published. I think she would have been very pleased.

I remember when I was a child and received my first tape recorder. I identify all too well with this young lad.

♦ ♦ ♦

The muted greens of their summer dresses melted into the bush like camouflage. I'm sure they know this. They wear green every day they come to sit, which is every day it doesn't rain from May until September. I know what they wear because I watch them from my house, about one hundred yards up the road on a small hill, and my room fronts on the cul-de-sac they always face. Sure, sometimes I used binoculars—who wouldn't—but the glint of sun on their swiftly moving knitting needles always betrays their presence. Even without the binoculars.

They sit in folding aluminum chairs, their backs to the

mulberry bush, day in and day out. It's taken me weeks to finally work up my courage, ever since we had to put Sandy to sleep, but I was ready. I wouldn't be able to see them, not today, not from my new vantage point hidden *in* the mulberry bush, but for the first time I'd be able to hear them. Watching their mouths moving through my binoculars I often wondered what two old ladies could find to talk about. Mom said they probably chatted idly, just to pass time. What's "idly"?

Setting down these facts in my trusty cassette recorder, the one I used to tape Mom and Dad's last big fight from the next room, makes me more sure of myself. Proof, they say, is, well, I don't remember the word but it's still proof. Like, playing back the recording of my folks last big—I mean really big—fight started the truce they've been on ever since. Even though they now try to hide my rechargeable batteries. The tape recorder also makes me feel like I'm not spying or anything but more like a real investigative reporter—which is what I want to be. All I'm really doing is training for the big time and the facts surrounding Sandy's death seemed like the right place to start. One day when I'm famous and win some big award and they ask me how I started my career, I'll be able to tell them it was when my dog went mad.

The slam of their door, the only one in the neighborhood not on a compressed closer, alerted me they were on the way. I couldn't see as far as their house, not without poking my head out, but within two minutes they were in sight. Each in her usual shapeless green dress. Even Mom said they must have a closetful, all different shades of green.

Mom also said she thought they were sisters, but wasn't real sure. Jimmy, who lived *right next door* to them, swore they were mother and daughter. He heard them talking on their back porch one night and one called the other "Mother." He wasn't sure which was which, though. All I know is that they're *both* old. All wrinkly with flabby arms and wiry gray hair cut real short. They both wear stockings rolled down below their knees. You can't see the rolls when they walk, but when they sit it looks really gross. Especially through the binoculars.

As I watched them slowly work their way to the mulberry bush, I recorded the facts of this investigation. It wasn't really Sandy going crazy after he peed on the old lady's knitting that started me thinking as much as it was Polly Stillman's hand. Sandy was pretty old, after all, about fifteen years, and for a mutt that's a lot. Just because he started foaming at the mouth and snapping at everyone there was no *real* reason to connect that with the old lady throwing her ball of piss-soaked yarn at him and yelling (it was the first time anyone ever heard her yell) for half the neighborhood to hear. What she yelled, though, had something to do with it—I mean, it made me start thinking that these little old ladies might be some kind of strange—but not everything. All she really yelled, Jimmy told me later—and he heard it himself—was, "You mangy cur! May the wrath of Negri befall you!" It was real odd. Jimmy said he remembered it because it sounded like something out of the Conan the Destroyer book he was reading.

The vet said it was rabies. I was real upset and told the vet what Jimmy said the old lady said and he gave me a curious look. Then he got out a big animal medicine book and showed me something about Negri viruses being in the brain of rabid dogs.

Seeing that they were almost close enough to hear, I wisely stopped whispering into my tape recorder. Investigative reporters don't get caught on their first real snoop—I mean scoop. Leaving the RECORD button down and the tape running, I scooted back a little more into the bush—just to be sure I was completely hidden. The soft hum of the recorder, which sounded real loud to me on the ground, would—I planned—go unnoticed by the old ladies. With a little bit of luck the soft bird trills and occasional traffic would be enough of a cover.

Listening to them set up their chairs seemed to take forever. Old ladies get real picky about the exact spot their chair is in, which way it faces, how close it is to the bush and exactly where each one's knitting bag would be. Waiting for them to settle in and begin talking, really talking—not this stuff about "move the chair a little to the left"—I started to think about Mrs. Stillman.

Mrs. Stillman was pretty cool for an adult. She wanted us to call her Polly, even though she was so grown up she had a little baby.

My mom said that Mrs. Stillman wasn't cut out to be a mother and she should have married a rich man and had lots of maids—that her house was always a mess and all she cared about were her long fingernails. But what Mom didn't know was that Mrs. Stillman, I mean Polly, always had soda in the fridge for us kids and lots of chocolate cookies. Just because her baby cried a lot was no reason to say she wasn't a good mother. The kid was a snotty brat. *Real* snotty. Always wailing with gross globs of stuff coming out of its nose. No wonder Polly didn't want to pick it up, or anything. I don't even blame her for swatting it now and again.

She gave it—the kid—a good hard swipe that day, right in front of the old ladies. I just happened to be watching through my binoculars and saw them waving their knitting at Polly, but no one heard what they said to her.

That night Mrs. Stillman lost her diamond ring in the kitchen sink—one with a garbage disposal unit. No one knows how the unit turned on while her hand was in there, poking around for the ring, but the ambulance driver told us that the four fingers that got sliced clear off at the first joint were too mangled to be sewn back on.

The click-clack click-clack of the old ladies knitting needles finally started and beat out a simple, hypnotic rhythm.

"Edna," the one to my right said, "it sure is a beautiful day."

I finally had a name!

"Sure is," said Edna, "and quiet, too."

Long moments passed as Edna and the other old lady sat and clicked and clacked their long shiny needles. Even from under the bush I could see the sun catch the silver spears and wink the tireless movements to me.

"You know, Hattie," I heard just as I began to drift off, and woke right up again! I finally had both their names, even though from the back I couldn't tell who was who. Come to think of it, I probably couldn't tell them apart from the front either. "We haven't seen that nice man who fed the pigeons every day. I wonder if he's gone away?"

"Tsk, tsk, Edna, you know that those pigeons were dirty filthy birds that brought disease and mites and shat up the bushes and windows," Hattie said. "Why would you want that man around anyway?"

"He was nice to us, Hattie. Why, remember how he'd tip his hat when he went by and always said, just as nice as you please, 'Good morning, ladies.' For some reason not many people talk to us, you know. It was pleasant seeing him, that's all." Having had her say, Edna picked up the rhythm of her knitting again.

"I heard he had an accident," the one on my right, Hattie, said.

"What kind of accident? He seemed such a nice, safe person."

"Choked on a Cornish hen bone. They're like small chickens, or pigeons. Happens a lot, nowadays. People choking and all. They even put signs up in restaurants on what to do when something goes down the wrong pipe. But he was home. Alone."

The sound of four knitting needles stopped as Edna and Hattie paused to reflect, it seemed, on the dangers the modern world held.

After a while the click-clack click-clack started up and, once again, I found myself being lulled by the sound, by the sweet smells of newly mown lawns and maybe even by the soft breeze and warm sun both finding their way to me despite my cover.

"Talking about people we haven't seen," one of the women said, but in my drowsy state I couldn't figure which one, "what ever happened to the man who drove by in that

# ACT OF LOVE

## by Kristl Volk Franklin

Kristl Volk Franklin, a native of Germany, emigrated to the U.S. as a child. With the help of TV shows such as *The Mickey Mouse Club*, *Sky King*, and *Broken Arrow*, English quickly became her second language. Although she has lived in in New York, Louisiana, Texas, and Oklahoma, she considers the South her home. A few years ago she began writing again, after a lapse of twenty years. Her work has appeared in *My Weekly*, *Piecework*, *Byline*, *Lives of Real People*, *Woman's World*, and *Women of the West*. She has published short stories and articles in the U.S. and Great Britain and has won numerous state and regional writing awards in Arkansas, Texas, and Oklahoma. A member of Horror Writers of America, she's currently working on a psychological suspense novel titled, *Hush, Little Baby*. Kristl now lives in Denver with her husband of twenty-two years and their three school-age children.

Kristl may have left the South, but the South hasn't left her. This story is very much Southern Gothic.

♦ ♦ ♦

There is a beginning to madness. A specific moment when time turns inside out to expose another dimension of existence. Some describe the process of insanity as falling headlong into a black pit, entering a different reality through a tear in the fabric of Self—a reality where the subconscious acts without constraints; where good and evil are extensions of each other and destruction is an act of love.

For Memory Anne Adams the madness began when she was twenty-eight months old.

The noises nudged her.

At first the sounds were low and guttural and then gained intensity until they woke her completely.

Rubbing her fists in her eyes, Memory sat up on her bed,



noisy station wagon? The wreck of a thing that used to backfire all the time? My word, every time it happened I thought someone was taking a shot at us."

"His was a sad case," said Edna, which meant Hattie had asked the question. "He suffered a severe gaseous disorder and just couldn't pass the gas. His stomach ruptured and they didn't get to the hospital in time."

"How sad," murmured Hattie.

"Isn't it the truth," commented Edna, sounding very wise.

There was something I knew I was missing in all this, but the sounds, smells and warmth under the bush began to work their way on me and soon I found my eyes closing. The last thing I remember thinking before surrendering to sleep was that at least I had my tape recorder running.

The dream was odd: Edna and Hattie stood at either end of my street waving their knitting needles in the air like two crazed orchestra conductors. I even dreamt the music. A swelling of all the stringed instruments I knew from music appreciation class with a hundred musicians following their lead, the movements soaring with each wild wave of a flabby arm. There were drum rolls and loud cymbal crashes every time one of the old ladies pointed her knitting needle at a house, or a person, or a car, or a cat or a dog or a fire hydrant that burst wide open—gushing water into the sky and drenching everything but the two old ladies.

I was soaking wet. It was raining, hard, and here I was, all alone, under the mulberry bush. The tape had finished and the machine stopped, who knew how long ago. I didn't even know what time it was now except that it was time to get home and dry off.

The warmth of my house, the promise of dry clothes and the smell of fresh brownies has got to be one of those rare treasured moments of life that people talk about. Especially the brownies. I grabbed a rich, thick chocolate wedge, still warm and bursting with walnuts, from the kitchen counter and dashed up the stairs to change before Mom spotted me. Lectures about staying out in the rain are *not* appreciated.

Hitting the REWIND button as soon as I had my door closed, I rummaged through my closet floor for the jeans I'd worn only three or four times and also lucked out finding a reasonably clean shirt. Stripping off the soggy set, I threw myself, brownie in hand, on my bed. The tape had rewound and waited to be played.

Pushing PLAY I again listened to the sounds of this very morning: my brilliant reportage of the facts, my breathtaking announcement that the old ladies were on their way, the endless sounds of them settling in for the day and my deductive masterpiece in finding out their names.

This time, though, the nagging questions I'd fallen asleep with not only surfaced but began to form into some pretty ugly answers. The old man with the pigeons who choked on the hen bone was Henry Muller, who most people liked. I remembered hearing about his dying last month. The guy in the car had to be that creep from the butcher shop who almost went out of business because he couldn't stop breaking wind in front of customers. His farts did sound like his car backfiring and he never did anything about stopping either.

They were quiet a while, which is when I must have fallen asleep—just the click-clack click-clack recording loud and clear. Then Edna, I think it was Edna, said something that made me stop chewing the last of the brownie.

"That boy," she said, "the one who lives up there at the end of the road." I could almost see her pointing with her knitting needles to my house. "Have you ever noticed the sun glint off his windows when he's watching us?"

"All the time, dear, all the time. I wonder what he does to make that flash of light."

"Well, I don't wonder at all. I know. He's using binoculars to spy on us, and who knows how many other innocent people he's watching when they least expect it."

"Binoculars? Do you really think so? Dear me. It's possible, I guess. And it *would* account for the reflections only happening when we know he's home."



"I told you I'm sure, didn't I? Anyway, he'd b
it. Those things can be dangerous, you know."

"Why, how could a pair of binoculars ever hurt

"The same way a magnifying glass can start a
know. The lens will reverse the sun directly into
and blind him. Maybe even burn into his brain a
him."

"That would be a terrible thing to happen to s
young boy."

"Yes, but would you rather he grew up to be one of t
filthy perverts we read about?"

"I guess not. But . . ."

And my tape ended.

a small cotton-ticked mattress that rested directly on the floor, and tried to see, tried to find her mother.

"Momma," she called out. There was no answer.

The murky late afternoon sun seeped around the edges of the heavy window shade covering the one window in her room and gave shape to her little rocking chair with Amanda, her doll, propped at an angle. But not even the sight of the doll nor the familiar colored shadows of her clothes hanging on pegs along one wall reassured her—these things no longer made her feel safe.

The noise came again. It was a howl this time that sounded like a wild, crazed animal in pain. She was scared. So scared. Where was her momma? She stuck her right thumb in her mouth and listened carefully to the sound. It was a low groaning and panting now and seemed to come from the bathroom down the hall from her room.

"Momma," she tried to yell again, but the tears choked the word in her throat and made it weak.

"MemORY." The voice started her name low, as if it were another groan, and then rose on the last syllable. It was Momma. Somehow Momma was in the bathroom with the noise. And she was calling for her.

It took only a second for Memory Anne to scoot off her bed and scamper to the bathroom, her bare feet slapping the cold wood floor. The bathroom's door was partially open and the light spilled out to the hall. But when she reached for the door, something made Memory Anne pause and still her hand on the glass doorknob. It wasn't only the sound that was horrible—she grabbed her nose and opened her mouth—it was the smell.

The odor was heavy and dank, like the many times Poppa and Uncle Larry had gone hunting and brought back a deer. The skinned carcass, glistening pink, had hung with the hind legs bound, pointing skyward, and the forelimbs straight down, with a stump where the head should have been. Uncle Larry would take his hunting knife and slit the body from between the hind legs, down the belly, through to the throat. The shimmering entrails boiled forth in the wake of the opening as if the dead animal were giving birth to its own innards. The smell was the same. The same smell of blood and cut flesh and body fluids now made Memory Anne hold the tip of her pink little nose, which Uncle Larry said looked like a sea shell. She pushed open the door to the bathroom.

A woman lay on the floor, the back of her head propped against the side of the deep, claw-footed bathtub, her legs sprawled out toward the entrance. Memory Anne recoiled and started to close the door—as if the scene in the bathroom was a mistake, a mistake she made by opening the door and looking in.

Like the time she woke up early from her nap on one other day and had gone into her parents' room. Two adults, without a single stitch of clothing on, had been writhing on the bed. To Memory Anne it was the strangest sight she'd ever seen—Momma's white legs sticking straight up from Uncle Larry's shoulders. Later when she asked her poppa about it, he didn't say a word. But she knew he was mad at her. Somehow, opening that bedroom door had been a mistake. Now, opening the bathroom door was also a mistake. If only she could shut it and start all over. Then the sight of Momma and the blood wouldn't be there.

"Memory." This time the name was a whisper. Memory Anne pushed at the door again. But, instead of looking first at the woman on the floor, she concentrated on other things in the room. Her small tube of Ipana and new pink toothbrush stood straight in her peanut-butter jar. The string shopping bag with her bath toys hung in its place next to her wood-framed potty chair with its own little lid. Her small toilet supported a limp arm; another arm draped over the closed seat of the big toilet. The woman on the floor lay panting, gasping for air, as if she'd been under water too long. Memory almost didn't recognize her mother.

Momma's face was white and swollen. Her eyes were squeezed so tightly shut it looked like it hurt. Her maternity top, the one she'd made out of dotted Swiss to wear around the house, was bunched under her arms, exposing the bottom half of her melon breasts. From there down she was naked. Her large stomach rose up and around and down the way it had grown these last few months.

Momma lurched forward and grasped her knees. Her mouth opened and her head went back. The noises started again—a deep throat moaning that sounded like the wind coming around the corner of Memory's bedroom.

"Momma?" she asked, but Momma wasn't listening. Something was happening. Something the little girl couldn't understand. Without knowing exactly why, her attention was drawn to the patch of short black hair between her mother's legs.

Memory Anne had seen her mother naked before. They often bathed together. She knew about the secret places on her mother's body, about the special openings that mommies had. But this was different. And this was a different Momma.

At that moment, with a great expulsion of breath, Momma flung herself back, her head thumping against the edge of the bathtub and her arms once again grasping the two toilets.

She lay so still.

"Momma? Momma, are you dead?"

Her mother opened her eyes and leaned forward, supporting herself on one elbow. "Memory, come here." She motioned to her with one hand. Memory edged closer.

"Listen carefully . . ." Momma began to say but then trailed off as her chest heaved again. She started to take deep breaths. "Go—get—Miss—Reed—" Her head flew back and a yell exploded from her.

At that Memory also started to wail. "Me don't want to . . . me scared . . ." The two cries—one from the laboring woman, the other from the frightened child, mingled, strangely harmonizing.

"Oh, God, it's too late," Momma yelled and then broke into sobs. "Help me . . . someone help me. . . ."

Memory Anne's own cries stopped abruptly when a peculiar sight distracted her. Something that looked like a small ball was coming out between her mother's legs. It emerged slowly, then slid back, then bulged again until it was almost out. On one side of the circle was a tiny nose and two tiny eye slits that were closed.

Momma reared up again, clutching at her legs which quivered uncontrollably. "Damn you, Carl . . . damn you to hell. . . ." She gave a mighty grunt and her face turned beet red. As she rocked back to take another deep breath, she yelled, "Damn you for doing this to me . . . you bastard . . . you left me . . . you son of a bitch."

With that, the object, stuck in Momma's special opening, slid out into a congealed puddle of fluid on the cold linoleum floor. Memory Anne stepped forward and crouched down to get a better look.

It had a tiny body, the same size as her doll Amanda, but the head was much bigger. It moved its mouth and mewled weakly. It was hooked to a slippery looking rope that came out of her mother.

The infant gave a couple more cries before it was still—still forever. . . .

Memory Anne cried when the three of them stood around the hole that Poppa dug in the back pasture. Back where the ground was low and soft and not good for anything else except burying.

Momma didn't cry at all. Not even at the sight of the small bundle wrapped in a worn-out quilt scrap or at the soft thud it made hitting the bottom of the hole when Poppa dropped it in. Of course, Poppa didn't cry either. And when Memory's own cries turned into sobs, Momma gave her a couple of sharp slaps on her bottom. The baby was better off this way, Momma said. The baby's head had been too big, not normal-like. The baby girl wasn't meant to live.

"At least, not in this world," Momma said, as if there were another place somewhere that some children were meant to live.

Memory Anne thought a great deal about that place where children were better off during her growing-up years at the farm. And she often went to that spot at the back of the pasture. When she was sure no one was around, she would lie on the little mound covered with sweet-smelling clover and look up into the open sky and take trips deep down inside of herself. She thought about what it would be like to be dead, cradled by the warm soft earth. It soothed her. Especially when she felt a particular violent episode coming on. (Spells, Momma called them.)

Three more infants, girls, were eventually buried near that spot. Memory named each one, including the little girl who died on the bathroom floor, Darian. Because the family had little money, and her poppa had no predisposition for such frills as hospitals and obstetricians, Memory was the only one present each time her mother gave birth. The remaining four surviving children she helped her mother deliver were boys.

After the birth and death of the first Darian, life changed for Memory and her mother. Poppa stopped going hunting. He evicted the Reeds, who lived half a mile down the dirt road from them and who had sharecropped the acreage that Poppa planted. He began going to town by himself once a month and purchased all the staples and extras the farm didn't provide.

Except for this once-a-month shopping trip and the rare occasions he was called to work at the gravel pits, Poppa never left the farm. No one ever came to visit at their place, either.

Not even Uncle Larry.

Memory Anne missed the lively young man who threw her up in the air and then caught her, all the while pretending he might not. He'd bought her a red hair ribbon and called her his pumpkin. Because of her orange-red hair that matched his own carrot top, she supposed. She missed Uncle Larry. When Memory Anne asked about him, Momma slapped her across the face, leaving a red mark of her fingers imprinted on the little girl's cheek.

"Don't say his name—do you hear me? Not ever—ever," her mother whispered hoarsely. With her face on fire and her ear ringing, Memory barely heard the rest of her mother's stiff explanation that Uncle Larry had moved to Virginia.

For years Memory thought about her uncle, who, as she learned as she got older, wasn't her uncle at all but a friend of the family's. She thought about him and other secret things whenever she could, especially when she walked her brothers down the country road that ran through their property to catch the school buss at the blacktop main road.

When Memory's brothers become a certain age, Poppa provided each boy with store-bought clothes and shoes and sent them for schooling on the days he didn't need them in the fields. Memory was nine when the three-mile walks down the road began. At first it was only she and Lance, who was three years younger, scuffing up little clouds of dirt on their way to the bus stop. Lance carried his new shoes, tucked in the sides of his overalls, whenever possible. And delayed the trip by making side sorties to pick dewberries that grew in wild tangles in the ditches. By the time Memory pushed him on the bus, purple was smeared across his mouth and tiny briar scratches crisscrossed his hands. Royce came next and, in his eagerness, always streaked ahead of them on the hot, red-dusty road. By the time Jake was old enough to trail along, Haven, the last boy, was still too little for school. Haven never did get to board the yellow school bus.

Memory held Haven's hand firmly to keep him from taking off across the fields after a jackrabbit or a poppin' jay. Jake trailed a few feet behind, dragging the lard bucket that held his biscuit and ham through gravel. Tears made clean paths down his dusty cheeks. Jake hated school and started crying the minute they left the house. How Memory yearned to take his place. School. It was a magic word to her. Sometimes as the boys filed on the bus, she imagined that Mr. Wheaton would lean out and yell to her, "Come on aboard, Memory Anne."

"But where is the bus going, Mr. Wheaton—I mean really going?"

"Why to a better place, Memory Anne."

But Mr. Wheaton never leaned out and he never invited her aboard.

Other than that bit of yearning, she didn't question the fact that she didn't go to school while her brothers did. The bus was empty when it stopped in the mornings and empty when it finished its run in the afternoons. She had no way of knowing that girls might be expected to attend school until the year when Lance mentioned something about it to Poppa at the supper table.

She'd been preoccupied with softening a piece of crumbled cornbread with warm pot liquor so she could feed toddler Haven. Momma was in the bedroom, sitting in the rocking chair. She did that sometimes. Memory Anne would get up in the morning and find her mother just sitting, her face toward the wall, staring at nothing. She stayed that way for days or weeks while Memory took care of the family and the chores, helping her mother to the bathroom and spooning food and liquids down her. This time Momma's belly was growing again, and her flesh hung from her arms like chicken skin. Memory was considering what she could force down that reluctant throat when Lance spoke up.

"Poppa, Mr. Wheaton ask me today how come a young'n as big as Memory ain't going to school." Lance's words came out in phrases between mouthfuls of collards and cornbread.

"Who in the hell is Mr. Wheaton?" Poppa asked sharply.

Seeing the fury gathering on her father's face, Memory looked away quickly. But the words "Memory" and "school" echoed in her ears.

Lance washed down a large bite with a gulp of buttermilk and answered prematurely, almost choking on a piece of cornbread.

"Mr. Wheaton's the bus driver," he finally got out.

Poppa didn't say anything for a long while. Memory hung close to the table. She wiped Haven's mouth, filled Poppa's iced tea glass, washed a few things in the sink, anything so she could hear what Poppa would say. It wasn't until he'd finished his meal and started to push away from the table that he said, "Listen here, Lance, I want you to tell Mr. Wheaton, or anybody else that should ask, the reason she don't go to school or go galavantin' off nowheres is because our Memory Anne is simple."

Memory stood stunned at the kitchen sink. Poppa fixed Lance with one of his stares.

"Schooling don't do her kind no good," he added. He made Lance repeat to him what he'd said to make certain the boy got it right. Then, satisfied, he slid back his chair and left.

Memory, frozen at the sink, washed everything that came under her hand, floored by this revelation. She knew what being "simple" meant; slow, dumb—not quite right in the head. But she wasn't simple! Why, by the time she had turned nine, Memory knew she could do everything a full-grown woman was expected to do. She helped birth babies, picked the garden, canned fruits and vegetables, fixed meals, tended children, washed, cleaned—everything her mother had taught her to do. She was a fast learner and smart, too. She'd taught herself to read and write just from helping Lance and Royce with their lessons.

She felt her insides churning at her father's words and the hurt was like worms in her chest—writhing and twisting until the pain made her dizzy and out of breath. When she couldn't stand it anymore, she dashed out of the house to the front porch.

Poppa sat on the edge of the porch with his legs almost touching the ground the same as always, as if nothing had happened—as if her whole world hadn't stopped. Lying beside him were rags, rods and things that he used in cleaning his deer rifle. Shiny bullets lined up in a row, like tiny soldiers, along the edge of the porch. The wood of the rifle stock shimmered like brown satin under his arm and the blue-grey metal of the barrel that rested in the crook of his arm gleamed softly. The muzzle pointed down at his feet. Poppa cleaned his rifle every night, right after supper.

Memory Anne squatted next to him, pulled the length of her shift over her knees, and wrapped her arms around her legs.

The night had a damp chill to it brought by a careless wind that blew across the open porch. The crickets and frogs screamed in the dark recesses of the night.

"Pop-p-pa," she stammered, her hurt crawling up into her throat, making it hard to speak. "Why did you say that?" No answer. Only silence from the dark-haired man cleaning his rifle.

She tried again. "Why would you say something like that—you know it ain't true."

The cries of the insects and other animals filled the emptiness between the two figures on the lit porch.

Presently, her father leaned over the side of the plank flooring and spat, sending a long stream of yellow tobacco juice into the night.

"Just listen to that racket," he commented, and sent out another stream of juice, smaller and more arched. The porch light caught the crest of it and gave it a sparkle like a rhinestone. "I guess it's fixin' to rain."

"I ain't dumb, Poppa," Memory persisted. She thought her heart might burst. In her mind's eye she imagined blood spurting from her ears and dripping from her nose and mouth. Is that what happens if your heart explodes?

"No, you ain't dumb, Memory Anne. You're plumb smart for a little gal." Poppa's voice grew dangerously soft and Memory sucked in her breath. "But I couldn't rightly tell them people the truth now, could I?"

"The truth?" The girl's heart pounded so hard the thin material binding her chest quivered.

"Why, Memory Anne—you know how you are, with your spells and all."

Her body stiffened. And she thought her heart stopped for a few seconds and then started pounding again. She had forgotten about her "spells." She always did until the next one. It's not fair, she screamed deep inside of herself. She never remembered doing the things they said she must have done; Momma catching her smearing a baby's dirty diaper on the walls in her parents' bedroom; one of the boys reporting that she stood trancelike at the edge of the barn's loft with a rope around her neck. And then the last time, Poppa found the soft rotting body of a mother cat and her seven newborn kittens when he got to the bottom of the grain storage bin, small pieces of Memory's red ribbon knotted around the scrawny necks.

Memory Anne didn't remember any of the "craziness" as her mother called it. Surely if you were genuinely mad, you'd remember it, wouldn't you? Inside of yourself you would know if you were insane. Wouldn't you?

On the porch the wind dwindled down to nothing and the mosquitoes came out in full force. Poppa slapped the side of his neck. "Besides, this is the place you belong," he mumbled. "No sense in you going off somewhere and whoring around."

*Whoring around.* The blood drained from her face and pooled around her heart. She felt lifeless.

So that was it. That's what this had been about all along. She should've known! Her muscles contracted, and she kicked out her legs stiffly in an effort to get up. She had to get away. Her foot caught against the row of bullet soldiers and sent them flying out into the yard. She had to get away from the sight of Poppa calmly and carefully polishing the rifle, the small piece of flannel caressing the barrel. With one long stride she leaped off the porch and ran into the darkness.

She felt destroyed, as if something had eaten away at her insides until there wasn't anything left to give her life. For at that moment, all the pieces fell into place and it came to her that Poppa would never let her leave—not as long as he lived.

But it wasn't because she was simple . . . or because of her spells.

It was their punishment, hers and Momma's. For being whores . . .

About every month or so, right after he came back with the supplies from town, Poppa did a little celebrating.

"Gotta cut loose somehow," he would mutter. "I'm tied to this goddamn house, you whore." He spat the words in her momma's face. "Can't go nowheres on account of I've got to keep an eye on you."

The celebrations always happened deep in the night, after all the little ones were in bed asleep. But Memory kept herself awake, knowing what was coming. Afraid to look but unable not to, she eased over the hot sweaty bodies of her brothers and crept to the door. The keyhole was the kind where if you squinted and angled just right you could see into the next room.

There was a large wooden beam that ran along the ceiling in the main living area. At the far end of the room, straight in the line of her vision, an iron hook projected from the bottom of the beam, close to the front window. During the day, a plant hung from that hook—a plant in a macramé plant holder that Momma had made when she and Poppa were first married. Now, the hook was bare, the dull metal dimly visible in the half light of the room.

He hung Momma from that hook. Time after time.

Her crossed wrists bound with twine; her arms overhead pointing skyward; her body stripped of its thin shift and underwear. The way the muted light hit the crevices and planes of her body with its sagging breasts and bloated belly made her look like the pink-fleshed deer he and Uncle Larry used to dress.

The things he did to Momma as she swung from that hook were things that Memory Anne took deep down inside herself.

He always started by straddling a chair he'd brought from the kitchen and then just sat, looking at the hanging figure for the longest time, taking deep pulls on the bottle of wine he held in one hand. His other arm cradled his rifle. Another swig at the bottle. And another. When it was empty he set it on the floor, loosened the front of his pants, and urinated into the bottle.

That's when Momma started to whimper. Not loud. Just a low, hurt, little whimper.

Sometimes, he stopped in the middle of what he was doing and with long quick strides came over to the door of the bedroom where Memory crouched behind the keyhole. Heart pounding, she barely had time to scurry back to her place on the crowded bed before the door eased open. She felt the light from the other room on her body and she felt him standing at the threshold, watching. But, after a few minutes, he always closed the door quietly and went back to the woman dangling from the hook.

One particular incident terrified the girl every time she witnessed it and closed every avenue of escape that she might have imagined.

"You thinkin' of leavin' me, whore?" he whispered hoarsely to her mother, on a night after coming home from town. "Thinkin' of sneaking off, you and that red-haired brat of yours?"

Abruptly, he straightened his knees, dismounted the chair, and stood next to Momma. She kicked out at him half-heartedly and he grabbed one of her flailing legs, pulling it up and over his shoulder. Then he took the long barrel of the rifle and forced it in her as far as it would go.

"This is what'll happen to you, whore, if I catch ya." He had to put one knee on the floor in order to reach the trigger. Momma arched her back and became motionless, her thin legs trying to find purchase on her husband's shoulder. She cried quietly and hysterically. The seconds passed with excruciating slowness, before he, finally, mercifully, squeezed the trigger. The click made a tiny sound. The sound of life. The death of hope.

It always ended the same. When he tired, he eased the rope down. The white, bruised body crumpled into a heap. Then, before he untied her wrists, he fumbled with the front of his pants again and mounted her—like the stallion

Memory had seen across the main road, rearing up on any mare that held still long enough.

Then it would be over until the next month, unless Momma was carrying. He never touched her then. But, right after the baby was born, it would start all over again the night he came home from town.

Poppa never bothered Memory Anne—or the boys, for that matter. Of course, there had been times when she was little and he'd cuddled her in his lap with his hand under her dress. He tickled her special places. One time he did it too hard and hurt her.

The next day all the knives in the house were gone. She first noticed it when Momma broke the carrots she was fixing for supper instead of cutting them.

"Don't you need a knife, Momma?"

"There ain't no knives anymore, Memory Anne."

"What do you mean?"

Her mother stopped a moment, pieces of carrot still in her hand, and propped herself on the edge of the kitchen sink. She stared out the window. There was nothing to see except acres of plowed fields stretching to the horizon.

"Has Poppa ever done anything . . . well . . . bad to you?" Momma said. There was a strange hesitancy in her voice.

"Oh, no, he'd never hurt me."

Her mother looked down into the sink at the bowl of potatoes that were soaking. Laying the carrot aside, she picked up a potato and began scrubbing at the brown skin.

"Last night you must of had a . . . nightmare," she said in a casual tone, her eyes hidden from Memory Anne. "And it started you off on one of your bad spells. You ran into the kitchen, grabbed the knife out of the cupboard and tried to . . . cut your Poppa. Said you wanted to slice his fingers off." She shook her head and selected another potato. "Land o'sakes, don't know what's gotten into you, child. These spells of your'n are gettin' worse."

Memory had many more spells after that. But Poppa

never held her in his lap or caressed her again and she and Momma never talked about the nights Poppa came home from town. . . .

The day the last baby was born was bad.

That morning Memory Anne took her time shuffling down the hot dirt road with her little brothers. The white of the sun burned through the thin material of her flour sack shift, but she barely noticed because she was lost in the depth of her thoughts. Thoughts that no one knew about. Thoughts she was afraid to put into words.

After the bus drove off, belching and grinding its gears, she stood for a long time in the sun, exhaust fumes in her hair and on her clothes and the heavy tarry odor of the soft blacktop road enveloping her—smells of another world. How easy it would be to start walking, and walk, and walk—and never stop, she thought. But, instead of heading down the main road, she turned to make her way back home, dragging behind her a protesting Haven. For all her thinking and planning, she couldn't imagine the world out there and how she could live in it. All she knew was the farm. And if she didn't go back, what would happen to Momma? Without her, what would Momma do?

By the time she returned to the house, her mother was already in hard labor. It would go quickly this time.

Memory had everything she needed ready at hand. She dropped a pair of scissors in a pan of water and put it on to boil. Sent Haven out to play. And went back into the bedroom where Momma grunted. Her mother raised up in the bed, knees flared almost even with the mattress, and held on to her ankles. Memory took a quick look under the sheet.

The padding under the buttocks was already soaked. She changed it, and when Momma relaxed after the last contraction, tried to see how far along things were.

One tiny foot hung out of the vagina.

"Somethin' wrong, Memory," her mother said between gasps. "It ain't never been like this before. I push and push and nothing happens."

"It's coming out the wrong way," Memory whispered. She looked at her mother's face closely and noticed for the first time the blue shadow around her mouth and the paleness of her skin—she looked as if every drop of blood had been drained out of her.

Fear greater than anything she'd ever known before flooded over Memory and left her drenched in sweat. She saw death in Momma's face—the shallow breathing, the gray sunken eye sockets. Her mother was dying. And, if her mother died—Memory Anne turned away from the moaning figure on the bed and stood by the bedroom window where she saw the light gleam from the metal of Poppa's rifle, leaning against the side of the tool shed—if her mother died, there was no telling what Poppa was likely to do. Still looking out of the window, she watched her father prop back the hood of the old Ford truck and tuck his head inside. Memory knew it was only his fear of her, a primitive, unspoken fear that she saw in his eyes, that stood between them and gave her a thin shield of protection. For there was a reason why Poppa "celebrated" in the front room instead of the relative privacy of their bedroom. She had figured it out long ago.

He knew she watched.

He wanted her to know.

And there was no doubt in her mind that one day soon Poppa's fear would not be enough to protect her on the nights he came home from town.

She looked again at the pale bloated woman on the bed. There was no reason, no reason at all, for him to want to lift a finger to save Momma.

The eighth baby, a girl, was delivered in the early morning hours of the next day and Memory knew she would be the last.

She washed the squalling infant in warm water and wrapped her in a small piece of flannel. The house was quiet. Poppa had headed toward town, to try to find a part for the truck, he'd said. The boys still slept; it would be a few hours yet before they'd have to get up for school.

Momma rested in her bed. She'd lost consciousness after her last feeble effort to push. Memory had to pull the small limp body out of her and a gush of blood followed. She'd packed a towel in the gaping vagina and the bleeding seemed to have slowed.

Tired beyond belief, Memory carried the baby with her to the living room window, next to the macramé plant hanger. The plant in it had been dead for a long time. She balanced the baby on her shoulder while she tugged at curtains heavy with country dust and pulled them aside.

The morning was just breaking. Light streamed through the mist formed by the warmth of the earth meeting the coldness of the night. It would dry up by breakfast, she knew, and another suffocating hot day would press on them.

The baby in her arms let out a lusty cry, surprisingly strong after her ordeal. Memory Anne held the infant up and in front of her, the tiny face toward the window.

"See there, Darian, that's the world out there." The baby sagged forward and Memory expertly turned her to hold her in the crook of her arm. Taking small steps, swaying in a rocking motion, Memory walked into the kitchen and began to sing to the child, "Hush, little baby, don't say a word, Poppa's gonna buy you a mockin'bird . . ."

Momma had prepared a cardboard box for this expected child and had lined it with a pad made of old material to serve as the mattress and a worn baby's blanket for cover. Memory stood in front of the box that was on the kitchen table, still rocking the baby in time to the lullaby. She hugged little Darian up against her shoulder, the small face that looked so much like her own turned against the cloth of her dress. She tightened her hand behind the head as she had with the other girl babies, pressing the face against her shoulder. The baby's hair felt soft as down.

The infant began to squirm a little.

Memory pushed harder. And sang, "Hush, little baby, don't say a word . . ."

Finally, when the little body stopped moving all together

and the arms and legs went limp, Memory very carefully nestled the dead child in the makeshift bed, just as she had with the other Darians. The tiny face looked peaceful above the faded yellow of the baby's blanket, as if the child were napping. Memory had to look closely to see the blue tint of the skin and the eyelids rolled half open. She tucked in the edge of the blanket around the doll-like feet. A smile curled the corners of Memory's mouth. Darian was in a better place now.

Memory Anne felt peace as sweet as anything she'd ever known, and she was no longer exhausted. She wanted to finish watching the morning come in, but before going to the front porch, she poked her head into her mother's room. The still white figure on the bed seemed dead. But she saw the quilt rise and fall with life and was reassured.

When she reached the porch, she hugged her breasts and briskly rubbed her arms, more for comfort than against any coolness the morning still held. She had to find a way, she thought again, for no telling how many times. A way to free them. She walked across the porch and sat on the cement steps that led out into the yard.

Gentle fingers of wind lifted the hair that looked as if fire lived in it away from her face. She raised her head to catch the breeze and closed her eyes for a moment, shutting out the world. When, at last, she opened them, a glint of light stung her. Something lay hidden in the grass by the side of the porch. She knew immediately what it was. Her breath caught in her throat and her insides clenched in a spasm. For a moment she felt lightheaded and the brightness of the morning swam in front of her. But she was scarcely aware of this, because the object she picked up from the grass demanded her full attention.

Her hand closed on the bullet and she slid it in the pocket of her dress. She glanced over to the tool shed where Poppa had left his rifle propped inside the door. Feeling the outline of the bullet through the thin material of her dress, she squeezed her eyes shut and saw a white body hanging from a hook and a rifle stock like brown satin. And heard a click.

Something inside her burst open and she felt a sweet sense of release that entered every pore of her body.

"There's a better place than this for you, Momma," she said out loud.

Six long strides to the tool shed. Two quick motions with the bolt. One bullet slid carefully in the chamber.

Memory Anne returned the rifle to its place inside the shed's door.

Now all they had to do was wait—wait for Poppa to come home from town.

# ARC LIGHT

## by Lisa W. Cantrell

Lisa W. Cantrell is a past member of the board of directors of RoVaCon Scholarship Funds, Inc., an annual science fiction convention (held in Virginia's Roanoke Valley) that supports seven academic scholarships, and is currently on their professional advisory board. She's a past Secretary for Horror Writers of America. Lisa has a business college degree, has worked as a legal secretary, and for fifteen years has helped run a small family business that specializes in building bulk storage tanks—hence her knowledge of welding and metal fabrication. She actually tried welding herself, but says she wasn't too good at it. *The Manse,* published in 1987 by Tor Books, won her the HWA Bram Stoker Award for Superior Achievement for a first novel. Her second, *The Ridge,* was published in 1989 by Tor, and her third, a sequel to *The Manse,* is tentatively scheduled for 1990. Her short stories have appeared in *Cricket: The Magazine for Children* and *Alfred Hitchcock's Mystery Magazine.* She conducts a weekly writers' workshop at a community college in Madison, North Carolina, where she lives. Married, she has a son who is a college student and jazz musician.

Who has not at one time or another been afraid of the dark? Lisa looks at that fear in a completely new light.

♦ ♦ ♦

Joe Hix is afraid of the dark.

Maybe it's because he lacks experience of it, having grown up in the half-light of the ghetto, where days hang smog gray and nights flicker pied neon. Joe came to know darkness mostly by inference—like the outside of his bottled world; a cloudy knowledge with little relevance to the way things were on his side of the glass.

Maybe it's because his brother locked him in a closet once. Joe had been little and groping and terrified. There'd been *THINGS* in the closet. He'd screamed and screamed until his mother came and hushed him with a slap.

Somewhere along the way Joe learned to avoid the dark, avoid it like a sour thought on a sunny day, by retreating to an inside place, a place of smiles and light where he could laugh and dream and see.

Only now that isn't working anymore. Now the darkness is trying to come inside with him. It's *alive.* And Joe is afraid . . .

♦ ♦ ♦

It rained all day. A droning downpour that congealed the air and beat dead areas into the brain. Joe was thankful to be off work, away from the cavernous tank fabrication plant with its tin roof that changed rain into an endless barrage of shrapnel, relieved to get out from under the heavy welding bonnet that lately had begun to smother him.

Bounding up the couple of rickety front-porch steps to the rooming house where he stayed, he swung open the screen door, letting it bang shut behind him, glad to be out of the rain and home.

(until he saw the stairs)

A long flight of narrow wooden stairs led to his room, each step worn smooth in the center: a trail from nowhere to nowhere hollowed out by the shuffling feet of countless boarders, a mute testament etched in faded oak.

(sometimes it tries to trap him, channel him into the groove)

They disappeared about halfway up, swallowed by a spongy darkness that hung there like one of the heavy rain-clouds from outside. Joe gazed into that no man's land and felt a familiar prickle at the pit of his stomach and the back of his neck. He could see himself climbing those stairs—the way he used to each night after second shift—jerking nervous glances over his shoulder and scanning the dark. He'd never seen anything, but he'd known it was there, the *darkthing.*

(sometimes it whispers to him)

waiting for him to pass, waiting to crawl behind him up the stairs. Stealthy. Foul. Edging closer with each step.

He'd taken a cut in pay to get on days.

Joe studied the pocket of darkness that was the upstairs landing, a premature shadowland created by the afternoon storm. Sometimes, when he thought about it, he could remember the good feel of moving here—a third-rate boarding house on a backwater road, pockmarked and wilting, but away from the streets and sounds and stinks of his old neighborhood, his old life. Maybe not quite out of the bottle but enough toward its mouth that he could breathe.

(only he doesn't think about it much anymore)

He was on the list for the next downstairs room to come available *old Cooter-man might die soon God knows he's been crawling toward it long enough at night hear him coughing and coughing and shambling along the hall to the downstairs john.*

Something touched his face. Startled, Joe glanced up at the lightbulb dangling by a cord from the downstairs ceiling. Like a skulking cobweb, its string had brushed his cheek. He'd forgotten all about it. He reached up and pulled it on. Yellow bug-light spilled around him, spattering the walls and stairs, melting the ice that had begun to chill his spine. There was another one upstairs. If he could reach it.

Outside, rain drummed the front-porch stoop. A sudden gust of wind filtered through the rusty screen and set the naked lightbulb gently asway.

Joe watched yellow light move up and down the stairs, ebbing and flowing to the rhythm of the swinging bulb. Little tentacles began to snake up the side walls, sucking them inward, daring him to try for the landing, try and make it to the upstairs cord.

He could sense the darkthing watching him, peering down on him from above.

(a nausea of feeling *not alone*)

and for a moment felt its breath, smelled its fetid breath.

Slowly he crossed to the staircase and took hold of the banister, lifting his left foot to the first riser. His heart began to pump, sluggishly at first, then faster . . . faster. Goosebumps shivered from the small of his back to a point just behind his right ear. His forehead glazed with sweat. His scalp shot needles toward his brain.

His right foot felt anchored to the dull wood floor of the entry hall and he leaned back heavily, resting his weight against the wall, one hand gripping the sweat-stained banister, the other rubbing a steady downbeat on faded jeans.

(it's watching, the *darkthing,* watching him, waiting, daring him to go for the landing and the upstairs light)

Ghosts from a hundred childhood graveyards whispered across the silence

*(sniveling little coward yellowback chickenshit chickenshit)*

until he slammed both palms against his ears and forced them back into their tombs.

Fumbling inside his jacket pocket, he yanked out the small flashlight that was his constant companion, aimed it up the stairs like a gun. His thumb froze to the cold metal switch as he pressed it on, waiting through the eons of that nanosecond for the light to shine. At last a scream of light burst forth—

—and caught something!

*Spotlighted it!*

Something that grinned a flash of defiance—then was gone, bleeding away from the stab of light, blending into the darkness until all that remained was a whisper-laugh that puckered the skin on the back of Joe's neck and sent him shrinking into his damp jacket seeking warmth. Then that, too, was gone.

He could go up now. Safe in the glow of his flash. Safe to the upstairs lightcord. Safe to his room where protection would gleam from every lamp and fixture until morning sunlight neutralized their puny effort. Then, perhaps for a little while, he could rest.

♦ ♦ ♦

He was going to be late for work again. If this continued he'd not only be off first shift, he'd be out of a job. Joe didn't want to lose his job. It kept him from being just another butt in the gutter.

He heard the final buzzer sound as he rounded the corner of the building and ducked in through the main gate. Offering a sheepish grin to the timekeeper, he fumbled through the stack of cards the man had gathered until he located his. Number one-four-two. Quickly punching in, he handed it back, wincing as the man stuck it atop the pile, where it glared his lateness to the world at large.

Being a class-A certified welder who had taken a pay cut to get on days might cushion him for a while, but not forever.

Grabbing his welding bonnet and gear from the employees' storage locker, Joe hurried to his work station, spiky legs eating up the distance and spitting out a hollow thud each time a heavy workboot met the cement floor.

"You're late again," said Larry Jefferson in way of greeting as Joe strode up to their place on line.

Joe glanced around, then back at the tall black man. "Where's the man?"

"Meetin', up to the front office." Larry handed him a fistful of welding rods. "Word's out the pinkies gonna be flowin'."

"Layoffs? *Jesus!* And I had to go be late again." Joe felt his gut heave. He quickly stuffed the electrodes into the rod pouch that swung from his belt and turned to his welding machine.

"Shit, man." Larry glanced up from the dial he was setting on his own machine and shot him an expansive grin. "No way they gonna lay you off. You the fair-haired boy."

"Cute, Larry." Joe pulled on his welding gloves and bonnet, temporarily hiking up the hinged faceplate so that it jutted outward from the headpiece like a hood. He began twiddling dials.

Larry chuckled softly, adjusting the welding helmet that rode atop his own wiry black hair. "On the level, Joey. You ain't got nothin' to worry about. Nobody here can lay a bead to the metal like you"—he held up a slender welding rod as though to illustrate his point, then fit it into the jaws of his electrode holder and clamped down—"'cept maybe me. Why you think they give you first like you wanted? Goodness of their hearts?'' He snorted in disgust. ''You was a *fool* to mention pay cut.''

''Worth it,'' Joe muttered, more to himself than to Larry.

''C'mon, bro.'' Larry donned a pained expression. ''You still rappin' that 'boogy in the dark' shit?''

*(chickenshit chickenshit yellowbelly chickenshit)*

Joe's insides hardened. And he'd thought Larry was different, talked to him some, tried to explain. He'd liked him from the first, liked his easy humor, liked the smile that always seemed to bring a piece of sunshine into the big, gray building.

But they were all the same—his brother and the other kids, those girls in high school, his mucho macho fellow workers—

*(chickenshitchickenshit)*

—all of them.

''Fuck you.'' Joe flipped down the faceplate.

Larry sighed, ''Look, Joey—''

But Joe had tuned him out, turned him off.

(they're all the same all of them)

''Fuck you,'' he repeated softly.

♦ ♦ ♦

Lunchtime was the usual round of bologna sandwiches and dirty jokes. Joe sat in a corner of the canteen area and quietly fed his sandwich to the company dog. He wasn't hungry. Neither was the dog. Or maybe Bowser just didn't feel like bologna today. Taking a few half-hearted nibbles, he abandoned the sandwich for a pork chop bone one of the other men offered. Joe scooped the remains off the floor and deposited them in the trash barrel on his way out.

The end-of-lunch buzzer sounded. Joe saw his foreman heading toward him, clipboard in hand. For a moment he froze, remembering Larry's talk of layoffs.

''Hix, need some welding out on the yard,'' the foreman said when he got within earshot. ''Big tank supposed to ship out this week. Get your gear and follow me on out.''

Joe's stomach muscles uncoiled. No pink slip today. With a deep breath of relief, he did as told.

A huge cylinder of stainless steel dominated the plant yard, shards of refracted sunbeams dancing off its shiny #4 finish. Fourteen feet in diameter, thirty-five feet long, it dwarfed the small propane tanks that were Joe's usual job assignment. He wasn't intimidated by the tank's size, nor the more exotic and expensive material of construct. Yet something seemed . . . not quite right . . .

The tank rested horizontally in a special set of power turning rolls that could rotate the vessel as needed. At the moment it was rotated so that the shell manhole was positioned about two feet off the ground. The manhole was uncovered. To allow entry—

A familiar shiver nudged Joe's spine, then slithered upward until he felt the hair on his neck come alive.

*(No! Not now! Please not now! And not here!)*

It couldn't be here—it wasn't *right* here. He had to keep here clean—for Chrissake! It was all he had left.

He stared at the small round hole in the huge gleaming shell, and the darkness that lay behind. A cloudy cyclopian eye in a bloated silver giant. Joe felt wounded. Sick.

"Gonna need an internal weld on the bottom head," the foreman was saying, and he gestured with his clipboard toward the bloated silver giant. "Equipment's already in place. Use the five-thirty-two stainless rod and set your machine—"

Joe tuned out. He knew what kind of welding rod to use. Knew how to set his machine. And he knew what waited for him inside that tank. It had been a game all along—nothing but a game. The *darkthing's* game. The darkthing—laughing at him, playing with him, feeding on his growing fear.

The foreman kept walking toward the tank just like nothing was wrong. Nothing at all. Joe felt numb. He had to force his feet to move. It made his whole body tingle. He couldn't feel the ground.

The foreman stopped at the tank and turned around. Joe

watched the man's lips move another minute or two, then watched him walk away.

He looked at the tank.

It greeted him warmly—avid onlooker to a play already written, a bit player whose role is preordained, a standing ovation to his fear.

And Joe *was* afraid. So afraid that he couldn't remember when he hadn't been afraid. It was like dying.

His eyes found the small, round eyehole. It seemed to be studying him, now, sizing him up. In the momentary stillness he thought he heard a low throaty chuckle rumble deep within the massive tank—

—and suddenly Joe was ravenous to see this thing that menaced him. Suddenly nothing was as important, nothing had ever held such meaning. No matter what the result, no matter what the cost, he burned to see his tormentor. If the darkthing wanted a fight he'd give it one. Joe knew how to fight. He'd fought things all his life. When had he stopped fighting?

Going over to the welding machine positioned next to the opening, he affixed the ground wire and turned it on. He filled his rod pouch with the proper electrodes then picked up the electrode holder that was attached to the end of a fifty-foot power cable. The cable was coiled neatly beside the welding machine, ready to be pulled out as the welder progressed farther and farther inside the tank, providing electrical current to the welding contact point.

Joe removed his welding helmet and laid it on the ground beside the manhole. Tucking the electrode holder under his left arm, he turned back to the opening.

Without warning, a challenge erupted from the bowels of the giant vessel.

Nodding once, Joe climbed through the opening into the tank.

The air inside the vessel was dank and slightly musty. It seemed to inhale toward the far end, creating an internal imbalance as though a vacuum was being pulled on the vessel, away from the opening, away from the light. *The darkthing holding its breath?*

Carefully playing out power cable, Joe moved into the darkness. The cable snaked behind him with a hiss of amusement. He glanced back and saw little dust motes swimming in the shallow light that clung to the inside of the manhole opening.

Pressure began to build as he moved farther in, the soles of his workboots having no real trouble finding purchase on the smooth gentle grade of the vessel's inner wall. Inch by inch he continued, snail-like, forging a corridor through the heavy gloom. His heart began to thud an echo to each step, louder as he crept along the cold steel shell, a dull drumbeat amplified by the hollow metal body surrounding him

(the monster you are now inside . . .)

He stopped. Inhaled slowly, deeply. Again. Again. The thudding shriveled to an undertone.

He walked on.

When he judged himself to be about ten or twelve feet from the end of the tank, Joe stopped and stared into the solid blackness. He could feel the darkthing waiting, watching

*(chickenshit chickenshit lily-livered chickenshit)*

*smiling* at him.

Joe smiled in return, a snarling grin that curled his lips back from his teeth and squeezed his eyes to narrow slits. The challenge reiterated itself, belching an egestion of impatience.

Drawing a single, slender electrode from his rod pouch, with delicate precision he placed it into the jaws of the electrode holder and knelt on the cold stainless steel. The act brought a feeling of reverence. And power. *He* was in control of this moment, threading the wand of destiny through his own magic spell.

Bending forward slightly, left hand touching in front of him as a reference point, he brought the active rod into contact with the metal shell, striking an arc. The circuit being fed from the welder outside, through the fifty feet of power cable, into the electrode holder and down the slender length of the welding rod was complete.

Blinding white light burst into brilliance before him—a million, *billion* suns in unison. Joe stared at the magnificent arc light, seeing its true splendor for the first time, undiluted by the protective lens on his welding helmet. Never had he known such raw power. Never had he seen so clearly.

*'Where there is darkness, let me sow light.'*

*'Let there be light.'*

He was God!

A ball of pure light danced before Him, spitting slivers of itself into the darkness, rending a million fiery pathways, rebounding against the now sparkling steel. Surely human eyes had never beheld such perfect light.

Joe's eyes began to feel dry and grit-filled as He gazed at the light He had made and the ultraviolet slowly began to fry the optic tissues. But that didn't matter. A symphony of ice-white splendor was being played at His bidding; a ballet of sparkling artistry in command performance. Nothing could withstand Him!

He could feel rage pound at Him from just beyond the core of light, a tidal wave of hatred—tinged with . . . *fear!* Yes! There was fear. It was *afraid*. The darkthing was afraid! Joe's laughter blended with the light. What a joke! What a marvelous, magical, wonderful joke. The taste of revenge was honey on His tongue. He didn't feel the little spatters of molten weldsplat that were singeing His arms, legs, torso. This moment of triumph was *His*. Even the pain that had begun shooting through His eyes to His brain could be controlled.

With casual arrogance, Joe lifted His head and focused on a point beyond and above the dazzling orb making its obeisance before Him. An outline was barely discernible. But it was enough. Slowly, Joe's new vision refined the image: delineated, sculpted, peeled back the layers of darkness like a shroud from a corpse.

those of the dogs he had brought with him. They were the biggest dogs LaVerl had ever seen. English mastiffs were what the Navvie called them.

"Don't much matter if they're Eye-ranian mastiffs."

LaVerl's voice was loud in the silent Jimmy. It startled him for a moment. "Whatever they is, they'll feed on Little Boy's liver afore he gets a chance to learn he's dead!"

Much as LaVerl feared and disliked his own dog, Little Boy had more than earned his keep these past two years. LaVerl could not afford to leave such a valuable meal ticket in a bloody mound of red clay in the fighting arena. And he could hardly refuse to let the pit fight. The Navvie had made sure to throw up his challenge in front of the other trainers.

LaVerl scowled. There was only one way out of it. The Navvie would be found dead in the morning, his throat torn open, supposedly by one of his own dogs. And Little Boy would be safely tucked back inside his hole, drying Injun blood mottling his tan muzzle.

The other trainers would have to destroy the Navvie's bulls. What with their trainer dead, it wasn't safe—no! Not by a long shot. LaVerl grinned. Not safe a'tall to let the Navvie's bulls live. LaVerl's brain swelled with pride at the simplicity of his plan.

He spotted the turnoff, a spongy outcropping of swamp grass and quickmud off to the left. He killed the Jimmy's lights and eased into the yellow shadows.

This was a dangerous business he was about tonight. If he wasn't damn careful, he could be the one with a missing windpipe in the morning. And that was if he was lucky and the dogs got to him before the Navvie.

LaVerl marveled at the ease with which the Navvie had moved in and taken charge. The trainers were a close-knit community, a perfect crew of cut-throat spoilers. One had to be born into their circle to belong. LaVerl himself had ridden in on his own daddy's coattails, following the old man to dog fights all over the neighboring counties. And when his daddy had died, the dogs had gone to him—a king's fortune to the people populating this mountain.



For a moment Joe put the world on hold; for a moment he disconnected nerve endings that were shrieking pain; for a moment every dissected piece of him flowed together in total understanding, pushing back the wall of darkness that marked the bounds of reason, letting in the light; a moment out of time . . . as he stared at himself.

The single welding rod sputtered, puddled to its end; the light faded to black.

Joe smiled. Serenity nestled down in him. He broadened his smile, feeling it, testing it. It eased the pain in his eyes. Of course. The bigger he smiled the smaller his eyes would get and the less pain there'd be. He could smile away his shrieking eyes.

(Someone is calling him)

Joe laid down his electrode holder, removed his rod pouch and gloves and neatly placed them beside the holder. He could feel his face glowing with the fire of his smile.

Picking up the welding cable, he held it loosely in one hand and threaded his way back to the manhole opening, hardly stumbling at all.

"Joey—?"

(Larry's voice)

"What you doin' in there, man? You done left your welding helmet out—Good God, Joey! Your face—it's all burned! It's . . . Sweet *Jesus!* Joe! Joey, your eyes! Oh, Joey, Mother of God! Look at your eyes! Look at your eyes."

Joe spread his smile around him. He curled it about his head, made a halo of it. He sent it before him. He shed it in his path. What did eyes matter? He'd seen the face of darkness.

"I ain't afraid," he whispered to them all. "I ain't afraid."

# THE PIT

## by Patricia Ramsey-Jones

Patricia Ramsey-Jones is an officer of the League of Utah Writers, a member of Horror Writers of America, and a member/critic of the National Writers Club. In her mid-thirties, she's the mother of two sons, and lives in West Jordan, Utah. Her short fiction has appeared in *Haunts*. Currently she's working on two children's books, a young adult novel, a mainstream novel of psychological suspense, and a full-length tale of supernatural horror.

"The Pit" was written after researching dog fighting when Patricia was employed by the Humane Society of Utah.

♦ ♦ ♦

LaVerl Pitkin glanced in the rearview mirror. He was sure he was not being followed. In this one moment of distraction, the Jimmy's left front tire plunged into a chuckhole. As his hips left the seat, LaVerl lost sight of his reflection. His head slammed against the ceiling, then the vehicle crawled forward out of the hole and plopped him back into the seat.

"Godforsaken Georgia backroads!" LaVerl rubbed the sore reddening spot above his right eyebrow.

The Jimmy passed out of a grove of dogwood and the newly revealed moon stabbed through the windshield at LaVerl's eyes. It hung bloated and yellow and sullen, its bulk contradicting the way it floated effortlessly in the moist sky.

"Fat as a tick in a blood bank," LaVerl muttered. That strange light would not serve the business he was about tonight, but that wasn't to be helped. All that really mattered was that the Navvie be dead by morning.

LaVerl scrubbed at the bristle of a ten-day beard. He wasn't particularly a large man, the muscles just beneath his skin were ropy from too many years of backwoods interbreeding. But his senses had been sharpened by that same



incestuous bloodline, his baser instincts brought closer to those of his predatory, four-legged ancestors.

His red hair was a ragged confusion of long strings at the neckline to spotty tufts that battled old scars at the scalp. Scars, whose origin was neither significant nor worthy of remembrance to a man with LaVerl Pitkin's violent history, the most pronounced of which slanted upward through the temple and canted his right eye at a jagged angle. His two front teeth were decayed nubs and the rest were cracked and stained with nicotine. At nineteen, LaVerl Pitkin looked easily twice his age.

The ring finger and pinkie of his right hand were missing at the second knuckle. This deformity had earned him the nickname of "Captain Hook" among the other trainers. LaVerl had no idea who that was, but Royal Harvey had told him it was some feller out of a kid's fairy story.

"Got too close to a crock 'n' got his hand chomped off clean to the bone!" Blackish-brown spittle from a wad of Macon chew stained Royal's lips as he talked. "Hear tell the croc liked the taste of that 'ole feller so well, he was always followin' him 'round for seconds. So the Captain—he feeds that big, ugly croc a alarm clock. That ways, he kin always hear that croc jest a'tickin' afore it gets close enough for another bite."

Royal had then punched LaVerl up alongside the head. "Maybe you oughta find a alarm clock for Little Boy. No tellin' when he might get in the mind for another taste." Royal cackled and brown spittle flew from his lips. "That is—if'n that bull's still breathin' after eatin' pi'zened meat like you!"

The remaining fingers of LaVerl's right hand curle around the steering wheel like a claw. The memory did n set well on a night like tonight. He had been lucky, ve lucky indeed, to leave just two fingers behind in Little Bo gullet and escape with his throat. Before this night w over, the Navvie would not be so fortunate.

The Navvie had arrived on the mountain a fortnight a A huge, hulking Indian, his mouth tilted downward i snarl that seemed permanently etched on his face,

But the Navvie had appeared out of nowhere, arriving in town with his dogs in the bed of a battered green Ford with rust-flaked running boards. Why, they had never even learned his real name. It was Royal Harvey who had started calling him the Navvie, for want of anything better. And the other trainers, in awesome respect, closed their eyes to the nonexistence of his mountaintop lineage, drew in their elbows, and sidled over to make room for one more in their circle.

LaVerl cracked the door. Steamy air poured into the cab. He skirted around brush, testing the ground beneath his boots like a cat on a mattress.

A tire iron swung from the claw of his right hand. He didn't like visiting the dog in daylight, much less in this eerie day-dark of the yellow moon riding on his shoulder. He hadn't been to the dog in three days and Little Boy would surely be half mad for food and water.

LaVerl spotted the rotted wood of the trap door that covered the ground above Little Boy's cage. His throat went cold. The tire iron shook in his fist. He toed the trap door with his boot, kicking it aside, and leaped backward. Always, at this moment, he half expected the dog to leap from its pit.

From the bowels of the hole, a rumbling growl floated upward. LaVerl crept closer to the edge.

Little Boy's eyes glowed yellow, whether from the moon or an inner blood-hate LaVerl couldn't be sure. His lips were curled back over long, white incisors. The ears lay flattened against his anvil-shaped skull, eyes spaced abnormally widely apart. His bobbed tail stuck straight in the air, stiff and bristled like the hair on the back of his neck, and moved not the slightest in a gesture of friendliness.

LaVerl's breath hitched in his chest. "Hey there, Little Boy." His voice was nothing more than a sigh. "I come to feed ya."

◆ ◆ ◆

LaVerl's equipment lay untouched since the last time he'd used it, wrapped in a canvas tarp beneath a thicket of blue elder. Threading the clothesline wire through a five-foot length of PVC pipe, he wrapped one end around his palm and formed the other into a noose to drop over Little Boy's head. With this stiff leash, he could lead the bull with a minimum risk of the dog turning back on him.

Royal Harvey had hooted the first time he'd seen this contraption. "How long ya think that bull's gonna let ya' push him round with that thing, Cap?"

LaVerl had still been nursing the freshly raw stumps on his right hand. Sudden anger laced his words with false courage. "Maybe you'd like to hand-feed him for me, old man! He's had the last piece o' me he's *ever* gonna get. That's right, Royal! You show me a better way to lead this bull and if'n you still have all of your loose change a'dangling there between your legs, I'll piss on my own daddy's grave!"

Royal's face was a grim mask. His breath shrilled from his nostrils. When he finally spoke, his voice was subdued, but lethal. "The day comes I can't control a pit, boy, is the day I set out my rocker with a bowl of mush and my false teeth a'hand. You don't belong in this business, Pitkin. A man what can't handle his own dog will see the day when one turns on the other and there won't be but one left to tell the tale." He spat a clot of tobacco juice dangerously close to LaVerl's boots. "My bet's on the bull, boy!"

But despite Royal Harvey's contempt, LaVerl feared Little Boy's unpredictable moods even more. The dog snarled in the hole, hurrying LaVerl about his mission.

Little Boy was pacing the perimeter of the cage like a mare ready to drop her foal, anxious to be about the business at hand. The dog stopped, looked upward, when LaVerl slid a wooden plank down into the hole.

"Hey there, Little Boy. I know your belly's a'wantin and if'n you'll just show some patience, Ole LaVerl'll see ya get somethin' to eat for long."

The dog bared its teeth, answering LaVerl with a low, threatening growl. LaVerl jerked the plank and lodged a jagged splinter in his thumb. For a moment, he was tempted to stop this madness, to leave the dog to starve to death in the hole. He withdrew the board an inch, then sighed. If he let the Navvie best him this once, his reputation would never be repaired. There was no turning back.

Little Boy sniffed at the plank. Sensing its familiar purpose, he pawed at the quavering board. Before finally planting the bridge between himself and the dog, LaVerl tightened his grip on the PVC pipe. The plank had barely settled in the earth of the hole when the dog was scrambling up.

LaVerl snagged Little Boy halfway in his ascent. The dog snapped at the wire noose, but LaVerl quickly wound the slack around his hand and pulled the pipe snugly against Little Boy's neck.

The bull's head swiveled around, the end of the pipe buried in the fur at his collarbone. His eyes met those of his master, lips curled back. As the dog snarled, the pipe vibrated in LaVerl's palm.

"Gotcha—ya mangy bastard!" LaVerl tried to conceal the trembling in his voice with a brusque authority. "You'll be eatin' soon enough. Soon's I decide you've earned your keep!" He shoved the tire iron down into his boot top and jabbed Little Boy with the pole. "Get goin'!"

Steam rose from the ground, spiraling upward as if magnetized by that strange yellow moon. The wire slipped in LaVerl's sweating palm. He longed to wipe his hands on the front of his shirt, but didn't dare loosen his hold on the dog for even a moment.

The Navvie had squatted in an abandoned moonshiner's shanty two miles in-wood. They would walk in from here. LaVerl didn't want to give the Navvie any warning and a reason to turn the English loose.

Little Boy set the pace, plodding silently ahead. Pausing every so often to catch a scent of squirrel or possum on the trail, he scrambled forward. The momentum of his muscular surges caught LaVerl off guard, yanking him precariously off balance.

A bullfrog rattled nearby. The heavy air trapped even the slightest of sounds, magnifying them in the still night. The frog sounded as if it were right underfoot. Little Boy's ears prickled. He scanned the woods beyond them, then snuffled and pawed at a copse of water hemlock.

LaVerl shivered as the moon skipped through cloud cover, casting dancing oily shadows on the ground below. Then it disappeared completely. As if a giant fuse had been blown, the woods went black. In tandem with the sudden darkness, a bird screamed, then gurgled hideously like a woman with her throat being cut.

LaVerl jumped and jammed the pipe into Little Boy's throat. "Get movin', you sonofawhore! We don't got all night to get this done. If ya don't get to steppin', I'll feed ya to the English myself!"

Little Boy stiffened, then raised his head. The clothesline wire was drawn deep into the pipe as he turned back to face his master. His snarling muzzle changed to a macabre grin. He pushed back at the offense against his bunched throat. Then, he stepped closer to LaVerl, bringing the wire forward with him. LaVerl's eyes widened as the wire tightened. The thin metal seared into his flesh.

Little Boy's jaws opened as he strained against the pipe. He stepped once again toward LaVerl. The wire had become firmly embedded in the skin around LaVerl's palm. His hand numbed against the razor-sharp pain. The missing fingers of his right hand throbbed in phantom agony.

LaVerl's eyes bulged as he realized the pipe had begun to bend under the will of the dog.

The bird screamed again. This time it sounded like hideous laughter to LaVerl. Little Boy's forepaws dug deep into the marshy ground. The dog panted and snarled as it lunged toward LaVerl. As if from a great distance—a safe distance, a distance where he was only watching this happening instead of living it—LaVerl heard the plastic pipe crack beneath the dog's weight.

"*Whoa* there, Boy!" His voice sounded calm. Much too calm for this deadly situation, he thought. He gripped the pipe with both hands, leaning into it with his belly. The wind flew from his lungs. The tire iron, out of reach, gouged into his leg below the knee. Then the pipe cracked again.

This second crack broke LaVerl's fragile membrane of calmness. "*Whoa, Boy!* I was only funnin' with ya! God as my witness! Ya know I don't mean ya no harm!"

His voice seemed faraway. His vision swam as the oncoming dog lunged forward through a watery haze.

Then, for some unknown reason, Little Boy stopped. He stared back at LaVerl from narrowed amber eyes. The wire loosened around LaVerl's hand, freeing a stream of dark, warm blood from the circular cut. The flowing blood pulsed from the wound with the rhythm of LaVerl's slamming heartbeat. Little Boy studied LaVerl as if seeking confirmation of his master's surrender.

LaVerl leaped at the opportunity to appease the maddened dog. "That's a good Boy!" His hand screamed from the sudden freedom of the choking wire. "Ya really had me goin' there for a minute. Whadaya say we get goin' again now? Huh, Boy?"

The dog glared at him. Trembling violently, LaVerl brushed at the sweat blinding his eyes and smeared a trace of blood on his cheekbone. "Okay, Boy?" He struggled to keep his voice deliberately soft and soothing.

Little Boy stared at his master for a moment longer. LaVerl felt belittled by the Bull's appraisal. Then the dog turned and stepped off once again in the direction of the Navvie's shack. LaVerl allowed the dog his lead.

Something had changed in that moment of rebellion, he thought. This had become Little Boy's mission, not LaVerl's any longer. The dog loped ahead, indifferent to the man staggering to keep the exhausting pace behind him.

Crossing the edge of a bog, Little Boy maneuvered through the sucking mud with a grace that belied his powerful frame, while LaVerl slipped and stumbled as he was towed behind at the end of the choker-pipe.

But LaVerl knew he was worse than a fool if he really believed that things had changed that much since Little Boy had taken charge. Little Boy had *always* been in charge and he always would be. Ever since that day two very long years ago that had more or less killed LaVerl's daddy.

♦ ♦ ♦

Billy Bob Pitkin took his first step toward death's embrace on his last trip to Asey Lee's still. Asey Lee was a one-time handler who had found breeding and selling the ferocious pits more profitable than fighting them. As a sideline, he picked up a bit of pocket change by providing the shine that flowed so generously on the mountain a few days before any match.

Billy Bob wasn't one of the usual patrons of Asey's potent brews. His tastes ran more to pure Kentucky Bourbon, and he kept a private stock secreted away in the tater hole, buried beneath stacks of cloudy Mason jars whose contents looked suspiciously clotted and unhealthy, sealed with lids that had blackened and corroded with age.

But every so often, purely for economical reasons, Billy Bob would fire up the Jimmy and make the long climb to Asey's cabin. And it was on this last trip to Asey's still that LaVerl accompanied his daddy.

Billy Bob's cousin, Gary, had decided to make an honest woman of his common-law wife, Opaline, who had borne him five children and was eight months gone with the sixth.

"Honest woman! Sweet Jesus's ass!" Billy Bob swore as they hugged the mountain on a tight hairpin curve on the twisting road to Asey's still. "Opaline'd never made a honest woman if the Pope hisself boiled her and pickled her in holy water for forty days and forty nights!"

LaVerl laughed. His daddy's disposition usually ran more toward mean and poisonous moods than the joke-telling, back-slapping frame of mind he was in on this day.

"If'n that welfare lady didn't promise to cut off the 'Aid to Dependent Children' what if she didn't see a weddin' license, Gary'd still be takin' the milk without buyin' the cow!" Billy Bob grinned and swatted at his son's head.

LaVerl ducked, pressing his back up against the other

side of the Jimmy. Billy Bob swung hazardously close to the edge of the road, speeding through a final horseshoe turn, and Asey's land shot into view. LaVerl, still in possession of all the fingers on his right hand, loosened his grip on the dashboard.

A sour-faced bitch, her tits swollen and dragging with milk, met the Jimmy as it approached Asey's house. She squatted on her haunches, scrutinizing the men inside the blazer. LaVerl and Billy Bob wisely stayed inside the Jimmy until Asey appeared.

"Get on, Sheba! Go let your pups suck!" Asey swung a booted foot at the dog. "I'd wager them fellers sure as squat didn't come all the way up this godforsaken mountain to jaw with an ugly old sow like you!"

Sheba obediently padded off behind the skeleton of a looted Nash Rambler whose yawning hood bemoaned its lack of salvageable parts. She turned just once, at the sound of the Jimmy's doors opening.

Asey and Billy Bob faced off, their bellies touching, their hands tucked down into their Levi's pockets.

"Well, Pitkin. Ya finally decided to come on up and take a gander at my champion litter?" It was more of a statement than a question. "Ya might find a pit that'd make ya proud for a change."

LaVerl goose-stepped backward at the slight to his daddy. He expected to see Billy Bob whip those lightning-quick fists from his pockets.

Billy Bob frowned, his expression darkening for just a moment, then he grinned. That smile reminded LaVerl of a gapper rousted from a sunny log by a careless boot. He could almost taste the venom in the deadly silence between the two men.

"Aw, Asey. You ain't never bred a dog up on this mountain what was worth his salt in the arena." Billy Bob still grinned. "Now Sheba—she's a likely enough bitch, but I hear tell there's some question about who the daddy of them pups is."

It was Asey's turn to frown. LaVerl watched as his hands

twitched ever so slightly in the recesses of his pockets. Any attempt at neighborliness had been lost. Asey's chin jutted forward. His head tipped back to meet Billy Bob's eyes.

"Whadaya want then, Pitkin? I ain't got all day to jaw with the likes of you!"

"I'm in the market for some brew."

Asey's eyebrows shot up.

Billy Bob continued. "Now don't go gettin' your bowels in a uproar. It ain't for me. Gary's marryin' up with Opaline and I need me a weddin' present."

"I should've knowed," Asey said. "You ain't got the taste of a bobcat in heat, Pitkin!"

They were on lighter ground now and LaVerl was relieved when Asey finally turned and led the way behind the house.

"Ain't nothin' the matter with my taste." Billy Bob followed. "I'm just in the mood for livin' a while longer."

Asey muttered something in return, but the words were lost behind his back.

Sheba met them once again at the corner of the house. The hair on her nape bristled in indignation. LaVerl could hear faint yips and mewlings coming from behind her.

"S'all right, girl." Asey shoved her aside. "They ain't interested in your brood."

But Billy Bob stopped and squinted at the tawny pups now wiggling out from a hole beneath the house. The biggest of the litter stepped independently away from the rest and snuffled at Billy Bob's shoes.

Squatting down, he scooped up the pup. The dog squirmed as Billy Bob examined the webbing between its toes. As he pried its tiny mouth open to glance at the roof of its mouth, the pup growled with surprising fierceness for a creature of its size.

"Black as coal," Billy Bob muttered.

LaVerl heard, but knew the soft words had escaped Asey. He also knew that a pup with a black mouth was destined to be a champion.

Billy Bob released his hold on the pup's fleshy nape,

dumping the dog in the dirt. It sprawled comically at his feet for a moment, then crouched into an attack posture. LaVerl almost laughed, but something in the pup's expression stopped him. It looked so serious and . . . almost dangerous in that miniature stance.

Billy Bob ignored it. He picked at his teeth with his thumbnail, then drew a piece of deer jerky from his shirt pocket. LaVerl knew the words were coming, but nevertheless, they sent a chill to his heart.

"How much?"

Asey grinned smugly. Another pup, the runt of the litter, joined its brother at Billy Bob's feet. "I should've knowed you'd pick that one. There's no mistake—he's champion blood."

Billy Bob sucked on the jerky, shrugging his shoulders in mock indifference. "He's okay. Might make a good second-line fighter."

Asey spat. *"Second line!* That dog's a champion if I ever seen one!"

Billy Bob shrugged again. "How much?" he repeated.

"Well, I don't rightly know if'n I'm in the mind to se—"

*"How much?"*

Asey squinted at Billy Bob. "Four hundred dollars."

*"Four hundred dollars!"* Billy Bob exploded. "I ain't never seen a pit *yet* worth four hundred dollars!" He turned his back to walk away.

"Three-fifty." Asey hurried.

"Two."

The pup still crouched at Billy Bob's feet. Its sibling scrambled over Billy Bob's shoes.

"You're a fool, Pitkin, if ya think I'm just gonna give this pup away!"

Then everything happened so quickly that if LaVerl hadn't been watching his daddy's face so closely he might have missed it.

Billy Bob drew the jerky from his teeth and released it through his fingers. The dried meat hit the ground between the two pups. The runt was quicker, snatching it up, and began to run for cover when the bigger pup hit him from behind.

Knowing it would be bested in a fight with the larger dog, the cur rolled over, showing its belly in submission.

The larger pup sniffed at the jerky, then lunged at the runt's exposed and plump belly. The runt screamed in surprise as sharp teeth punctured his skin. He struggled to regain his feet, but the larger dog ripped deeper with a seesawing motion.

It was all over in less than a minute—before Asey could interfere. LaVerl shuddered as the larger dog sniffed once again at the jerky still clutched in the dying pup's mouth. Then, disinterested, it turned and sauntered away.

Billy Bob smiled at Asey as he pulled his money roll from his back pocket. He peeled several bills away from the roll, dropping them as they separated from the stack. The bills fluttered to the ground and covered the convulsing body of the runt. Sheba whined and licked at the pup's bleeding nose.

"You *did* say four hundred, didn't you, Asey?"

Later, as Billy Bob climbed into the Jimmy, a jug of moonshine slung beneath one arm and the pup cradled in his other, he gazed down lovingly at the dog.

"Little Boy! That's what I'm a gonna call ya!" He roared at the irony of the name. "Little Boy!"

The pup looked up into Billy Bob's face and snarled.

♦ ♦ ♦

LaVerl shivered in spite of the humid heat. That had happened just two weeks before his daddy died. LaVerl had never forgotten it and never quit hating his daddy for dying and leaving him alone. Why, he wouldn't be in this mess this very minute if Billy Bob were still alive.

"Damn you, Daddy!" he swore. "Damn *you* for gettin' this devil and then goin' and dyin' on me!" He sobbed and was ashamed that the memory of his daddy could still make him cry like a baby.

Little Boy turned and glared at LaVerl as if the mention of

the devil had struck a cord in his own black soul. He turned again and pulled LaVerl behind him with a vengeance.

Two weeks after the purchase of Little Boy, Billy Bob Pitkin had been drinking hard for three days. Around midnight of the third, he tilted a bottle of Kentucky Bourbon to his lips and drained the last golden drops.

The table he sat before tipped to its side as Billy Bob lunged to his feet. LaVerl knew enough to keep his distance.

"Gotta shake the dew from my lily," Billy Bob slurred as he crashed toward the door.

But somewhere on his trip to relieve himself that night, Billy Bob had decided to climb down the tater hole to his stash of Kentucky Bourbon. And sometime since his last trip down there, two of the wooden steps had been removed. Maybe it was too dark and maybe Billy Bob was just too drunk to see the missing steps and that awesome chasm winking below him.

At any rate, he fell to his death, and LaVerl thought he had heard, from inside the house, the awful crack of Billy Bob's neck when he hit.

As a matter of fact, he thought he could hear it again now in the trees beyond them.

LaVerl knew, with all his heart, that Asey Lee was somehow behind the missing steps. But nothing had ever been proven (a man like his daddy could count more enemies than friends) and Billy Bob Pitkin was buried alongside LaVerl's mother in the cemetery on Windy Ridge. And Little Boy was all his.

Little Boy stopped, one ear cocked above his head, and strained forward against the lead. As if this silent communication had been transmitted, a series of howls split the night a few seconds later. The Navvie's English had sensed their arrival.

Little Boy turned on LaVerl for the second time that evening. Their eyes locked; Little Boy's no longer threatening, just demanding. As the bull advanced, the wire tightened again, assaulting the torn flesh of LaVerl's palm. Wincing,

LaVerl loosened the slack and the wire spun out, opening the noose around the dog's throat.

He stroked the tip of the tire iron protruding from his boot top and slowly unwound the wire from around his hand. Little Boy shook the noose free from his head. LaVerl took one cautious step backward.

The Navvie's English had grown delirious in their baying. The air hummed with their howls. Little Boy crouched before his master. LaVerl backed up again.

"Not *me,* Boy! 'Member what we come here for?"

Little Boy bared his teeth. Saliva glistened like bits of broken glass on his muzzle.

"Ya mind me now, Boy!" LaVerl's hand crept toward the tire iron. "Ya mind me!"

The bull scanned the wood beyond them. Then, whirling around, he plunged into the tree barrier that separated them from the Navvie's shanty. The moon glinted once on his russet fur and then he was gone.

LaVerl stared into the trees where Little Boy had disappeared. He fought against an urge to run, somehow sure that was what the dog wanted him to do. "Little Boy? You out there?"

Then the howling of the English was cut short. Not with a lowering of tone or tempo. It just stopped. LaVerl's skin crawled. After sensing an intrusion into their territory, only one thing could have made the English quiet like that. The Navvie had sensed their arrival also.

"Little Boy? Where are ya?" LaVerl's instincts screamed as he was pulled irresistibly to the tree line. A cicada buzzed very near his head, then trilled off into the night. LaVerl ducked and slapped at his ear with his mangled hand.

The shanty was eerily illuminated by the yellow moon. Warped boards had been slapped on an invisible frame. Jagged splinters of glass protruded from the misshapen window frames. The porch had decayed and sagged in one corner. Although there was no sign of life, LaVerl was certain that the Navvie was there . . . and waiting.

He took one step toward the shanty and froze. A pen he hadn't noticed before had been built at the side of the porch. Constructed of the same remnants as the shack, it blended perfectly with the haphazard structure that had spawned it. The moon picked at a reflection inside the pen, teasing and tempting LaVerl for a closer look.

He blinked. Three pairs of eyes stared back at him from inside the pen. In horror, he recognized them for what they were.

The English sat quietly, assessing his approach. A feeling of suffocating pressure entombed LaVerl as he realized he had been drawn from the safety of the tree line. He stood paralyzed in the Navvie's dooryard, mesmerized by the hypnotic stare of the English.

"Little Boy!" The words were trapped in his constricting windpipe. The danger here was real and solid. LaVerl was not fooled by the passivity of the English. He felt the physical presence of an evil so alive its heartbeat entered his own chest and threatened to squeeze the very life from him.

Eyes narrowing, he cocked his head to one side. The mountain had become devoid of sound as if each insect, bird, and animal had joined in the conspiracy of silence. The English never took their eyes from him in their massive, statuelike postures.

Something was terribly wrong here. But LaVerl felt too numb and logy to figure out what it was.

Then a branch creaked behind him, breaking the terrifying silence. LaVerl whirled around, turning his back on the English. The trees stood barren, blackened by the mysterious depths of the forest beyond. Sweat blossomed on LaVerl's forehead and trickled into his eyes.

"Little Boy! *Dammit!* Where are y—"

And suddenly he was choking. Strangling from a steel grip wrapped around his throat.

The Navvie towered above him, one arm thrown almost casually around LaVerl's neck. The other hand held him firmly clenched between the shoulder blades like an errant pup. LaVerl surged against the suffocating hold. He jerked his head upward and met the face of the Navvie.

The Indian seemed to have swelled in size. He towered above LaVerl by almost two feet. His loosened hair, freed of the customary braids, stung at LaVerl's cheeks. The Navvie's eyes were closed. An expression of almost orgasmic ecstasy tipped the corners of his mouth.

LaVerl was pulled upward. His toes brushed the ground in the Indian's deadly embrace. As his face was drawn closer to the Navvie's, his vision swam.

He felt the Navvie's breath pulsing on his forehead and he opened his mouth to trap the precious air from his captor's own lungs. His lips grazed the smooth flesh of the Navvie's chin.

Then he bit down, grinding the Navvie's skin between his teeth. The Navvie's eyes opened wide in surprise. Tasting blood, LaVerl bit down again.

The Navvie shook his head. LaVerl's cheekbone cracked against the Indian's chin but, like a persistent terrier, he refused to release his hold.

The Navvie's arm loosened around LaVerl's throat. A rush of air swept between his teeth and scorched his lungs. His vision cleared instantly. Twisting violently in the Navvie's grip, he felt himself falling. His feet touched the ground again. His knees buckled beneath the weight.

LaVerl sprawled to his stomach, gagging from the sudden sickening overload of oxygen to his lungs. Above the sound of his own ragged gasping, the dooryard had come alive. The English barked and lunged madly in their pen. Birds chittered and screamed from the trees. LaVerl's eyes roared with the popping of his eardrums.

He realized that all of this was happening in less than a moment. Then his head was jerked back as the Navvie grabbed a handful of his hair and yanked him to his feet. LaVerl's arms flailed as he tried to strike at the force behind him. They were moving. The Navvie was dragging him backward.

The barking of the English grew wilder.

Louder.

Closer.

And then LaVerl realized the Navvie was dragging him toward the pen.

*"Little Boy!"* he bellowed. His screams were drowned out by the madness of the English's howls.

LaVerl was flung through the air. His back slammed against the rotten wood of the dog pen. It groaned and threatened to collapse beneath the impact. The English leaped into the air and clawed at the barrier separating LaVerl from their snapping jaws.

"Little Boy!" he screamed again, his voice garbled with terror. *"Seize,* Boy! *Seize!"*

The Navvie yanked LaVerl over the top of the pen and pressed him headfirst into the din of maddened dogs. One of the English leaped for LaVerl's face. Its teeth clicked the air, barely missing LaVerl's ear.

The Navvie probed for LaVerl's right eye with his thumb. LaVerl's back scraped the edge of the pen as the Indian pushed him further downward. Another of the English plunged at LaVerl's face. Its teeth snagged in his cheek, tearing a flap of flesh away to muscle.

LaVerl squealed. Arching his back, he thrust his body upward against the Indian's relentless pressure. His arms thrashed as he tried to find a grip to anchor his body. He was sliding once again over the edge when his hand struck metal.

Out of the corner of his eye, he could see the English gathering into a tight knot and eyeing his exposed throat. In desperation, he curled the fingers of his disfigured hand around the cold steel protruding from his boot top.

The tire iron slipped in the bloody raw wound of his palm. It dangled from his fingertips and threatened to leave his grip. His body teetered precariously on the edge of the pen as he raised the bar in his fist.

The yellow moon winked from the metal. The Navvie turned his head an instant before the bar smashed down into his skull. Stunned, he threw his head back and roared like one of his own vicious dogs.

LaVerl drew his knees up and kicked at the Navvie's chest. The Indian stumbled back, instinctively covering his face with clenched fists.

LaVerl dropped to his feet and charged. He whipped at the Navvie's face with the tire iron. Bone snapped as the bar bounced from the Navvie's wrist. He crumpled to his knees, his left hand limply grazing the earth.

LaVerl raised the tire iron in both hands above his head. His full weight followed the bar crashing down.

The blow struck the Navvie squarely on the back of the neck, then vibrated back up the bar. LaVerl's front teeth spliced the tip of his tongue. The tire iron flew from his hands. With an agonized groan, the Navvie sprawled on his face in the dirt.

LaVerl leaped away from the body. The English, sensing defeat, were silenced once again.

The Navvie lay face down. His long, black hair fanned the earth around his head like a malevolent caul. Sweat blossomed on LaVerl's face and bit into the open flap of his cheek. He began to shake wildly. His teeth chattered. Keeping one eye on the lifeless form of the Indian, LaVerl massaged his bruised throat.

The English whined and pawed at their pen. LaVerl hunkered to his heels, watching the now-submissive dogs. He gingerly probed the raw flesh of his cheek. It raged in protest at the disturbance. He used the pain as a catalyst and rose once again to his feet.

"Little Boy!" he shrieked. A bird mimicked his frantic cries. "Little Boy! I know you're out there! *Goddamn you!* Get here—NOW!" Blood from his ripped tongue filled his mouth and garbled the shouts.

The yellow moon spun in the black night. The English pounded against their warped pen.

"Little Bo—" LaVerl's voice cracked to a sob. The echo from the woods beat his breath back. "C'mon, Boy! Gotta get 'way from here! Gotta get to home!"

A soft breeze picked up and caressed LaVerl's torn face. The English began to bay. He turned to glance once more at the Navvie.

Then he ran.

♦ ♦ ♦

The humidness of early evening had been replaced by a predawn sweet mist. Night had a way of driving down the lush overripeness of the mountain. It lay under cover until dawn when the heat of the sun forced it steaming to the surface once again.

The moon had mellowed from a stark ochre sacrifice to a soft lemon creme. Even the cicadas and tree frogs seemed to have called it a night.

LaVerl stopped to listen, bent over, and clutched both knees. He drew a deep breath to halt the wheezing in his lungs. He couldn't be sure if the footsteps behind him were real or the imaginings of his own fevered heart. At any rate, the elusive tracking sound stopped whenever he did, cloaked in the shadows behind.

His teeth scraped the raw tip of his tongue. Wincing, he pressed his fingertips to his temples.

"You're a feeb, boy!" It was his daddy's voice and it didn't matter that Billy Bob Pitkin was almost two-years cold. He had said these same words often enough while he was still alive. "Even the miscarriage of a Cajun slut's got more sense 'n you!"

It was true. He'd gone and let Little Boy run off. The very reason he was here tonight was now gone. The very reason why he'd almost gotten himself killed.

"Little Boy!" he bellowed.

"Boy . . . Boy . . . Boy . . ." An echo taunted him.

A rabbit, startled by the break in early morning stillness, broke cover and bounded across open ground in front of LaVerl. It disappeared again in a copse of brittle shrubbery at his left.

LaVerl straightened. Fatigue spread through his limbs, draining his will to go on. He resisted the urge to collapse on this spot, to sleep off the nightmare chewing at his heels.

He shuffled forward, not bothering to lift his feet any longer. The mist grew more dense as he neared the bog where Little Boy had staged his rebellion earlier in the evening.

Spindles of steam still rose from the stagnant water, weaving its way in and out of the patchwork fog. The marshy ground gave beneath LaVerl's feet and drained his energy further. His breathing was labored and ragged as he plowed through the quickmud and finally onto solid ground once more.

The mist broke for a moment and the moon blazed down on the swamp. Then, just as quickly, it was swallowed again by the damp shadows.

LaVerl paced his steps to his heartbeat. The ground vibrated beneath his feet. But there was a strange cadence to the sound LaVerl couldn't quite put his finger on. Something not quite right, somehow not quite matching his own movements.

It was then that he realized that this was no heartbeat. It was footsteps—real, not imagined this time, stalking the woods behind him.

A moist breeze washed the back of his neck. Adrenaline instantly pulsed to his nerve endings. He forgot his weariness and, charged by fright, ran.

The mist circled around him. The footsteps behind quickened, breaking into a gallop. LaVerl twisted his head and tried to glance over his shoulder as he raced deeper into the fog. His pursuer was close, but still shrouded by the heavy mist.

Suddenly, he was falling. His feet had tangled with an obstruction jutting from the earth below. As he tumbled forward, his elbow smacked the ground and sent a shower of sparks shooting through his crazy bone.

His eyes widened as he recognized the board left protruding from Little Boy's pit, but the momentum of his body pushed him onward. He hit the bridge with the full force of both knees, his back wrenching against the fall. Snatching at the edge of the pit, his fingers grasped, scraped, missed. The board cracked just once under his flying weight, then split in two.

LaVerl's arms pinwheeled as he pitched forward to the base of the pit. There was a snapping sound as he hit. The sound of dry kindling broken across a knee and then LaVerl's leg flamed with white-hot pain. What little air that remained in his lungs was driven from his chest with a *whoosh*.

His vision turned gray. He felt himself drawn to unconsciousness when the footsteps stopped above him.

Slowly, LaVerl raised his head.

Little Boy stood at the edge of the pit, his paws planted firmly apart.

He gazed down at his master with an expression no longer menacing, but curiously detached. The moon crossed behind the dog and seemed to peek down over Little Boy's shoulder with that same curiosity.

LaVerl twisted his shoulders, struggling into a sitting position. His leg blazed with the movement. His vision threatened to darken again. Moaning, he slumped against the side of the pit. Sweat gathered at his hairline, causing his scalp to itch maddeningly. The dog's yellow eyes shifted with each movement, but his stance never changed.

LaVerl glared up at the bull. Pain swiftly turned to rage. "Whadaya think you're starin' at, ya mangy bas—"

Little Boy's muzzle lowered toward LaVerl. His lips peeled back from his teeth. An alarming growl rumbled from his throat.

"Easy, Boy!" LaVerl raised one hand toward the dog. "Easy!"

Little Boy's snarl seemed to turn into a grin. LaVerl's temper flared again. "Listen, Boy!" His tone held an undercurrent of fevered frenzy. "I'm hurt. Ya hear me! *Bad* hurt!"

The dog still grinned.

"Ya gotta help me, Boy! Gotta help me get outta this hole and get to home!"

Oh, how his daddy would have loved that. LaVerl could just picture Billy Bob Pitkin doubled over with laughter, his cheeks flaming, eyes tearing at the fun of it all—askin' Little Boy for help!

"C'mon, Little Boy," LaVerl wheedled.

The dog's eyes narrowed. His gaze was glazed with amber dullness. LaVerl was reminded of a dying runt, its blood staining the dirt around its torn body.

Little Boy turned from the hole. His hind feet sprayed dirt into LaVerl's upturned face.

"Wait! Ya can't leave!" LaVerl screamed. "Don'tcha understand? I'll die down here!"

Little Boy paused and stared down into the pit. LaVerl flinched at the dog's expression of scorn.

"Please," he pleaded. "Please don't leave me alone!"

Little Boy turned for the last time. His bobbed tail twitched once before the moon creased his back with golden light.

LaVerl stretched one arm toward the sky. The sound of Little Boy's padding feet faded away.

"Please," he whispered. LaVerl was left alone with the yellow moon.

And later, somewhere deep in the swamp, a dog howled.

# A RAINY EVENING IN WESTERN ILLINOIS

by Rebecca Lyons

Rebecca Lyons is a former Chicagoan now living in Boulder, Colorado, with four cats, a ton of textbooks, and several musical instruments. Although the bulk of her time is spent pursuing doctoral studies in environmental chemistry at the University of Colorado, the rest of the time she writes. She enjoys cats, folk music, and good beer, and is sincerely and incorrigibly addicted to chocolate. She has written science fiction and fantasy for many years, and has previously published stories and poetry in *Moonscape, Sorcerer's Apprentice, Aliens and Lovers* (an SF erotic poetry anthology), *Owlflight,* and *Starwind.* Two fantasy novels are in the works, as well as a SF novel.

Rebecca says this story developed from one of her own nightmares; so when you hear the patter of rain on your car roof, think once more of this atmospheric tale.

◆ ◆ ◆

There's a certain electricity about a Midwestern storm. You can see it advancing from a long way off, across the tabletop of the plains, like an evil, black wall, pushing the wind and the smell of ozone before it as it passes over the Mississippi into Illinois. When the lightning forks down into the cornfields, it sends a shiver up my back, and the hairs on my hands and the back of my neck stand on end.

I was driving south on 94, from Rock Island-Moline back in the late spring of '65, to visit Linda—sweet, blonde Linda, who still wore a pony tail and my jacket from high school. Far away, though, I could see the mother of a Midwestern storm approaching. It blackened the southwestern horizon and was moving squarely into my path. Outlying lone thunderheads had already dumped sheets of rain across the windshield of my little green Triumph before moving on and letting the sun shine again. Even as I watched, the westering sun broke through, glinting through the slanting sheets and causing a rainbow, which shimmered briefly and died. I'd put the top up long ago and was twiddling the dial of the radio trying to pick up something besides static.

"When I go to sleep," I sang against the thunder. "I never count sheep. I count all the—" I picked up the Everly Brothers from Rock Island and left the radio on for a while, lighting a ciggie and cracking the window a little. I was going a good steady sixty-two miles an hour. With the rain-slick pavement, I didn't want to chance going faster than that. I hadn't had the Triumph quite a year yet, and I had wrecked the Chevy before that.

The radio went static again. As I reached over to fiddle with it, I heard a beep and a red 'Vette pulled around me going maybe seventy-five, eighty miles an hour. He had the top down, and the wind was mussing his Beatle haircut. I reflexively pushed my hair back from my face. He looked like a sissy, and I couldn't for the life of me figure out what the girls saw in that type. Probably had a garage full of 'Vettes at home and could afford to waste one.

Lightning flashed dead ahead, making the radio snap and sizzle. It looked like we were through with the outlyers and were heading dead into mean mama. He'd regret having that top down, that's for sure. At any rate, he was soon out of sight. I found a Shirelles song—no British invasion for me—that lasted until the lightning flashed again.

Soon it was coming down in buckets. The wipers couldn't keep it off the windshield. I had no idea whether the sun had set or not, the black clouds had cut it off so thoroughly. I slowed down to forty, thirty-five, thirty, and then to a crawl, careful to keep away from the ditches at the side of the road.

I was thinking maybe I should just find a place to stay—I only had a couple of bucks on me, but right then a dry motel bed sounded like a good investment—when I saw the 'Vette again.

I could see the skid marks even through the rain, and butt end up in a ditch sat the Corvette. I shook my head and turned the radio off, coasted by him several yards, and stopped by the side of the road. Looked like the stupid fool had done a good job of cashing in his chips for good, but I figured the least I could do was to go back and check. I pulled the flashlight out of the glove compartment and shrugged into my windbreaker, not that that would do much good in this downpour.

It couldn't have been that long ago. One wheel was still spinning. I threw away my sodden cigarette butt and flashed a light on the scene.

"God." He must have been thrown out of the car into the ditch, then had the car land on top of him. He was pinned upside down beneath the car, which was kind of crumpled. All that was visible were his head, shoulders, and right arm. Rivulets of blood ran from beneath his shirt, down his neck and face, to dribble into his hair and be washed away by the rain.

The wonder of it was that he was not only still alive, but conscious. He might have heard me or might have been reacting to the light, but he turned his head in my direction and flopped his right arm at me. His mouth was open. Rain and blood dribbled in and then out again.

"Help me. Oh, my God, please help me."

I felt a little sick. He had that gray, vague look of a man who's already a corpse but just doesn't know it yet. I didn't really think I could do much for him, but I felt I owed it to at least try.

"I'll get help," I yelled at him through the storm. "Wait here." Stupid thing to say. "I'm going to get help." He didn't answer, but he blinked.

The car took a few seconds to start. It doesn't like sitting in wet weather, especially with the lights on. I drove ahead until I could make a U-turn. There was a town five miles or so back down the road, Jerseyburg or Corntown or something like that. I remembered seeing the sign. They might be able to help. I took the road fast but cautious. I didn't want to end up like that poor mother under the 'Vette. The low spots on the road were already filled with water, and I had to pump the brakes a couple times to get them to work right. Maybe that's what happened to him.

It was a tiny burg, maybe a couple dozen houses, but there were lights on in a diner. I drove up in front, stopped, and rushed in.

I stood getting my breath for a moment. There were about half a dozen people there: a teenage couple in a booth, an old fat man at the counter, a couple of old women playing cards at a table, and a middle-aged woman with horn-rim glasses behind the counter. The jukebox was blaring out Jerry Lee Lewis, thank God.

"I gotta use your phone," I blurted. "It's urgent."

Nobody moved for a second. I could've punched them. Finally the woman in horn-rims waved a hand vaguely toward a corner. "Well, there's a pay phone over there . . ."

"Pay phone? Dammit! This is an accident! I mean, this is an emergency." Part of me was saying it was petty to worry about a dime when a man lay trapped under a car in the rain, but I didn't like their attitude. At least the kid didn't have a Beatle haircut.

"Well, it won't do you any good," said one of the card players, a frowsy old woman with gray hair and a green housedress. "The phone lines are down all over the county. Some of the electric lines, too, I've heard, clear to Galesburg."

"They are?" Horn-rims turned to the phone behind the counter, picked it up, and listened for a moment.

"Just what we need, to lose our electricity," the other card player was saying. "And the radio said there were flash floods downstate."

The green-housedress woman shook her head. "I'm surprised it held out till this late in the season."

"You're right, Melba. The phones are out," Horn-rims said. "I can't raise a thing."

"Look—" I began.

"An accident, you say?" The old man had been staring at me, and now he spoke. "What kind of accident?"

"Remember those bad storms in March?" Melba, the green-housedress woman continued.

"Yes, sir," I told him. "Bad car accident. Guy hit a ditch about five or so miles down 94. Now he's trapped under his car."

The old man tossed his napkin on his plate and clapped a hat on his head. "Well. Kate, if the lines come back on, you ring for help." She nodded. "I'm heading to Deputy Price's office. He's got a radio; he can make a call on that. Mikey?" He turned to the teenage guy. "You get your car and meet me there. You may have to drive for help. Get going. No, Bethy. You stay here."

"I know some first-aid," the green-housedress woman offered.

"Thanks. Melba, but I think we'll do all right." The old man and I went out of the diner into the black of the storm. "Young man, why don't you head back up to the accident and put your lights on so we'll know where to stop?"

"Yes, sir." I started toward my car.

"Bad accident, huh?" Mikey said to me. "Pretty cut up?"

"Yep, pretty bad, it looked to me."

"Mikey!"

"I'm going, I'm going."

It was slower getting back. The electrical storm had slackened, but it was full dark, and I didn't want to miss the Corvette. I also didn't want to go into a ditch myself, and three times I had to test the brakes to make sure they worked.

There it was, butt end up. I coasted on beyond like I did before, stopped the car, and put the lights on. Probably run down the battery, but I had no choice. I grabbed the flashlight, ran to the 'Vette, and stopped.

The rain poured down for a full minute as I stood staring.

"Oh, my God."

The light shone on a black pool, pelted with rain. The

ditch had flooded, filled up with water. The Corvette was almost entirely submerged.

I switched the light off. There was nothing I could do for him now. I couldn't help but think of how it must've been, though, being pinned that way, with the blood dribbling down, and the water creeping slowly up, covering his forehead, submerging his eyes, his nostrils, then his mouth. I shivered, teeth chattering, and coughed as if I could feel the water filling my own lungs. With another shiver, I turned toward my car, my little green Triumph. Most likely that wasn't the way it was. No doubt he'd died soon after I'd left, he'd looked half dead anyhow. Probably slipped away within minutes, never even felt the water creep up. . . .

Shuddering, I stopped, my hand on the fender. I was probably getting a cold, or worse, maybe the flu. Being soaked will do it, that and being tired, and no food.

I turned, wondering when the others were going to get here. No use now. Lightning flashed, and I peered into the dark it had left.

"Mikey?" I could've sworn . . . no, impossible. I hadn't heard a car, hadn't seen lights. But he'd seemed slender, not like the old man. Thunder rolled in the north distance, and lightning flashed farther away. I was sure there was someone there, though I couldn't see him in the dark. It gave me an odd feeling.

I shook it away. Someone from a neighboring farm, perhaps. I straightened and took several steps closer.

Lightning flashed nearby, thunder cracked, and I screamed, a harsh, hoarse sound. I knew him now—the leather jacket, the Beatle haircut, and the gray face of a man already dead. The mouth was open, rain running in and out, and the eyes were open and looking at me. I was glad I had not see them too closely.

"My *God*!" Turning, I ran for the car, slipping on the pavement. I got it open and jumped in, thankful now that I'd put the top up, not like the Corvette. . . .

"Please start. Oh, God, please make it start." I didn't look behind me. I cranked the starter. The car went chug,

chug, chug, and died. The battery was low because of the lights, and it didn't like water besides. "God, please start." I wanted to cry. Chug. Chug.

I turned it off and sat, pressing the gas pedal, hoping I wouldn't flood the engine, trying not to let my teeth chatter in case *he* might hear. With a swallow, I tried the car again. Chug-chug-chug. Chug-chug-chug. I turned it off. Maybe next time. Lightning flashed again, the rain momentarily heavier. Where were Mikey and the rest?

I put my hand on the keys again, trying not to rattle them with my shaking fingers.

There was somebody beside the car, by the passenger side. Did I lock that door? I couldn't remember. I tried the car again. Chug-chug-chug. Chug-chug-whirr. Chug. "Oh, my God. Oh, my God. Please help me. Oh, my God." I heard a noise, and remembered that this was a convertible—oh, my God, did he want my car?—I'd heard that . . . that the nails grew after death, was it possible . . . do corpses have claws? I tried the car again, trying to run the thin line between goosing it enough to make it start, and flooding it or running down the battery.

I didn't want to look, but I had to. He was bending down, looking into the window. There was that gray face, the open mouth, rain running in and then out. He raised his right arm—was that a claw?—and looked at me. I couldn't help it—hand frozen on the ignition key, I met his eyes.

There was somebody hollering with terror and it was me, and mixed with the smell of rain and ozone, there arose an acrid smell of piss. I could feel my bladder release and was ashamed, but couldn't stop it any more than I could stop the hoarse madman's screams that were coming from my mouth. I had met his eyes, and *there was something gold glinting and moving in his eyes that should not have been there.* My hand spasmed on the key, and the car roared to life.

My foot had been pressed down on the gas pedal, and the car screeched out of there, skidding on the wet highway. I jammed on the brakes, and it screeched again and did a full turn. I wrinkled my nose at the smell of piss and scanned the horizon, hoping it would be empty.

There *he* was, standing right in the middle of the road. I gunned it and bore down on him. He didn't move. I didn't look at him, not even when I felt the sickening thump that meant I'd hit him. I tried not to look at him when he was sprawled across the hood of the Triumph, face pressed against the windshield. For some crazy reason, I turned on the windshield wipers and kept bearing down the highway, full tilt, veering this way and that, skidding all over the place. He stayed there, till I felt a scream rising up from my lungs into my throat, the final scream that would drive me over. . . .

Then he just sort of came apart, like he was a bag full of garbage or mud. He fell apart. Some lay in clumps on the hood; some got on the windshield and streamed away in rivulets, from the rain and the windshield wipers. I couldn't help but think of the rivulets of rain and blood that had dribbled into his mouth and then out again. Then suddenly there were lights and sirens and horns. I stamped on the brakes.

"What the f— Son, just what do you think you're doing?" It was the old fat man, getting out of the deputy's car, as I opened the driver's door of mine and sat there, mouth open, gulping like a fish. "Driving the wrong way down the road like that, in this weather; you could've killed someone!" There was the deputy's car, another sheriff's car, an ambulance. Mikey was getting out of his car, his eyes wide, staring.

"He was there." My voice was as reedy and shaking as an old man's. "He was there." My voice wouldn't steady out. I pointed down the road. My hand shook, too.

"What the hell are you talking about?" demanded the old man. "Who was there? The guy in the accident? I thought you said he was pinned under his car."

The deputy had gotten out of the car and stood listening. Now he took a flashlight and ran down the road, followed by the paramedics.

"He was there," I insisted, and stood up. My legs shook, too. I tried to smooth the front of my jeans. I smelled like piss and I knew it. I hoped the rain would soak some of it away. I hoped, too, that it would wash away whatever was on the hood of my car. I didn't look to see.

"If he was pinned," I heard the deputy say slowly, "there's no way he could've gotten out." I glanced down the road. We were closer to the accident than I had thought. The deputy just stood there at the side of the road by the Corvette, shaking his head at the black pool that reflected the light of his flashlight. "Nothing much we can do here. Not till the rains stop and the floods go down." He shook his head again.

"But I saw him." I took a few steps forward and tugged at the front of my jeans. Mikey just stood open-mouthed, staring first at the deputy, then at me.

The deputy turned to me. "Who? Who did you see?" He walked back toward me, swinging his light so that the glare hit me in the face. I flinched and turned away. "I thought you said he was pinned beneath the car."

"He was. I—" I could hardly tell them I'd run him over. Again I shivered, thinking about how he had come apart like that, like a bag full of mud.

"He could've been pinned," the old man said, "then found his way out when the flood started up. Thing like that give even a dying man impetus."

I shivered and turned from them.

The deputy glanced at me, then nodded. "In that case, he might still be wandering around injured somewhere, and we'd better find him before he stumbles into another flooded ditch and drowns for real." He turned to the other deputy, who'd been listening from the other side of the car, one foot propped up on the fender. "Paul, we'd better keep searching for a while. Radio for some more men. He might be wandering around the highway somewhere." He glanced up at the sky. "Rain's slackening off a little, anyway." He looked at me for a long moment. "Look, son, have you eaten this evening?" I shook my head. "Look, why don't you sit over here in the squad car. There's a blanket there and a thermos of coffee, and there might be a doughnut or two left." He guided me over. "Just sit for a couple minutes and rest." He led me into the car, handed me a blanket, a thermos, and a box with a dry doughnut and a half in it. There was no way out of the back seat, I noticed. I sipped at the coffee, nibbled at the half a doughnut, and felt miserable.

They were talking out there, he and the old man. I could hear snatches of it.

"Something frightened the boy, Ben," the old man was saying. "You saw him."

"Yeah, well, if you were seventeen and saw someone half dead wandering around in a storm, it might frighten you, too."

"I'm nineteen," I mumbled, and felt ashamed again. They thought I looked like a kid. Linda always said she thought I looked twenty-one.

The other deputy yelled something, and Ben yelled something back, then turned back to the old man.

"Maybe we ought to take him back to town, Ben," the old man was saying. "Give him a bed for the night, one of Kate's meals. Boy don't look too good."

"I thought you'd think that, you soft-hearted old coot, but consider this: there might well be something funny going on, and he might be it. Ever think that he might be a little over the deep end himself?" The old man didn't say anything. "Would you really want him around your wife and daughter?" I wondered if Bethy was his daughter.

I knocked on the window, and they glanced at me. "I'm all right," I told them. "I'm all right. Can I go home now?"

They glanced at each other, then Ben, the deputy, came over, opened the door, squatted down beside me, and smiled. "Listen, son, why don't we take you back to town, give you a decent meal at Kate's place, some coffee, then you come down to the station, make a statement. You know, report the accident, tell what you saw. Then I see no reason why you can't go home tonight. Where do you live?"

"Moline."

"I see. You go to school there?"

"No."

He nodded. "I see. Well, that's not too far away. I see no reason why—after you've made a statement and given us your name and phone number—why you can't go home tonight. Do you, Andy?" He looked at the old man, who shook his head.

I stood up, handed the thermos to him, and sneezed.

"Best get you out of the cold, eh?" He slapped me on the shoulder. "We'll give you an escort back, make sure you don't run into any ditches." He chuckled. I didn't think it was funny.

I opened the door of my Triumph and paused while Paul called Ben over for a moment. Suddenly a thought stopped me cold. I slammed the driver's door and hurried over to the passenger's side.

There was a tear. There was a tear in the roof on the passenger's side of the Triumph. I started to shake again, and a sound, like a moan or a whimper, began to form deep within my throat. Andy, the old fat man, was looking at me funny. I glanced down at the hood. The rain had washed it clean.

I got into the car. I looked for some ciggies, but the rest of the pack was on the floor and had gotten wet.

I skipped the meal at the diner, hungry though I was, even if it was free. I didn't want to sit there and smell of piss and have them all *know*. As it was I fidgeted all through the statement at the station, messing up my story and getting strange looks in return.

I never saw that piece of road again. I went back north to Moline from the town that night. I didn't stop seeing Linda, of course, and eventually drove south again, but by a different route, and never when it was storming bad. I occasionally wondered about stopping back at the town and finding out if they really did find a corpse at the bottom of that ditch, but how could I ask? And would they tell me the truth? Besides, I never did find out the name of that burg. I patched the tear on the Triumph and sold it. Bought a Volkswagen Beetle that I kept until they stopped making them. I got my hair cut into bangs, too, after a couple years.

The storms announce themselves from a long way off in parts of western Illinois. Flat as the proverbial pancake. And when the storms blacken the southwestern horizon and the lightning forks down into the cornfields, it sends a shiver up my spine and makes the hairs on my arms stand on end.

But not just from the ozone and the electricity. Not anymore.

# COMING BACK

## by Ginger LaJeunesse

Ginger LaJeunesse has been a professional artist since the age of sixteen and has sold poetry to various magazines. She's also been a carny, electronic technician, singer for a rock band, and antique store co-owner. Presently employed by a major telecommunications company, she works with computers. A single parent with a teen-aged son, she makes her home in San Jose, California. Ginger has a large rambunctious canine with a taste for shoes, and a mouse who lives in the stove. She collects turn-of-the-century children's fairy tale books, fantasy art, animated films, pre-1930s' jewelry, American art pottery, and Frisbees.

A mother's love, we all know, is strong, but the answer to just how strong is provided here.

♦ ♦ ♦

It's one of those wild nights. You know the ones I mean, with the midnight wind howling through the trees. The moon gazes down from a sky full of stars, and I feel sixteen all over again. The wind flings my hair around my face on the walk over to the pool hall. By the time I get there I'm one big itch looking for a scratch. There's this crazy musician-type, all long hair and legs, leaning up against the bar. I feel my jeans melt into me just looking at him.

He comes over to where I'm standing right inside the door, comes over slow, like he isn't interested. "Let's not stay inside," he says. "The night's too fine. Let's take a ride over the hill."

He throws his jacket on a guitar-case in the back of a really great car. A 'Vette or something. We roar off into the night, laughing like kids, like sixteen.

The highway over the hill is great. Twisting, turning,

banks all the wrong way. A challenge to every kid with wheels. When you're a kid you know life is forever.

We hit the first big turn and I lean forward to find a good station on the FM. Something we can sing to. Something crazy. Old Steppenwolf or early Springsteen, before he became the Boss and got respectable. I find the perfect song: "Stairway to Heaven." Going around the turn the rear tires slide a little, and I look at the speedometer. Sixty-five on the nose. I say, "Are we going too fast?" He laughs. I laugh, too. This is great. This is life. Trees rush by so fast all I see is a dark green blur.

He takes the next turn at seventy. It *is* too fast. The rear tires break loose. I have just enough time to think *Oh shit!* and we're sliding toward the edge. There's at least a hundred-foot drop. Enough time to think *What the fuck am I doing here anyway?* And then I'm dead.

One problem here, folks, is that I'm not sixteen like I'm feeling. I'm thirty and I got a kid waiting at home for me. He's eight and we're one of those single-parent families you read about. I can't be dead. Not now. Who the hell is going to take care of Jason?

Yeah, I know I should have thought about it sooner, like before I got in the guy's car. So don't lecture me. Just remember back to when you were young, when the wind sang in your blood and you had to go and go.

I'm not the best mother in the world, but I always look out for my kid. So I resolve, and it isn't easy, but I have some time, being upside-down at the bottom of a canyon. I just won't go. Not yet. Maybe later. After I find someone for my kid.

I'm restarting my heart when the paramedics get there. One crunches over to the driver's side. "This one's a goner, Dave. Pass me the Hefty." I think about the musician for a second and then go back to my heart. Nothing. I try some more. I hear someone lean in on my side, faintly, like through cotton wool. I can't see at all. "This one looks bad, too. Bring that flashlight over here." He gropes for my wrist, fumbles around in the dark. "Okay. Hold that light."

He feels for my pulse. "Nope, nothing here either." He lets go and backs away. His voice fades. "It must have been a hell of a crash."

Goddamnit, I will *not* be dead! They come back, shaking open the body bag. I will my heart to beat, my blood to flow. *Come on,* I tell my insides. *Live.* Just for now. Please.

The same voice calls for the firemen. Heavy feet come over to my side of the car with what sound like tin snips. Jaws of life, I remember. They scrunch and the door is open. The firemen take me out, not too gentle. Must think I've croaked. Another one, a woman this time, leans over where I'm lying in the dirt. I smell her perfume. *Check me, lady,* I beg silently. *I'm not gone yet.*

"Are you sure she's dead?"

"Sure, I'm sure," says the first one. "She has no pulse, Karen, nothing. Why?"

"I dunno, Mike," the babe says. "There's something . . . Her forehead is wet. Dead people don't sweat, do they?" She squats down and grabs my wrist.

"It's fog, Karen." He starts to walk away.

"No, not the fog." She probes my wrist. *I'm trying,* I tell her, but she can't hear me.

Mike comes back over. "Anything?"

"No . . . no." She sounds disappointed.

"She's dead, Karen. Give it up. You can't make her alive again. Get used to it. People die every day."

Easy for him to say, he's not lying in the dirt. Karen keeps hanging onto my arm like a terrier with a rat. She gets a pulse. I'm alive again. Sort of.

"Mike!" She's excited, yelling. "There's a heartbeat!"

"You're crazy."

"No, I'm not." She's got her fingers so far into my wrist she's about to cut off my circulation, which just got restarted. "She has a pulse! Slow and thin, but there." She straightens up and starts shouting for help. IVs and lights and a stretcher, right out of *Emergency*. Mike hunkers down beside me and takes my wrist again. Thud, I feel against his fingers, thud, nothing, nothing, nothing . . . thud.

"I'll be damned, you are alive," he says, softly. Only I hear. He brushes bloody hair off my forehead. "Quite a fighter, aren't you? I thought you were gone." He backs off, and someone slides a needle in my arm. I blink. My sight is returning, but all these people are still only shapes in the dark. A stretcher gets under me and we're finally in business. *About time,* I think. *A girl could die out here.*

They swing my stretcher up slow, so as not to bang me against anything, and winch me to the top. On the way up, I glimpse a bag, crazy-musician size, beside the twisted corpse of his car. I don't even know his name.

♦ ♦ ♦

Don't ever end up in the emergency room late on a Friday night. It's awful. People moaning and puking and dying everywhere.

I'm better now. My heart's thumping great, and I can tell the blood is flowing because the cut on my head is bleeding all over me. They wheel me in on a gurney; that part's okay. Red lights flashing, the IV hanging on a pole beside me, Mike patting me on the arm telling me I'll be fine.

A nurse comes over. She calls an aide, and they start cutting off my jeans. "Hey!" I yell. "These are fifty-dollar jeans."

"Honey." She glances at me and keeps on cutting. "You're lucky to be alive. Don't worry about your pants."

I see her point. They finish getting my jeans off and start sponging. "I have to call home." I try to get up. She shoves me down. "I have to call my son. He's only eight. He's alone."

"You aren't going anywhere." She frowns at me. "Alone?" Looks around. "Someone will call your son." She hands Mike my purse.

The doctor comes over to my gurney. "We'll have to admit you for observation, young lady. You got pretty banged up out there."

"No!" He stares at me, surprised. Oops, too panicky. I try it again, calmer. "I'm fine now." I start to get up again, and the nurse glares at me. "Really, Doctor, I'm okay now, just clean me up and let me go home. I have a little boy to take care of."

"I can't let you out yet." He writes something on my chart. "One night for observation and we'll see how you're doing in the morning. Okay?"

"No, it's *not* okay." I'm belligerent now, but can't help it. I have to go home. "I'm leaving, and I'm leaving now!" Out of the corner of my eye I see the nurse pick up a needle. The doctor nods. *Uh-oh,* I think. No drugs for this girl. I might not wake up. The nurse heads my way, needle gleaming. "Wait!" I say. "I'll be good. No drugs, no pills. I . . . I'm allergic to everything." The nurse stops. The doctor shrugs. I relax a little. They motion to the aide, and he moves me into a ward for the night.

I stay awake the whole time. I can't let my body sleep. It's easy for a while, what with all the groans and smothered tears, some of which are mine. What a mess. At dawn it quiets down and I squeeze my eyes shut to rest for a moment. When I open them again the paramedic, Mike, stands by my bed.

"You were dead," he says.

"Nah. Not even close."

He shakes his head. "When I checked you the first time you had no pulse, nothing."

"You weren't trying hard enough." *What is he doing here,* I wonder. "Karen, now she's got fingers of steel." I hold up my wrist. Purple bruises make a bracelet.

He stands there and looks unhappy. A nurse bustles in. I swear they're trained to do that. Bustle and bitch. You know, always in a hurry and always mad. I guess if they act mad at you it doesn't hurt them so much if you up and die.

The nurse asks if I need a bedpan. I shake my head. Nothing works like it used to, not even that.

"I have something for you." Mike has blue eyes. I always was a sucker for blue eyes. And blond hair. He has that, too.

"What?"

Mike looks at my face. "I'll be back in a minute." He leaves.

I remember that I still haven't called home. Jesus! Jason must be going crazy by now. I sit up, get my elbow under me. "Nurse! I got to call my kid."

She turns, holding a bedpan meant for someone else. "But your son is here. Mike went to get him."

I gasp. "Get me a mirror and a comb. I don't want to scare him to death." She hands me my purse from the table. I dig out a small mirror and look in. Someone else looks back. I put the mirror back. Whoever that person is, she'd frighten Godzilla.

The door to the ward opens and my son hurtles across the room. I grab him and hug him hard. He's got tears running down his small face. "Gee, Mom," he finally says. "You look awful."

"Thanks, Jason." I already knew that.

"What happened, Mom?" His face crumples like a used tissue. "I was so scared. It got late and you didn't come home and then Mike called."

I guess I look surprised. "Who?"

"Mike, the para-doctor-guy. You remember, the one who saved you. He said you'd been in an accident. Then he came over and stayed with me until morning. Then we came here to see you."

I'm in shock. "Mike went to our house?"

"Yeah, Mom, and brought *his* kid, too. And this morning we stopped at McDonald's and he bought breakfast for all of us."

More shock. "Breakfast?"

"Yeah, but I couldn't eat very much." Another tear leaks out of his eye. "I was still scared."

"I know, baby. It's okay now." I kiss his soft freckled cheek. "Everything will be all right."

"Will it?" It's Mike again. He's better than a rabbit out of a hat.

"Yes," I say. "Everything will be peachy once I get the

hell out of here." I hit the bell for the nurse. She comes—you guessed it—bustling in. "I want my doctor."

"He'll be here later this morning."

"I want him *now*."

"Why?" Mike butts in.

"Because I'm outta here, that's why. I'm gone. I'm history." That's too close. I feel tears start. I tell myself not to blubber like a damn baby. "I have things to do, Mike." I turn to the nurse and say, sweetly, "I tell you what. If you go get my doctor now, I won't pull this IV out of my arm."

She glares at me, but I win. She leaves, no bustle this time. I better not end up in this hospital again.

Doctors don't bustle. Ever. They don't have to. Look at Marcus Welby. He never did it once. The doctor who stalks in five minutes later is no exception.

"Hi, Doc." I smile. My face feels funny but everything stays attached. "I want to be released."

He comes over to the bed and takes my wrist. "Your pulse is not very good, young lady."

*Understatement of the year, Doctor.* "I still want to be released. I feel fine. And I have a son who needs me home."

The doctor glances at Jason.

"Well?" I say.

"You were in a very serious car accident last night, uh . . ."—he looks at my chart—"Debbie. The driver was killed instantly. You have multiple abrasions and contusions. Some blood loss, too. And a very weak pulse."

Cuts and bruises, I translate. Can't help those. The pulse I'm working on. Constantly.

"She does seem better now, Doctor, considering how she was when we found the wreck." Mike again. He's appointed himself my watchdog, I guess. He sure is cute. "It's almost miraculous." Oops, he's getting warm now. I'll have to be careful. I look at him narrowly. He grins back.

"It was a bad crash, Debbie," the doctor is saying. "Sometimes the victim of such a crash doesn't make it through the first night. They die of shock."

"Well, I made it, Doc. I didn't die of shock." Not last night anyway. "And now I want out."

He looks at Jason again and then at my chart.

"I'm all he has, Doctor. I have to go home."

"No relatives you can leave him with for a few days? No friends?"

I shake my head. "No, none at all." Unless you count guys with lots of leather who ride big Harleys.

"Tell you what," the doctor finally says. "I'll come back this afternoon. If you feel this strongly about it then we'll reevaluate." I love the way he talks.

"In English, is that: if I feel okay I can go?"

"No. If *I* say you're okay you can go."

"It's a deal."

He leaves. Mike follows. I hug Jason harder. I make up my mind to be okay by that afternoon. It can't be any harder than what I've done already.

♦ ♦ ♦

Jason looks at me across the kitchen table. "Are you sure you're all right. Mom? You still look awful."

"I'm fine, baby." I brush hair back from his forehead. He needs it cut. I think about my sister. She has hair the same red as my son. It runs in our family. I think of Mom and Dad, retired and living in Nowhere, Nebraska. I sigh. "Finish your cereal, Jason. It's almost time for the bus." I can't keep him home from school, though I'd like to. Things need to be as normal as possible.

"Sure, Mom." He swallows the last spoonful of Frosted Flakes and races out the door, grabbing books on the way. Just another day for him. Kids adapt so fast. I look at the phone. This is not going to be easy. I dial and hope my sister's not home. No such luck."

"Nina? This is Debbie. How's things going?"

"Fine, Debbie. What's up?"

All right, she's in a good mood. "Well, I have a serious question for you."

"Serious? You?" She goes off into gales of laughter. I

wait. Now is not the time to start a fight. "Okay, okay. What's the question?"

"If something happened to me, would you take Jason?" I wait again. There is silence on the other end. This is long distance, but I don't worry about paying the bill. I cough a little. My throat feels funny. More silence. I think about Nina's lifestyle. Weekends in Tahoe. Trips to Spain. If I could do all that I wouldn't want to take on an eight-year-old either. And I've known for a long time that my sister doesn't really like kids. Neither do I, for that matter, but the one in question is mine, and that's different.

"This is a hypothetical question," she finally says, "isn't it, Debbie?"

"Of course, Nina. I'm only thirty." Boy, is she in for a surprise.

"Well, if you can't find anyplace else for him. Put me last on your list when you make your will." She giggles. "You still have that silver shirt, the one you go dancing in? I want that, too."

*You can have my whole fucking wardrobe if you'll just take my kid.* I almost say it out loud but catch myself in time. Jason wouldn't be happy there anyway. After I hang up I sit and stare at the phone. I'm reaching out to call my mom when it rings and almost scares me to death. I know, not funny. I pick it up.

"Hi, Debbie. This is Mike."

"Mike?"

"Yeah, Mike. You remember me. From the hospital."

"I remember you. You took my son to McDonald's." I feel guilty. I never thanked him.

"I'd like to come over and see how you're doing."

"Well, okay. But not for too long." Maybe I'm not being Princess Charming, but this guy is taking up my time, which I haven't got mass quantities of.

"Debbie, I really like you and Jason. You have a lot of spunk—a lot of moxie, as they used to say. I've never seen anyone stand up to Dr. Rhodes the way you did. I'd like to be your friend. I think you need one right now."

"What the fuck do you mean by that?" He's getting too weird again, too close.

"Don't get mad, Debbie. I just want to help."

"I don't need help. I don't need you or anyone else. I never have. Go away!" I slam down the phone. It doesn't ring again.

I stand up and go look for a dictionary. What the hell is *moxie*? It feels odd to walk. I do it, but stiffly.

◆ ◆ ◆

"Can I have some ice cream, Mom?" Jason puts down his fork. "I'm all done with dinner." He glances around, a puzzled expression on his face. "What's that smell?"

"Must be your socks, fella. You should change them once in a while."

He goes to the kitchen, taking his plate. I grab mine and follow.

"There's no ice cream."

"Oh damn!" I put my plate in the sink. "I forgot to go to the store." Jason stares at my plate. Then at me. "I wasn't hungry," I say. I shove a box of cookies at him. "Here, have these." He takes the box. "But I wanted ice cream," he says on his way to the TV. Too bad, Jason, I think. We don't always get what we want. I wanted to live forever. I hear him turn the TV on. I lean my face against the refrigerator. It's nice and cool. I should put more perfume on. Maybe it will help.

*What do you do about Jason now, Debbie?* Who the fuck knows. I think about my mom and dad again. Retired. And they don't like kids either. I always knew that. Especially when they told me they would never babysit for me so don't bother asking, Debbie, you do understand, don't you? Sure I do.

I should have remarried. Just because the first guy was a bastard doesn't mean they all are. I should have done it years ago. I can't go out and find someone to fall in love with me. It's too late for that. I think about Mike. How nice he is and how great he was with Jason. Even after I was a shit to him. And he's so cute, just the kind I would have gone for. But I don't feel too romantic now. I don't feel sixteen anymore, not even thirty. The cold from the fridge soaks into my cheek and stays there. I feel pretty dead.

The doorbell rings. "I'll get it," Jason yells. He opens the door. "Hey, Mom. It's Mike."

"Tell him I'm not . . ." I say, but it's too late. He's already in the living room. I move my body around the corner and stand there, looking at him. He really *is* cute. Why do I always end up on the short end of the stick? Where the fuck was he three days ago? I know, out scrapping bodies off the road.

"Sit down," I say. I'm trying to maintain. It's getting harder as time goes by. I sit, too.

"Debbie," he says, "do you have any relatives who can help you?" God, he does get right to the point.

"I got a sister down south."

"Will she come and stay with you and Jason for a few days? Until you're back on your feet?"

"Probably not." I stare at the bruises on my wrist. It would be a waste of her time anyway. I haven't much feet left to get back on to. "She's into Lears and limos. Not kids."

"Your parents?"

"They're retired and don't live around here anyway."

"What would have happened to Jason if you hadn't made it back from the accident? Where would he go?"

As if I hadn't been asking myself the same question since being upside-down in that blood-soaked canyon. This guy is getting real close to home. Why? "You get personal, don't you? You don't even know me."

"I know more than you think."

Jason is looking real interested in this conversation. I notice it's his bedtime. "That's it, kid. Wash up and hit the sack. Now!" I add, when he doesn't move. He scrambles up and shoots down the hall.

Mike is watching me watch Jason. "You're not so tough," he says.

"He's all I've got. I'm all he's got."

"And that brings me back to my question. What will you do?"

I try to say something. I even open my mouth but nothing comes out. Then to my complete and utter humiliation I start to cry. That function still works. And then I can't stop. Mike comes over and puts his arm around me until I'm through. I hiccup a few times, like a baby. Dear God, I think, don't let him notice anything. I wonder if I put enough perfume on.

"I'm sorry, Mike. I don't know what happened." I reach for the Kleenex on the table. He hands me the box.

"I know what happened. You're at the end of your rope and you don't know what to do. You were nuts to get released. You should go back to the hospital and be thoroughly checked out. You're worse off than you'll admit. I think you're in real trouble."

"I can't go back to the hospital. I can't explain, either."

Mike doesn't look happy. "Okay. You can at least go back in a couple of days and let the doctor look you over."

"No!" I yell, and stand up. He looks surprised. "Look, Mike," I say. "I appreciate whatever the hell you're trying to do for me. But please, let me take care of myself." *Why don't I let him help me?* a voice inside me asks. *Just for once, let someone in. Before it really is too late.*

"And your son?"

"And . . . and my son." I feel tears prick my eyelids again. *Moxie, Debbie.* I tell myself. It means courage, according to good old Webster.

Mike leans forward. "There was something you were saying, out there in the dark, about not being able to go yet. Because of your son. You kept saying his name over and over again." He pauses, not quite looking at me. "Maybe I'm way out of line, but I have a boy of my own, a little older than yours. I started wondering what would happen to my child if I left someday and never came back."

"That's easy, Mike. You croak, your wife raises the kid." Simple, for most people.

"My wife died a couple of years ago," he says. "There's my parents and hers, but they're getting old, just like yours."

"Mike, what exactly are you trying to say?" I want this game to end. I'm too tired to play anymore. It's an effort to breathe. I remember a book I read a long time ago, in school. It was about lepers. Every day of their lives they check their bodies to make sure that no fingers and toes have fallen off. They can't feel anything so they have to check. I know I'm falling apart. And I want to. But I have to finish one thing first.

Mike looks directly at me. He smiles and I think maybe this is the right thing to do. What choice do I have? A foster home, ward of the court, strangers caring for my son?

"Tell me about Jason," he says and takes my hand. "Tell me what he likes in school. Who his friends are. What he hates to eat." I bend my head, stare at the rug. "Tell me, Debbie." He sounds encouraging. "You know how important this is."

♦ ♦ ♦

I do know how important this is, Mike. I came back a long way for this. I don't know if you figured that out or not. It doesn't matter. I know I trust you, though I'm not sure why. Gut feeling, perhaps. I don't have much choice anyway, do I? You were there when I needed you and stayed even when I told you to fuck off. There's a word for that, Mike, you know what it is.

My insurance stuff is in the top left dresser drawer in my bedroom. So are all of Jason's important papers. Birth certificate, immunization, all that bullshit. I had a will made today. It's in the drawer, too. If there's a hassle just show the sons-of-bitches the will and this letter.

Tell Jason that I'm sorry. He's the best kid anyone could ever want. Love him for me, Mike.

I can't hold on much longer. My dad used to say, *Where there's a need, there's a way*. I have the need, but I'm losing the way. It's hard to keep breathing and my pulse stopped twice this morning. You'd be proud, though, I learned how to take my own. Tell Karen I'll always have the bruise she gave me. I'll carry it to the grave.

And give my sister the silver shirt. Tell her to think of me when she wears it dancing. When the wind whistles through the trees and the stars glisten down and she feels sixteen all over again. Please tell her.

# I KNOW WHAT TO DO

## by Yvonne Navarro

Yvonne Navarro grew up mostly in Chicago, although she spent a few years living in Nashville. A legal secretary, who lives outside of Chicago now, she types 113 words per minute, and has had short stories published in *The Horror Show, Haunts, Deathrealm, The Gauntlet, Twisted,* and other small press magazines. She is a member of Horror Writers of America and is always working on one of a number of novels. This is her first professional sale.

This is one of the lightest stories in this volume, but it is by no means humorous—unless you have a deep-down dark streak as I do.

◆ ◆ ◆

We moved into the apartment in March. I hadn't liked the place since the first time we saw it, but I didn't tell Maggie until after it was too late to do anything. I don't know why, maybe I wanted to have something to hold over her head. It seemed like she'd controlled everything since we got married: the money, where we lived, what we ate, everything. If I'd said how much I hated the place—and I think I did drop a couple of obvious hints—she would have sat across from me at the kitchen table with that "let's talk about this in a reasonable manner" look on her face and explain how we were saving money (twenty-five bucks a month, big fucking deal), the landlord at the old place was going to sell the building and then the rent would go up, on and on, until I ended up agreeing with her anyway. By keeping my mouth shut I had future artillery if I wanted it.

Not that I don't love her, I do. I wouldn't have married her otherwise, not after the shit I went through with my first wife. In fact, if you wanted to use Maggie's psychobabble, the ex probably had a lot to do with my attraction to

Maggie. Security, a sense of organization, her always knowing what to do—sounds like a bunch of crap for a man to be saying, doesn't it? Like the old expression goes, you had to be there. Spend a few years with my ex and you'll understand.

The place was all right, I suppose. It was hard to compete with my old apartment and its golden wood floors and wall full of unblocked east windows. The new one was standard inner-city Chicago: dark and somewhat smaller, with a building on the east and an alley on the west. It was a first floor, too, and it made me nervous to think how easy it would be for some punk to break in, whether or not we were home.

We moved in.

The dog acted weird right from the start.

♦ ♦ ♦

"Get out of there!"

At 5:45 in the morning I wasn't expecting any loud noises and I nearly overturned my coffee when Maggie yelled. The small hallway that was the connecting point of most of the rooms was mostly in shadows, but I could still make out Chanci's gangly black shape with her head poked into the bathroom.

"What the hell is she doing?" I asked.

The dog made the mistake of stepping into the bathroom and Maggie was down the hall instantly to plant a solid whack on Chanci's rump. *"Out!"* The animal backpedaled and ran for the living room, nails slipping on the linoleum. For a second I thought she was going to trip and fall flat and I groaned inside; the dog was so clumsy it was embarrassing.

Maggie glanced into the bathroom and looked around, muttering to herself about dog hairs. It was still early, so I decided to keep my opinion about white throw rugs to myself.

"What was she looking at?" I asked, reaching down to tie my boots.

"I don't know," she said, flipping on the light. "There's nothing in here—wait! Oh, Jesus." She sounded disgusted.

"Now what?" I looked at the boots doubtfully. There was some serious wear around the backs; I figured by the end of the week I'd need a new pair and wondered if we had the money. Out of that same paycheck would have to come Dolly's alimony payment. With a name like that you'd think I would have known better.

"I think we've got cockroaches."

I got up and went to the bathroom door. "Where? Did you see one?" The room looked clean to me—too clean. That's the effect when you use too much white, like in a hospital. Personally I always went for blue.

"I think so—I mean I saw *something*. It ran under the bathtub."

We had one of those old-fashioned claw-foot tubs, the kind with about four or five inches of space under it. I got down on my knees and peered underneath, but it was too dark to see anything. That was another thing that went against the place: one stupid fluorescent light in the bathroom. I hated fluorescent lights and my list of grievances was growing longer. There was something way in the back, but I wasn't sure; maybe just a hole in the plaster around the baseboard—the building wasn't exactly in great shape. I stuck an arm under the tub and groped around for a few seconds, knowing that no cockroach on this earth is going to let me catch it. I've lived in worse places and roaches were old territory to me.

Something bit me on the forefinger.

I mean really *bit* me—fire spread up my finger and through the palm even before I could yank my arm out from beneath the tub. *"Son of a bitch!"* I screamed, jerking up from the floor and grabbing for the faucet. Garbled thoughts of scorpions under the tub ran through my head.

"What happened? John, are you okay?" If Maggie thought *she* was frantic, she should've had the feeling of burning napalm going through her hand like I did. While the icy water cooled the stinging, the water pressure made it throb nastily. Being a stonemason has gotten me a few fingers sandwiched between slabs of granite, but man, I'd *never* hurt this bad. Air hissed in and out from between my teeth, but I'll give Maggie one thing: she knows when to keep her mouth shut. When I didn't answer, she just stood there and waited, working her hands together nervously.

After a few minutes, the water seemed to do the trick and I turned it off so we could examine my finger. The only thing we found were two tiny, swollen places, one on each side just under the edge of the nail—maybe that's why it hurt so much—where minute chunks of skin were gone. But the bites weren't even bleeding, or if they had the water had washed it away. While I still didn't know what had done it, I was relieved. Visions of mice and rats swirled in my brain; I didn't know if mice carried rabies or not, but with no teeth marks on my hand I wouldn't have to worry about it.

"Do cockroaches bite?" Maggie asked doubtfully as she dabbed Polysporin on the wound and wrapped it with a Band-Aid.

"I've never had one bite me before," I answered. "Though I have read that in places where there are major infestations, like in housing projects, they'll eat the eyelashes off sleeping babies." She gaped at me, and I realized I'd made a mistake.

Her face twisted. "That's revolting!"

What can I say? It was too late anyway; as I left for work she was hauling bucket and rags and pine cleaner out of the pantry. I figured in the hour before she'd have to get ready for work she'd have our white bathroom smelling like a hospital, too.

♦ ♦ ♦

The next morning I saw it. Maggie was in the kitchen packing my lunch and thankfully didn't see the dog crouching half inside the bathroom door, or Chanci would've probably gotten a couple of whacks for doing it two days in a row. I couldn't stand to see that—Chanci may be big (she's half Lab and half Great Dane), but she's nothing but a silly puppy in a ten-year-old body. And normally well-behaved: she doesn't bark, bite, or crap in the house. It seemed a shame for her to get cracked just because the bathroom had bugs and she was curious.

Though I could understand why! The damn thing was huge, maybe as long as my thumb, a couple of inches at least—no exaggeration. It went scuttling backward under the tub when I reached around and flipped the light switch, but I could have sworn that it was only about half a foot away from the dog—like it wasn't afraid of her at all.

Well, Mama didn't raise an idiot, and I'd be damned if I was going to stick my hand back under the tub. To be honest, the memory of that pain was enough to make me hesitate about kneeling down and looking, but in the end I did, after glancing out the door and making sure Maggie was still messing with my lunch box. It would really make her crazy to think there was a roach crawling around the bathroom she'd practically sterilized yesterday. I thought I saw it, way back in the corner—the same spot as yesterday, when I'd stupidly tried to grab it.

I got back up and strolled into the kitchen without saying anything, first making sure that Chanci was in the other room to stay.

"I think I'll pick up some bug spray on the way home," I said.

Maggie whirled. I could see her fingers clench around the peach that was slotted for today's dessert and resigned myself to bruised fruit. "Did you see another one? Where? In the bathroom again?"

"No," I lied. "Just a precaution. We never did catch that one yesterday. Unless you. . . ?" She shook her head. "That's goes to show you. It'll probably come back, maybe with a family." She scrunched up her shoulders and shivered. "We'll start spraying, every day at first, then once a week. That'll kill them off and keep them gone."

♦ ♦ ♦

Friday morning I sat at the kitchen table—sometimes it seemed we spent our lives at the kitchen table—and made out Dolly's check. Maggie paid the other bills that were due and pushed a few aside that she figured could hold out another week; I could feel a breeze in a few places in my boots, but new ones would still have to wait. The alimony was the only bill I had to take care of personally and, after four years, writing that check still hurt to the heart. While Maggie didn't complain—which wouldn't have made any difference—she refused to write the check out and made me mail it myself.

Dolly was living on public assistance down in Missouri with her two sons from a previous marriage, a couple of pre-teen Nazis who liked things like dissecting live frogs and pulling legs off grasshoppers. One-fifty a month isn't much until you supplement it with twenty-five percent of my weekly take-home pay and double child support from some other guy. It's hard going to work when you know that ten hours a week is for some bitch in a backwoods Missouri town where eighty bucks will rent you a farmhouse for a month. And here I was, a working Joe who couldn't afford a new pair of boots.

It's a good thing I'd just finished my signature when the dog howled or I might have dug right through the paper. The pen went flying out of my fingers when I jumped up. Both Maggie and I ran for the hallway. My attention had been centered on the check and my ex, and I hadn't even seen Chanci creep all the way into the bathroom. Now she came rolling out as if something had knocked her off her feet, paws flailing at her nose. She slipped on the linoleum and went down, yowls getting louder as Maggie grabbed for her collar and I grabbed for anything.

Maggie finally threw herself across the dog and pinned her to the floor. Chanci's howling filled the apartment as she struggled wildly and whipped her head back and forth. I already had an idea about what had happened.

"What's the matter with her, John?" Maggie cried.

"Hold her!" I shouted, lunging for her head. I guessed right away that one of those cockroach things had bit her on the face; what I couldn't figure out was how we were going to calm the old girl down before she had a heart attack.

I also hadn't counted on the damned thing still hanging on to Chanci's nose.

The three of us scrambled around on the floor for about thirty seconds or so—I admit I didn't know what to do. I sure as shit didn't want to grab that thing with my hand, but I had to do *something:* Chanci's head was jerking in every direction and I could see flashes of the insect's dangling black body—it showed no signs of letting go. Her yowling was getting worse; I was afraid it was *chewing* on her.

*"John!"* Maggie sounded on the verge of hysteria.

"Hang on—I'll be right back!" I ran back into the kitchen, sliding on the floor and cracking my knee as I came around the cabinet and yanked out a drawer. Behind me, Maggie's cries of *"Stay!"* were getting hoarse and Chanci's yelps were coming faster.

*"John, I can't hold her!"*

Both hands plunged into the midst of the aluminum gadgets and searched frantically . . . there! A pair of tongs with serrated edges. I barreled into the hallway, pointing the thing like a gun, as if just the sight would drive the creature away, but no such luck.

"She's getting loose!" Chanci had almost squirmed out from under Maggie and I could see places where the dog's nails had raked welts into my wife's skin. I sprawled on top of the animal's back end and reached around Maggie, who was trying unsuccessfully to hold Chanci's thrashing legs; any second now I expected my lovable mutt to chomp into one of us. Pain has a way of changing a personality.

I outweigh Maggie by a good fifty pounds, but that dog was still bucking under me like some kind of wild horse. She opened her mouth and showed those old yellow teeth, and I thought, *Here it comes!*—but before it could I shoved my left fist into her throat and forced her head as far back as it would go against Maggie's arm. I ignored Maggie's shocked protest and reached over with the other hand and clamped the shell of that thing with the tongs, dug in hard and pulled.

It came off fast, but the amount of resistance against my arm muscles made my stomach twist in sick sympathy. The noise Chanci made sounded more like a screaming baby than a dog, and Maggie screamed right along with her. It wasn't until I pulled my fist out of the dog's mouth and stood up with that thing on the end of those tongs that I realized I'd hollered, too.

Chanci scrunched herself into a corner and pawed at her nose, with Maggie crouched beside her trying to talk soothingly. I saw spots of blood dripping down the tongs and half-fell into the bathroom, intending to flush that thing right down the toilet. As I reached for the lid my right hand bumped against the sink and the tongs opened a fraction too much.

The roach fell to the floor and made for the bathtub.

*"Motherfucker!"* I bellowed. My work boot came down with a hundred and eighty pounds of crazed construction worker in it and I *danced* on that little son of a bitch for a full ten seconds. Then I slumped against the sink and tried to catch my breath; the tongs had gone sailing into that unfriendly area under the tub. Maggie was still talking softly to Chanci; I don't even think she heard me swear over the dog's whines. She might play the stern master, but the charade didn't fool me: that dog's grizzled face and big brown eyes made her melt inside.

I rinsed my face and hands at the sink to get the sweat and dog smell off, then dried myself, grabbed a hunk of toilet paper and squatted down. It was an ugly thing, even bigger than I remembered, with sharp mandibles sticking out from each side of its head—maybe it wasn't a cockroach at all, but some kind of beetle. No wonder the bug spray hadn't worked; this sucker looked tough. I leaned closer and almost gagged. There was some kind of translucent egg sac tucked under its rear end; tiny black things pulsed inside.

*Gross,* I thought. *Let the sewers handle it.* I knew I'd have to do it quick or I'd lose my nerve; the thought of those babies twitching around with only a few layers of paper between them and my fingers made my balls shrink. But I couldn't leave it on the floor and go after the dustpan—if Maggie saw that egg sac she'd go nuts.

I reached for it.

It ran.

Toward me.

Memories rocketed through my mind: a handful of fire, Chanci squirming on the floor in agony, the grainy feel of tearing dog flesh as the tongs did their work. My legs went out from under me and my rump hit the floor hard, boots kicking furiously. The left one, thank God, connected and knocked it back a foot or so; the beetle-thing darted under the bathtub.

"What're you doing in there?"

The sounds from the hall had changed. Chanci's protests had softened to whimpers; I heard Maggie's slippers make small slapping sounds and clambered to my feet and hit the toilet handle before she came around the door. "Did you kill it?"

"Yeah," I said, trying to squelch the shakes that were working through my hands. "I flushed it down the toilet."

"That's good," she said almost cheerfully as she turned away. "I hope we don't get any more of those nasty things."

*Jesus,* I thought. *What am I going to do?*

♦ ♦ ♦

The dog was okay, though she stopped sticking her face into the bathroom. Her nose was a little shredded, but like my finger there was no permanent damage. The way she looked at me after we finished dabbing at her schnozz with peroxide, it was like a kinship. We both knew what it felt like to have something try and eat you, and it had nothing to do with sex either.

Saturday and Sunday are Maggie's days to sleep late, since she gets up with me at five during the week. I'm an early riser even on the weekends, generally dozing on and off for a while, then getting up and leaving Maggie to rest for a few more hours. That's the time I do a few things around the house—whatever can be done without much noise—take care of business, so to speak. If there's nothing that needs to be done, I'll just watch television, cartoons or maybe an old movie on cable.

Pre-dawn Sunday I had business to take care of. I stood outside the bathroom door in near darkness, staring into that little room with no better light than what came from a feeble nightlight in the kitchen. But it was enough. My hands held sophisticated hunting tools: a piece of paper and a glass jar with a lid. If I couldn't kill it, then I'd catch it and trust my gut feeling that there was only one of those creatures, a mutant. A single indestructible beetle-thing in this whole fucking world and it had to be in my house—life's a real bitch sometimes. What I did know for a fact was that there wouldn't be just one for long, and I had to catch that thing before it gave birth.

I'd tried this same gig Saturday and gotten nowhere, though I hadn't given up until I'd heard Maggie moving around in the bedroom. I figured what I needed was live bait.

Taking my house shoe off was the hardest thing I've ever had to do, next to actually putting my sweating, defenseless foot down on the cold tile of the bathroom floor. If it wanted fresh meat, it would have to come out almost to the door; I couldn't bring myself to get any closer than three feet from the tub.

I *felt* it before it attacked—some kind of primal sixth sense kicked in and saved my ass, and I'm not fool enough to claim I wouldn't have screamed if it had bit me again. I smacked that jar open-end down on the floor, so hard it was a damned miracle it didn't shatter. Then I just knelt there, breathing hard, water dripping off my head like it was ninety-five in the sun instead of a winter-chilly morning in a dark bathroom. Vibrations ran through the jar and into my hand, making my skin crawl, and dread pulled my lips thin as I slid the paper between the jar and the floor and flipped it upright, twisting the lid on without bothering to take away the paper. I was too afraid.

At about the same time as I switched on the light, I thought how silly it was for a grown man to be afraid of an insect. Mandibles clicking, the thing in the jar started slamming against the glass in a futile attempt at escape, and with both relief and revulsion, I saw the egg sac was still connected and throbbing with unborn life.

Maybe my fear wasn't so stupid after all.

♦ ♦ ♦

By Monday afternoon I was afraid lack of oxygen would kill it, though I hadn't risked drilling even the tiniest hole in the lid because of the impending babies. With a couple of hours to spare before Maggie got home, I took my time retrieving the jar from its hiding place among the camping gear in the building's basement. The thing inside seemed paralyzed for about five minutes, then began ramming energetically against the glass. I figured it must be like a person who keeps running headlong into a foot-thick concrete wall and stopped worrying. If me stomping on it didn't destroy it, neither would a few days of thinned-out air, though the cold in the basement had made it sluggish. Chances are it would probably die off in cold weather like other insects.

I turned up something else from the basement: a little box that had once held a new lantern glass. It was just the right size for the jar, with a little extra room for padding—some of those great little air bubble sheets were still inside. I put it all together carefully and addressed it using block letters and a backhand slant that didn't resemble my usual scribbling at all, though I really didn't think it would matter.

I was much calmer now. Organization, a sense of security

and always knowing what to do, things patiently modeled for me by Maggie. Knowing how to take care of business, that was the key. I shook the package gently; not a sound could make it past all those air bubbles.

The clock showed I still had an hour before Maggie got home. I could walk there and back and still have time to shower.

♦ ♦ ♦

"Hi," I said happily. "How much to mail this first class?" The woman behind the window didn't smile back at me when I pushed the box forward, but I didn't care. She dropped it on the scale and I winced slightly.

"Dollar-fifty."

"Fine," I said. "Let me have it in stamps, please. And a 'Fragile' sticker, too." That earned me a dirty look, but I still walked out of the post office with a big shit-ass grin on my face.

♦ ♦ ♦

A warm wet April breeze blew in the door with us. We'd been out for Saturday brunch, nothing fancy but still a treat considering our budget. Maggie checked the mail, and I walked on inside and opened the blinds in the front room; for a second the sun broke through the cloud cover and shone in the window, sending bright stripes of light bouncing across the carpet. The place I'd once hated finally seemed like home.

"Look at this, Johnny," Maggie said as she flipped through the envelopes. She always called me Johnny when we were getting along really well. "The alimony check came back unclaimed. I wonder what's going on."

I just smiled.

# THE DROUGHT

## by Lois Tilton

Lois Tilton, a part-time instructor in philosophy at a local community college, has been writing for about five years and has sold short stories to *Dragon, Weird Tales, Aboriginal SF, Space & Time,* and *Sword and Sorceress.* She has finished three novels and is working on another. She lives in Glen Ellyn, a Chicago suburb, is married, and has two kids and a cat, known collectively as the "Forces of Evil."

For the last two summers much of the United States has suffered through drought conditions. That reality only makes this fiction all the more horrifying.

◆ ◆ ◆

The elephants were dying.

It was late October, and the rains were late coming to the parched savanna. During the dry season the elephants had dug seepholes into the sandy streambed, but now even this source of moisture was threatened as the water level receded.

The barren red sands near the seep were littered with bones, dessicated and bleached to fleshless white. More recent carcasses were drying to leather under the sun, bones only beginning to protrude from the shrinking hides. Vultures and marabou storks clustered on the gray hulks, tearing at the rotting flesh.

The living animals listlessly roamed in search of food or shade, but starving elephants had long since stripped the surrounding country of edible vegetation. The trees left standing on the slope above the seep were leafless, shadeless skeletons, a few shreds of bark still clinging to the deadwood.

As the sun's heat baked the arid sands, the naturalists continued their observations of the animals around the failing waterholes. Hendrick Van Den Berge finished photographing one of the accumulated broken heaps of bones. "This must be the elephants' graveyard," he had tried to joke yesterday, but his laugh had died under Dr. McNulty's glare.

Near the roots of a toppled acacia tree on the slope, Hendrick saw vultures tearing at the body of a small elephant. He approached, thinking the animal had to be newly dead. The blood was still welling from gashes in its trunk and ears.

Then, as a bird's curved, sharp beak plunged into one of its eyes, the elephant's trunk twitched. It was still alive!

He cried aloud in shock and grabbed up a dead branch, swung it at the vultures, driving them back. They shrieked defiance at him, flapping their wings. Hendrick saw Geneva Rhodes come running toward him through the brush.

"What . . ." she started to ask, but then her eyes fell on the elephant.

Hendrick looked sick. He had never before seen the vultures feeding on a still-living creature. He lowered the stick and gasped, "Did you *see?*"

Geneva sympathetically put a hand on the younger man's shoulder. "It happens," she told him. "You just have to get used to it."

"God," Hendrick said, his voice shaking, "its *eyes!* There ought to be . . . We can at least put it out of its misery."

There was a rifle back in the Land Rover, but Geneva unhappily shook her head. "I'm sorry," she said, and he heard regret in her voice, "but we can't interfere. Dr. McNulty . . ."

Hendrick turned to discover that the diminutive elderly naturalist had come up behind them. Her eyes were narrow in the seamed brown leather of her face. Dr. Alicia McNulty was a prominent advocate of nonintervention in wildlife management.

Hendrick looked back down at the elephant. Its sides heaved shallowly, soundlessly. Just a few meters away, the birds malevolently rustled their feathers, waiting.

"Come on," Geneva said, pulling on Hendrick's arm. As they walked down the slope, the triumphant scream of a vulture behind him made Hendrick shudder.

All the rest of the afternoon, his eyes kept returning to the acacia tree and the flapping mob of birds beneath it, their cruel, hooked beaks tearing at the elephant's flesh. Its living flesh. But there was nothing he could do, no way he could interfere.

At last the shadows lengthened and the long afternoon came to an end. During the ride back to their camp, Dr. McNulty said nothing to Hendrick. He had only joined the two naturalists yesterday, on assignment to photograph the effects of the drought on the reserve's wildlife. But later, after they had finished their dinner and were resting around the campfire, she cleared her throat.

"Young man . . ." she began. The lecture detailed McNulty's views on the consequences of misguided efforts to subvert the natural process. "It's best to let things run their course," she concluded. "There were droughts in Africa long before men ever tried to interfere."

Later, Geneva took Hendrick aside to explain. "She's seen this so many times, you have to understand. At Tsavo Reserve in 1971, when six thousand elephants died . . ."

He nodded. He knew populations could grow too large, that the vultures served a necessary purpose in the natural order. He knew that the baby elephant was doomed. But why did it have to suffer those long, painful hours—days—of dying? What harm could a single act of mercy have done?

He finally said goodnight to the other two and crawled into his own small tent to undress for bed. The night air was cool and comfortable after the day's heat, but Hendrick found himself tossing on his mattress, unable to sleep, unable to escape the image of the helpless baby elephant. From the distance of the night came the calls of predators, and he thought he could hear screams from creatures dying in pain.

Finally he gave up trying to sleep and pulled on his

clothes and boots, crept out of his tent. He took the loaded rifle and began to walk. Dr. McNulty might order him off the site, but he couldn't let it go on.

It was no more than a couple of kilometers to the place where the baby elephant had lain dying. The African moon was full and bright, illuminating the way, yet Hendrick stumbled several times over unseen obstacles in his path. Some of them were bones. All Africa was a boneyard, Hendrick thought. Possibly he was walking over the remains of some ancestral hominid, some species millions of years extinct.

Near the overturned acacia he heard the high, chuckling cries of hyenas and saw the flash of eerie, luminous eyes as one of the beasts raised its gore-masked face and looked up at him. He held the rifle ready. The hyenas were unearthly in the moonlight. He could hear their snarls and the crack of bones.

The pack was tearing at the belly and hindquarters of a carcass that lay buried underneath them. He was too late. He hoped the end had come for the baby elephant before they began to feed.

Suddenly weary, Hendrick turned to walk back to the camp and his tent. But he had hardly gone more than a few dozen paces when the shape of an elephant materialized in front of him. Although he knew how silently the huge creatures could move, its sudden appearance froze him with shock and fear. The beast was a luminous white in the moonlight, its trunk was raised and its ears flared wide. Then a scrap of cloud floated across the moon, and when it had passed the moon-elephant was fading, blowing away like a bank of fog.

Hendrick had no recollection afterward of walking back to the camp or falling asleep. He woke the next morning sweating inside the oven of his tent. Light flooded into his eyes. He blinked. Geneva was holding aside one corner of the tent flap. "You'd better get moving," she told him. "She's just about ready to leave."

Hendrick let out his breath—that so-vivid dream! Then

he saw that he was wearing his clothes, even his boots. He passed a hand over the blond stubble on his face—there would be no time to shave. He could remember, now, that he had gotten dressed, had gone out there. And seen . . .

But no, that was impossible. He crawled out of the tent, pulling his sunglasses out of his shirt pocket. The sky was already bright, cruelly blue, the sun a blinding disc of heat.

"No sign of the rain," said Geneva, shaking her head. "I was in the Hwange Reserve during the '82 drought. If the weather doesn't break soon, this could be worse. Last night, I dreamed—"

Then Dr. McNulty called out, "Well, are you both ready?"

Geneva picked up her notebooks and gear, and Hendrick crawled back into his tent to get his camera equipment. He was confused. Had it all been a dream, then? The hyenas? That moon-pale elephant looming over him?

He had to know. When the Land Rover got to the streambed, he went back to the overturned acacia. His heart beat fast for an instant as a vulture looked up and flapped its wings, screeching. But the baby elephant's carcass was torn open and part-consumed. The hyenas had been there.

"So," said a voice behind him, and Hendrick started. Dr. McNulty knelt to examine the carcass.

"It was inevitable," he admitted.

"The young always go first," she said. "The weakest. This one probably wasn't even weaned. And the water level at the seep is too low by now for it to reach."

Then she touched his arm. "Look."

While they watched, and Hendrick took shot after shot with his camera, an elephant cow came walking slowly up the slope toward the small carcass. Its backbone and pelvis stuck out sharply under its sun-cracked hide. The birds retreated. The cow's trunk swung back and forth in distress. Then it moved to the other side of the overturned tree and stripped off a couple of lifeless branches, carried them back to lay across the baby elephant's body.

"What's it doing?" Hendrick whispered in awe.

"That one is the mother," McNulty replied. "They'll do something like that when one of them dies."

They walked back down to the seepholes. For the next few hours Hendrick photographed the animals as the doctor pointed them out to him. Hendrick was impressed that she recognized each animal in the region as an individual, knew its age, its history, its condition.

But he shook his head when she told him that his young elephant had lain dying by the tree for three days before the vultures found it. How could she be so indifferent to the creature's pain? He turned his camera on the largest bulls, digging their tusks into the dry, unyielding sands. Some of the animals had dropped to their knees to try to reach their trunks to the water.

"They look like they're praying for water," he said softly.

Dr. McNulty snapped, "You're anthropomorphizing!"

Hendrick flushed in anger and turned to photograph the tumbled heaps of bones down by the seep. Elephant graveyard or not, the bones fascinated him, their massive size, the skulls with tusks cut away by nomadic ivory scavengers. They looked strangely human, like the remains of giants.

Was it anthropomorphizing to think that a suffering creature could hope for relief? If they could invade his dreams . . .

That evening Hendrick felt exhausted. He was careful to take off his clothes before lying down. The moon was still bright and full. It shone through his tent. Its light was cool, unlike the searing light of day.

The brightness grew, filling the tent with heat . . .

He woke, sweat-drenched, aching. He was fully dressed again, his boots on, and his clothes were gritty with sand. He shut his eyes and groaned, remembering. The elephant had stood under the moon, immense and pale in the moonlight, watching as he knelt on the sand, digging for water, scraping the sand away with his hands.

Geneva was sitting on a camp stool drinking coffee when he came groggily out of his tent. Her clothes were dirty with sand. She stared at him, then slowly reached to hand him a cup. There was sand packed under her fingernails.

She spoke first. "The elephants were crying for water. I went to the river, but it was dry. I started to dig . . . Then I woke up. Like this."

Hendrick nodded. "The night before, I thought I had really gone out there. But then I saw . . ."

Geneva's hand, holding the coffee, was shaking. "It can't be real," she whispered, "but—"

Just then the Land Rover drove into the camp, Dr. McNulty at the wheel. She braked the vehicle and looked from one of them to the other. Geneva stood up. "Alicia, can I ask you—did you happen to have any . . . strange dreams last night?"

Dr. McNulty started. "Dreams? No, absolutely not!" Then she snapped, "Do you two think we can try to accomplish something today?"

Hendrick saw Geneva's face go red with embarrassment and realized the obvious implication—he and she together. He flushed, too. She was at least thirty-five, he had never considered . . .

But denying everything would make it worse.

That day the scene at the failing waterholes was a vision of hell. Animals lay dying, too weak even to search out the meager shade. Vultures perched on the carcasses, wings spread wide, naked heads striking deep into dead and dying flesh. The sight of the carrion birds made Hendrick feel sick, but no one could keep them away from so many dying beasts.

Screams filled the heat-shimmering air as the elephants fought over the drying waterholes. Two massive tusked bulls charged each other. Hendrick watched, appalled, as a smaller animal was knocked down and trampled by the heedless giants. It tried in vain to heave itself to its feet, but at least one leg was broken. Finally the injured creature lay its head down on the sand.

The naturalists had shown him the scattered, splintered remains of other animals that had been trampled to death in similar circumstances near the streambed. Some of them were decades old or more. The elephants were grinding the bones of their ancestors into the sand. But the bones were fleshless and white. Their suffering was ended long ago.

He watched the victorious bull drop to its knees and extend its trunk deep into the well. It knelt for a long time, and when it got back to its feet, the end of its trunk was dark with moisture. When it walked away a number of other animals rushed forward. One cow pushed aside its own half-grown calf in an attempt to reach a place at the seep. The young animal cried out weakly. It continued to circle around the well until an older elephant charged it in irritation, bellowing.

Geneva came over to Hendrick, abandoning her observations. "It's as if thirst has driven them mad," she said. "Turning on each other." She looked eastward, in the direction of the monsoon. The cloudless sky was a merciless, blinding blue.

That night in camp Dr. McNulty confronted them. "I can understand," she said, looking at Hendrick, "how the effects of the drought might upset someone who is young and not used to seeing this kind of thing. Even"—she turned to Geneva—"a more experienced observer. The things we're witnessing aren't very pleasant. But I'd like you both to remember that our observations are important, that what we learn now will have a bearing for future crises. I'll expect you both to remember that tomorrow and keep your minds on your work."

Hendrick was embarrassed as he watched her walk over to her tent. After a moment he got up and went to the fire to start a fresh pot of coffee. When he brought Geneva a cup, he asked, "Do you think she has . . . the dreams?"

Geneva shook her head, she didn't know. They sat at the table, speaking of small things, distant things, anything but elephants and rain. Neither of them wanted to sleep, to dream.

Then the moon rose, full and white, illuminating the savanna. Hendrick stared. The elephant stood glowing in the light. It raised its trunk, trumpeted its summons soundlessly.

He stood, followed.

The elephants were standing at the seep. Their circle opened for him. Hendrick knelt. With his hands, he began to dig into the moonlit sand.

The moon elephant stood apart, white as bleached bone, watching him. Hendrick kept digging, scraping out sand with his bare hands, but the barren sand refused to yield up moisture. Finally he straightened. "There is no more water!" he cried out. "There has to be rain! Don't you understand? Rain!"

He beat with his fists on the sand.

His eyes flew open, met the brilliant glare of the sun, already risen. He sat upright. Geneva lay slumped across the table, her head lying on her arms. He shook her. She woke, gasped. Together, they stared at their broken-nailed, bleeding, sand-encrusted hands.

Dr. McNulty came out of her tent. Her mouth tightened when she saw them, then she turned away. Her clothes were clean. And her hands.

Geneva pushed away from the table. "What's happening?" Her voice was high, strained.

Hendrick began, "The elephants, maybe they—"

"No!" She backed away from him. "I don't want to hear it."

Hendrick went to his own tent to clean up. None of them spoke in the Land Rover as they drove the short distance to the seep. In the harsh daylight the memories of the moonlit sand seemed unreal. It could only be a dream. He clenched his hands into fists. Blood trickled from one scraped knuckle. Fear was starting to take hold of him. How many more nights, digging his fingers into the arid, unyielding sand? Desperately he turned his face to the east. Would the rain ever come?

There were fewer animals on their feet at the seep this morning. Thirst-maddened beasts scattered sand as they tried to dig for water, roaming from one dry hole to another.

Dr. McNulty climbed from the Rover and briskly started down toward the streambed. "I want to check those holes," she said.

Suddenly Hendrick looked up. "No!" he cried, jumping out and running after the older naturalist. "Don't go down there!"

Without warning, one of the bull elephants at the seepholes lowered its tusks and charged. "Look out!" Hendrick yelled, and McNulty's head jerked around, but before she could run the animal was on her. Her body was thrown into the air. The bull raised its trunk in a trumpet of rage as she hit the ground. It charged again, but then drew up suddenly, just in front of where she lay.

Geneva rushed up to Hendrick, jerked his arm. "We have to do something!"

He hesitated. Alicia McNulty lay broken on the sand below. The bull was turning its back. It walked over to the nearest seephole, lowered its head and began to dig.

Dry-mouthed, Hendrick slowly approached the frail human figure. A hand stirred. She was still alive. But then the bull looked up from the seephole, flared its ears and charged.

Hendrick fled upslope, yelling for Geneva to run. When he halted, panting, and looked back, the maddened creature was stamping the ground beside the injured naturalist, raising a cloud of dust. It was not going to let them near her. They would have to drive it off or kill it first.

"I'll get the rifle," Geneva cried, running to the Land Rover. But in a minute she called, "It's not here!"

"You've got to go back for it!" he yelled. "I'll stay here in case there's a chance to get to her."

The Rover's motor roared into life and Geneva sped off toward the camp. Hendrick looked back down the slope. Once again the elephant was digging. Sand flew in a frenzied spray. Some of it fell on Dr. McNulty.

He wondered how seriously she was hurt. There were

certainly broken bones, perhaps internal injuries. He bit his lip, watching the animal at the seep. It knelt down to reach more deeply into the hole. Hendrick waited tensely for it to leave. He was sweating. The blazing sun was driving the moisture from his tissues. Alicia McNulty lay exposed to the pitiless heat, no more than two hundred meters away.

He sensed a nearby presence and turned his head. The moon-pale dream elephant stood beside him, silently watching the helpless woman.

Hendrick had to try. He took a single step. The bull at the seephole lifted its head, threatening. He halted, stood still.

The sun slowly traversed the glaring blue sky, higher, burning even more intensely. Hendrick glanced at his watch. Where was Geneva? She should be back by now!

He looked back to the seep, then his breath stopped in horror. A vulture was descending to the sand next to the still figure. It lowered its naked head, its cruel, slashing beak . . .

"No!" he screamed, running down the slope.

The bird's head lifted; it flapped its wings. But the bull elephant was back on its feet. Ears wide, tusks lowered, it charged again. Hendrick swerved, managed to sidestep the rush, but the animal turned around, unbelievably quick. He fled up the slope, running for his life, until he was in among the dead and dying trees. He could hear the splintering of wood behind him. Finally the elephant trumpeted, turned around and headed back down to the seep.

Hendrick stared down at Dr. McNulty. The elephant's charge had frightened the vulture away. He exhaled with relief. But then he caught his breath once more as a winged shape dropped to the sand, followed by another.

Where was Geneva with the gun? Sobbing curses, Hendrick looked wildly around, seized a knob of bone and hurled it at the scavengers. The carrion birds screeched and backed away. Yet, now, more were starting to descend.

Hendrick threw another piece of bone. He crawled across the sandy ground, seeking more. There were at least a dozen vultures around the injured woman now. His arm was starting to ache as he kept throwing chunks of bone, rarely hitting the birds. They were getting bolder. A vulture's long neck struck out like a snake. The bird jumped back as Hendrick's throw hit it, but now there was a dark red hollow where Alicia McNulty's eye had been.

Hendrick screamed and ran toward her, heedless of his safety. Then he stumbled, fell on his face. As he struggled up, he stared, then dropped back to his knees. The massive, bone-white shape of the dream elephant stood between him and the birds' victim. Its head, its gleaming ivory tusks, were lowered, and its eyes spoke to him: *Don't interfere.*

Beyond his sight, but not his hearing, the carrion birds fought for a share of the flesh.

♦ ♦ ♦

Geneva braked the Land Rover to a skidding halt and jumped out, clutching the rifle. The sandy basin of the seep was unnaturally silent. Elephants were standing on the sand, facing eastward, their trunks raised as if they were scenting something on the air. She started to call out, then saw Hendrick on his knees, head down, hands covering his ears.

She ran to him, frantic, shouting, "I couldn't get to the rifle! There was an elephant in the camp, I . . ."

Then her voice died away as he lifted his face. Slowly, she looked down toward the seep. Vultures clustered on the sand, ripping at some bones and tatters of cloth. She put her fist to her mouth.

Now Hendrick was staring into the east. Geneva turned. Together they watched the sky begin to darken with rain-bearing clouds.

# THE NIGHTMARE'S TALE

## by Tanith Lee

Tanith Lee was born in 1947 in North London, England. She attended grammar school until the age of seventeen, was a library assistant for four years, worked at various jobs, and then spent a year in art college. In 1974 DAW Books bought her novel *The Birthgrave*, and she became a full-time writer. Almost forty books and some hundred short stories of hers have been published, and four radio plays and two television programs have been broadcast in England. She has been awarded the British Fantasy Award and the World Fantasy Award. Her stories have appeared in *Shadows, Night Visions I, Women of Darkness* and other well-known anthologies. At present she is working on a "very large and extremely horrible" fantasy novel *The Blood of Roses*, for Arrow Books. She lives in Kent, surrounded by one cat and half a hundred plants.

This is again another excellently written and evocative historical story by Tanith.

◆ ◆ ◆

This story was told me one evening in a café by the river, near to the Ruined Bridge. The dusk was blurred by fog and, somewhere below, where the bank ended and the water began, the vague torched eyes of barges were creeping up and down, slow and fearful, with now and then the mournful warning of a gong. In the café, the fog had entered, too, and with the primal oil lamps and the smoke of cigarettes, gave us the atmosphere of Venus. An old man was brought over suddenly with the ominous announcement, "Here is a fellow can tell you a few histories."

They sat him before me and there he was, creaking in his overcoat. I filled him a glass, and idly invited him to begin. He started to talk of the Revolution. He looked ancient enough to have known the participants, when a boy. Not until he was well into his third glass, did he squint at me slyly and say, "But the strangest stories come after the Revolution ended. When they washed the City clean of blood, and put the axes away. It was then."

After which he launched directly into a narrative that had something in it of a Shakespearean drama, and something of the nature of a myth. I did not know if I, or he, believed it. Punctuated by the eerie flickers from the river, dispersed through the lamplit fog, it clung inside my head. False or real, it had its own truth. I set it down; now you must judge for yourself.

## I

Of the many thousands who had died in the murderous blood-tides of Revolutionary times, there had been a young poet and his innocent wife. Their names and lives may be found elsewhere, he a dark and clamorous man, she pale as a swan, following her husband to the scaffold in the white dress of a bride. They left behind a child then only two years old. This offspring was brought up by a surviving sister of the mother's—in those days it was not unusual when one member of the family was confiscated for the gallows for the rest soon enough to be dragged in tow.

The woman, who shall be called Andromede, raised the little boy in the best fashion she could and, at the proper age, saw to it that he was educated to the highest and nicest degree she could afford. Along with the nourishment of his body, clothing of his person and tutoring of his mind, she also saw to it that her sister's son was fed, garbed, and schooled in the most incredible amounts of pure bitterness. It may have been that she herself was once in love with Jean de St. Jean's father, the poet, or that she had loved her sister excessively. Or it may have been simply the fact of the terrible shock she had undergone when all her familial world was swept away in the space of two or three horrible months: something had made of Andromede a powerful and insidious instructor in the lessons of enduring hate.

How she did it can only be guessed. One half imagines that, instead of saying grace before a meal, some other words were spoken, rather in the way of the antique toast, "*Death to my enemies.*" Or that, over the beds were hung samplers which read: *You shall seek out the wicked and destroy them.* And, *An eye for an eye.*

Probably, when she knelt down like gray marble in the church at the end of the street and the child asked for what she prayed, Andromede may well have replied: "For *justice.*" And probably also she indoctrinated the little Jean with anecdotes of his parents, their vivid talents and virtues, their fairy tale love, and their death.

For eighteen years, until the age of twenty, Jean de St. Jean grew to manhood in that shadowy city of aftermath, in the wreckage of a revolution, going about between a grim stony school with turrets and cobbled yards, reeking stoves, mealy books, and a maze of crowded dirty, crooked streets that led up into an apartment whose windows peered across a joiner's court at a high wall. Three rooms, which were thick with dust in summer and wet with cold in winter, with a stove that smoldered and reeked even worse. If there was generally sufficient, it came at the cost of something—some gnawing, obscure pride to do with a state pension, a recompense for the unspeakable, which could never be enough. And he grew up, then, forcing his way toward the light like a plant in flinty ground, Jean de St. Jean, the poet's son, breathed in, along with the damp and dust and church bells from the street's end and the invisible samplers of hatred, an exquisite yearning for he knew not what. But it was not ambition or carnality or fame or happiness. And one day, one morning, by accident, he discovered its being and what it was. It was revenge. And like a luscious berry, God had put it in his hand.

He rushed home to the mean apartment of his aunt, along the knotted streets, his heart in his mouth, and bounding up the stairs flung wide the door.

"Anny!" he exclaimed, which was his pet name for Andromede the hateress. "Anny, you won't credit—"

Andromede came from her bedroom, where she had been tightly pinning up her hair. For the first time in eighteen years she felt the full spasm of fear. She stared into her nephew's face, and saw him for what he was, as if, until this moment, he had been partly hidden from her. He was a man, with the hair of her sister in a sun-caught cloud around his face, and his eyes dark and clamoring.

"Whatever—" she began.

He held up his hand to silence her.

"I have seen," said Jean, in a wild, cold voice awful to hear, "a *thing*, a *monster*, walking in the garden of the Martyr Church."

"I don't understand you, Jean," said Andromede. She did. She shook from head to foot and her bowels had turned to water, exactly as had happened eighteen years ago on the night the Citizen Police hammered at the door.

"It was Dargue," said Jean. *"Dargue,"* he repeated.

Then he fell silent and stood looking at her. It would have been difficult to say which of them had gone the whiter.

Dargue was the man who had been directly responsible for the execution of the poet and his wife. It was he who denounced them and, later, by adding his signature to the warrant, he that ensured there would be no escape. He had supposedly been drinking wine and as he wrote his name, a spot of the drink fell beside it like a drop of thin blood. The document had since been displayed, with others of its kind, and perhaps Jean had even seen it. Of course he knew the six letters that composed the D-A-R-G-U-E. And, too, he knew the man by inner sight, having had his appearance and mannerisms described uncountable times over. That Dargue had, as Jean, aged eighteen years, did not prove a deterrent. He had been away all this while, like a fiend in Hell, revelling in the illicit riches the Revolution had given over to him when, in the last days of its madness, he fled.

"He has been living in the Colonies," said Jean, referring to the far-flung possessions of the City as if to another planet. "An island . . . Black Haïssa. He has a house there. They jokingly say, he has three wives. Nègre women."

*"I don't want to hear!"* screamed Andromede abruptly, clasping her hands over her ears.

"You must, you must," pleaded Jean. And going to her, he put his arms around her and held on to her just as he had when a child. For her own various reasons, Andromede had never been a caressing, physical woman. Her return to an embrace, especially an importunate one, was awkward and labored. Now she did nothing at all, but stood there in her gray marble mode, waiting perhaps for all this to end.

"Anny," said Jean, "listen carefully. I'm not a boy now. You know I'm well educated, thanks to you, but have no prospects in this rotten corrupt city. I've had it said to me already, my best chance . . . would be to try my luck in the Colonies." He paused, and when she did not respond, hurried on with: "There are fortunes to be made in the islands."

"Yes," she said, stupidly, sounding almost asleep. Her hands had fallen back to rest on his arms as he held her.

"There's the money you put by for me. Let me have it, Anny."

"So you can take yourself to the Colonies?" She stole a glance at him. Her eyes were stunned rather than bleak. Was he going to leave her?

"Yes, so I can go there. Don't you see? Where *he* is."

"Why?" said Andromede.

It was astonishing, after all her work upon him. After eighteen years of a single lesson perfectly repeated and learned by heart. Now, when he replied, solving the mathematical formula in its preordained and only way, now she could not make head or tail of it.

"To kill him," said Jean de St. Jean. "What else?"

Andromede had the correctness of soul at least to bow her head and not to protest again.

"He's to return to the island shortly. Out there," said Jean, "in that *lawlessness,* it will be easy."

"Yes, it's easy to kill."

"Anny, it's what we wanted in our dreams, and here's my chance."

"Yes."

"You'll let me have the money, then?"

"Very well. I saved it for you, Jean."

"For *us.* For *them*—my father. *Her.*"

"Yes."

"You mustn't grieve. In a year I could be home. We might be rich. You'll have a carriage, and beautiful clothes—velvet for church."

"Silly," she said, brokenly.

She tried to smile. Maybe she even tried to take on again her serpent's craning, the foremovement of its venomous strike, the attitude of her insatiable hunger for justice, retribution, the getting of eyes for eyes. If so, she failed in that, too. The smile was meaningless and unconvincing, but she pressed it on her face from that morning to the dawn ten days later when Jean caught the boat from the old Quay of the Angel, and was borne out limblessly toward the jaws of the sea.

Andromede, standing at quayside, amid the plumes and hats and tears of others come to wave someone away, was dry and upright, like a thin blasted tree. It was her pride not to weep until she was at home, alone there amid the dust and cold and shadows, listening helplessly for the sound of his footsteps on the stair, for the snatch of a song he might now and then sing, the dropped book, the rustle of his coat, his *"Anny, here I am,"* his *"Goodnight, God bless you, Anny."* She told herself she would never see him again, and in this she was quite right.

♦ ♦ ♦

The journey was a lifetime. It passed across seasons, geographical barriers, climates and spatial zones. Months were consumed by it. You could not embark on such a journey, and complete it, unaltered. And yet, with all its doings and happenings, its events of seasickness, storm, calm, boredom, the visitations that were foreign ports—progressively more and more foreign as one advanced, moving tableaux that swam up from the depths of the ocean and slid away again behind like the white wake of the moon by night—the fishes that leapt, the stars that revolved, and the whole reasonless, rocking environs of the sea itself—such things eventually classified themselves into mere living, ordinary existence. For Jean experienced them and survived them all, and to some extent they were lost on him in any case, for he was already in pursuit. His hunt had indeed begun at the Quay of the Angel, when he learned which boat, and which ship, were to carry Dargue a week before him.

It was, however, as though the entire passage comprised and was framed within an after-image: that of sailing through a bottle of pale skies and water holding rain, coming gradually out of the bottleneck into a violent sunset burning in heaven like stained glass.

Although this time the conflagration died as quickly as it blew up, going down beneath a curious cloud.

"There," said Jean de St. Jean to one of the less disreputable of the crew, "what is that?"

"Haïsa," the man replied. He added that they had anchored eight miles out, and would not be going in until sunrise.

Jean was left to observe the cloud darken in a sheet of drained fire, and then to darken and harden on, blacker than the star-sprayed sky.

There were mountains on Haïssa. In fact, Haïssa was, it seemed, made of mountains. There was something in the island Jean had not expected, as a young man intent upon his quest and his vengeance. The island itself had importance. It possessed some kind of sentience, dimly discernable across the rhinestone rollers, the reefs and the night.

As he stood at the ship's rail, Jean became aware of another being on the deck.

It is almost impossible to describe the way in which the

awareness stole over him, especially in view of what followed. The sensation grew rather in the manner in which a man may come to feel he has some illness, amorphous at first, the faintest disinclination, ebb of the spirits. Yet presently depression is reinforced by a score of other slight intrusive signals. At last he must acknowledge the onset of the fever that will lay him low.

Jean bore the feeling, which was not exactly of being watched, more of being waited upon, for a count of five or six minutes. These would have seemed interminable, except that all the while he was trying to argue himself from his certainty. Frankly, he did not for a moment think anything human or explicable was with him on deck. He knew, from the evening's previous sounds, and a by now familiarity with the general noises of the vessel, crew, and passengers, the position of all men and objects. Even the ship's dog had become detectable to him during the voyage, as it lightly padded through its rounds. *This* presence was of one who had not, until that hour, inhabited the ship.

Finally, Jean turned, and scanned the area about him. The moon was rising, the heavy lush moon of these regions, which on its nights of waxing seemed full of sweet juice. The deck glowed and was laid bare, the masts and bundled sails, the cabins and hatches, the station of the great wheel. No one was there in all that stretched instant of moonlight. The vessel was like a floating coffin on the ocean. Only Jean remained at the rail. And nearby somewhere—invisible—and untenable and nonexistent—the other.

Jean crossed himself. It was an involuntary action, a reflex of boyhood. But when he did it, he thought he heard a soft, long, low laugh go pulsing around the deck. This laugh, if it even occurred, was suddenly in all places at once, and gone as suddenly and utterly. Jean had grown very cold, but he was not afraid. He said, under his breath, "I know you. What have you come to tell me?" But that, too, was only his instinct, for he did not know, either what was there with him, or what he had said to it.

Nevertheless, there came a swift flash, like a star falling or a light quenched somewhere between himself and the next item of solid material, which happened to be one of the masts. What it was he did not see, although it seemed afterward that it might have been the reflection of a face, glimpsed as if in a mirror. It was a peculiar face, too, more a mask, that was at one and the same time black and white, but whether the black was laid over the white or the white on the black, Jean could not make out.

And then he found he could move, the air had soaked back to its usual tepid warmth, and he started to hear real sounds from the ship, and to behold some sailors over by one of the hatches smoking their pipes, and the watch motionless, aloft. The other thing was gone.

The young man went down to the saloon to take his supper, trying to put off a vague sense of shame that apparently naturally replaced the supernatural sensation that preceded it. Below, he drank more than he was used to with his meal, and went to bed amused at himself and engorged by notions of his arrival at the island in the morning, where his search would commence at once for Dargue.

♦ ♦ ♦

The ship entered port an hour after dawn. For whatever other reason, it was likely Haïssa had earned the epithet "black" in one way from her looks. Behind the harbor the town straddled a vast swooping slope that expended itself abruptly, miles off, against enormous uplands cumbered in jungles or forests, which showed jet black against the vibrancy of the sky. Beyond these nearer heights yet more gigantic cliffs scaled up, thick with vegetation and trees, until distance reduced the panorama to transparency. In two or three spots a solitary waterfall shone like a straight white column of smoke. The town itself was by contrast pastel and tawdry, the ripe smell of it drifting out across the harbor with the stink of fish and fruit. Parrots, in cages on peeling balconies that overhung the water, screamed. Although he had seen black men as he neared the island, Jean had never gazed on such a quantity. Their species was so different he could not fit them into any comfortable niche. It was easier to detail them as some form of higher and less tractable animal. The brilliance of their teeth shocked him, as did their women, walking barefoot on the sharp stones and broken shards above the shipping, with metal necklets and colored scarves circling their waists and brows. The women of Jean's landscape had figures made of laced bone and hair like raveled silk. These had pelt or fleece upon their heads. Their breasts swayed with the rhythm of their steps as they walked, like cats.

Had he not been imbued by his purpose, the young man, alone and mostly penniless in this alien world, might have given way to preliminary panic. But he was armored, was Jean. And in his armor he went ashore and, carrying his bag himself, went up the first curving street from the port, between the balconies and birdcages, across a square of big-limbed trees pendulous with gourds, under the stucco and the palms and over the steps, clung with orchids, that led to the upper town of Black Haïssa.

And the cat-women passed him in their skins of velour, and higher up he saw the ones who were half cat and half human, swarthy near-white, driving in their carriages with fans of feathers in their carved ringed hands. And he saw the gentlemen, too, lounging by the barbers and the hotels in striped waistcoats, and some of these were black and some not quite black. But the whites had gone to the very surface-top of the town, like froth to the top of coffee, and there were to be noticed, pieces of mosaic among the plantains and palm trees, froth-white mansions with faded names, colossal gardens gone to seed, Passion flowers and flowers that ate flies, snakes in dry fountains, and giant spiders hung among the vines, weaving with their legs.

But the visor of his armor was down across the eyes of Jean de St. Jean, the poet's son. He knew the word *Dargue*. That was what he had come for. He climbed up because that was the way the streets and steps led him, and the hanging parks of Haïssa Town. Dargue was a man of substance in this place, and should be simple to find.

And Jean knew an aching urge to see him again. It was nearly poignant. As if, in looking at this man, he could perceive, lifted miraculously out of time and decay, his two parents, whose faces he knew only from some little paintings kept in Andromede's apartment.

♦ ♦ ♦

Jean had of course conceived a plan, partly conceived it in his home city in the days after sighting Dargue. Aboard ship, during the ocean months, he shaped the plan—or was shaped by it, perhaps. The fuss that some of his fellow passengers made over him—as a young hopeful setting forth to try his fortune (naturally the true purpose was not revealed to them), and the general talk of the way of getting on in the islands—molded the plan further. It became outrageous and possible. It appealed to Jean by its audacity, its very terribleness. For what he eventually proposed to do was to approach Dargue directly, rendering him the false identity that he, Jean, had already adopted for the voyage out—it was one of the few provisions the poet's son had taken to protect himself. And, having so engaged his enemy, Jean would stand before him and beg for an occupation, flaunting the good City education, making of himself a charming and valuable prospect. That Dargue should take him on, employ him, as a secretary or assistant of some sort, was so balefully ironic, Jean did not believe it could not come to be.

Installed in Dargue's very household, privy to his secrets, which rumor suggested were often dark, debauched, dangerous, Jean foresaw a hundred opportunities both to ruin and, ultimately, to commit murder.

How the murder was to be accomplished, this he did not know, and had never visualized. It was a shadow act performed in dream. *That valid.* He trusted the hour and the means would be given to him.

Jean made his inquiries after Dargue at Haïssa Town in the manner of the young hopeful off the ship, a fellow citizen, speaking a common tongue, clever, and prepared to be industrious. Quite quickly he had his directions, to a mansion out along Oleander Road. It was a two-hour ride, which to Jean, on foot and with his bag in hand, would furnish an afternoon's walk.

◆ ◆ ◆

Oleander Road was not a road in any sense of a city street. It was a broad avenue of earth that rambled out from the edges of the town, and curled itself away for miles through the hills. It was barricaded by banana trees, and continually encroached upon by the forest, a swollen, lubricious wall of leaves and trunks that bulged inward with incredible potence, alight with sun, with bird noises, and the quiver of insects. The air was warm, it seemed to run down in rivulets, so that everything to be seen wavered. Along Oleander Road, at considerable distances from each other, the old houses lay off the track, behind spilled paths, rough-haired lawns, and plantings of cocoa and tobacco. In one place there was even a milestone, but it indicated the leagues back to Haïssa Town.

Shade was thrown all over the road, and shots of sun. The shambling route went always higher and higher, and began at length to show, through windowpane openings, sky and sea below.

Drenched in sweat, Jean walked the road. His bag came to weigh like the weight of the sins of the one he sought.

There was nothing else he could do. It was out of the question to turn back, and he never debated that he should. He went on, sometimes turning his head to catch the weird bird cries of the forest, or slapping at some blood-sucking thing that had bitten him. It was a type of hell, this walk. He had not foretold the punishment, but neither did he resist its infliction.

The shade pool on the road deepened and spread, and a breeze started that shook the huge hammered-iron leaves of the plantains. It was evening and, abruptly, on his left, Jean saw the notice that indicated the estate of Monsieur Dargue.

He felt a start of the pulses, as though he had encountered a lover unexpectedly.

The garden of Dargue's house was positively enormous and dense with the coming of darkness. The overhanging shrubs and trees seemed hung with heavy coils of snakes. A scent began of strange, pale-colored flowers. The stars were piercing the sky like drops of silver sweat or blood bursting out upon a thin black skin.

Jean wandered through this tangle of night, and behind the little fires of flowers the house suddenly appeared, two stories of masonry in a cage of verandas lighted by oil lamps, which hung on it like ripe fruit.

A dog commenced to bark and howl drearily. Jean stood beside a fountain and saw the mansion of his enemy before him, and everything became for a moment unreal. It was as if he did not even know who he himself was, or his own name. As if he had forgotten the name of his father, and why he had come here. The word *Dargue* was meaningless.

The moment was frightful to Jean. It actually frightened him, but more than that, it caused him to struggle with some faceless adversary, and to win.

After that the house was Dargue's house, and he must get to it at once.

Perhaps he became aware as he drew nearer that there was a hush on the building. The dog had left off its dirge and the crickets were very loud. One lighted window burned in the second story, nothing else. The lanterns around the veranda seemed to grin. Beyond the house stretched the fields of the estate, but no lamp moved there; it might have been a primeval swamp.

Jean rang the bell, which was quite ordinary. He had to wait some while, and was reaching out again for the bell-pull when he heard a kind of dragging step coming toward him through the house.

Jean was conscious then that something had gone wrong.

The door opened. An elderly black man was craning out, peering up at him. He had the face of a beautiful marmoset, which themselves resemble the princes of another world. But he was so old and bent, and maybe had had to bend his inner self also, that he looked at Jean with a timorous indifference, saying nothing.

"Dargue. I am here to see Monsieur Dargue," said Jean stridently, his voice too noisy, like something that escaped him.

The old man continued peering up at him.

"I've come a long way," said Jean, and suddenly realized that he had. He trembled.

"Monsieur Dargue," said the black man, softly.

"Yes. Tell him—"

"No, Monsieur," said the black man, "I can't tell him. Monsieur Dargue is dead."

The whole night caved in upon Jean. Shadows, trees, darkness, stars, all came rushing down, pouring in through the top of his skull. He dropped his bag somewhere in the maelstrom. Then found himself leaning against the wall.

The servant man still watched him, still indifferent, but saying now in a craven way, "He take ill on the day he come back. He take to his bed. Then the doctor come. Then the priest come. Then Monsieur Dargue, he dies. He dies last night."

In the silence that followed the servant's recital, Jean heard himself say, equally softly, "But I've come such a long way. I came to find him."

"He dead, Monsieur."

Jean said, "Yes."

And then the servant seemed to try to reward him for his compliance.

"He is lying out on the bed. You want come in, Monsieur, have look at him?"

A rush of nausea. "No," Jean said. "In God's name—"

When he recovered a little, the servant had closed the door, and audibly made his dragging progress off again through the house.

For a few seconds Jean leaned on the wall and wept. It was the ghastly disappointment of the passionate child, whose desired gift has been snatched away at the last instant, literally out of his hand.

Worst of all, he did not know in the least what to do next. He had been almost four months tending to this; more, his entire life had in some sort latched on it. But the dream act was already performed. Even as he had stood on the ship's deck, scenting the odor of Haïssa across the night, even then. Death himself had preempted the frail revenge of Jean de St. Jean. Face to face with his own mortal inconsequence, the young man turned from the house of his enemy, a shell as meaningless as if gutted by fire. He trudged away, not quite knowing what he did, through the serpentine garden.

## II

On Oleander Road, near midnight, Jean beheld a strange procession.

He supposed he had sat down at the road's edge, as he might have done in some country lane of the north, above his city. Here there were snakes and poisonous toads, hairy lianas, vampire insects—but he was past considering them. He did not sleep but sank into a stupor, in which he was aware of moisture, the dew of old rains dripping down, and things that hastened over his hands. The moon crossed the road, and when it was gone, through the dark a throbbing seemed to come, like the pulse of blood along an artery.

Jean gazed with dull eyes. Presently the curtains of night were parted, and from some obscure avenue among the trees of the forest, a troop of men and women emerged on the road. They looked themselves black as the night, and would not have been easy to see, but for the fact many of them wore light-colored garments that shone in a skull-faced flicker of lanterns. Jean noticed that several of the women carried bunches of some plant. It was not unfamiliar, perhaps he had seen it growing wild here and there, an ugly shrub, stringy, like an uncombed horse's tail.

The leader of these people was a tall man dressed in white. He stalked ahead as if alone, staring directly before him. He held a whip with a bone handle. There was also a girl who lugged in a wicker cage two or three black birds that jumped and flapped, but their outcry was lost in the drums and a deep, ceaseless murmuring that went with them up the road.

Jean was aware, incoherently, that he looked on something that maybe it would have been better he had not seen. There was an overt secrecy to the procession, which seemed to make no attempt to hide itself simply because, by an inexorable law, it must not be witnessed.

When the vision had disappeared into the tunnel of the road, going in the direction perhaps of Dargue's estate, Jean stayed motionless, listening after the fading drumbeat, until it mingled with the beating of his own heart in his ears.

When he moved again, it was with a stupified caution. He was not afraid, but he suspected he should be.

He stumbled on, and with no further encounter, came eventually back to the brink of the town. Here, earlier, he had found a possible lodging. Having climbed the wall, he slept in the garden of this place, for he would not rouse them at that hour; the prohibitions of his upbringing forebade such a thing. It was almost dawn in any case. The sky's membrane palpitated. Beneath a mango tree with savage leaves he fell and, using his bag for a pillow, began to tell himself mindlessly over and over what he must do. That all there was to do now was to seek labor, as a clerk, or even at a meaner occupation, earning his return passage to the City. What else could he attempt? For he was like a somnambulist roughly wakened. The dream had misled, he had lost his way.

Although he could not sleep, every now and then the image of the procession on Oleander Road went swaying through his thoughts, scattering them.

Had the procession been going to the house of Dargue?

But they had told him on the ship, that the black race of the islands hated the white race. The last wave of the Revolution, breaking there, had freed the slaves of Haïssa, but made of them instead mostly serfs. And those that had become black masters in their turn, hated, too, in a more perilous, educated manner, anything that was pale, even where darkness ran just visibly under the skin.

This was a land of nightmares, this country he had woken up in. He must get home. Anything else was futile. He was broken.

♦ ♦ ♦

It is probable Jean went mad that night. Of course, he had been tinged by insanity for years, for all his life. But like a deadly flower it burst open in him then, in the hours on the road, going back, cheated. Beneath the mango in the garden of the lodging house.

This is not to say his madness was incurable.

When day arrived, he heard persons stirring in the house, and went and claimed his room there. Next, having washed himself and shaved, he went into the town to look for employment. He did all this very correctly, and like a man with no soul. There is a name for this condition in the islands, and he was to hear it quite soon.

In the afternoon, when a bruised light hung over the town, the outrider of the storm which at that season usually occurred daily, Jean de St. Jean was sitting in the dusty little office of someone who might be willing to give him some work. He had been waiting an interminable time, which was in reality only a few minutes, and his nerves were urging him sluggishly but repeatedly to get up and leave, for this could be no use to him. Then, the door opened, and a black man entered.

He was dressed as a laborer, and his personal scent was strong, like the musk of the panther. He looked directly at Jean, and, without a word, jerked his feline head toward the street.

Jean saw this, and said, "What do you want?"

He had not achieved the proper purblind arrogance of the white in Haïssa, or the proper uneasiness either. He reacted as he would have to something unreal yet fundamentally inimical. To a threatening and *superior* thing.

The man did not answer him, but poised there, plainly expecting Jean to get up and go out with him.

Jean was so exhausted, so demoralized and unhinged, that in a moment this was exactly what he did.

When they were on the street, Jean said, "But—"

That was all.

They went down and down, through a kind of corkscrew of streets, where vines and palms poured over walls, and the houses came to be built of planks and tin. Finally there was a space, and a rickety hut with a tin roof and the black man pointed at its door.

"Who are you?" said Jean.

The black man laughed. He looked like a god when he did so, lawless and all-wise. Then he spat on the ground and walked off another way, and Jean was left there, at the bottom of the corkscrew, with only the door in front of him. So he pushed the door wide.

Inside was the dusk again, redolent with such stuff as cooked rice, blood, spice, tobacco, washing, and rum. He could make out no furniture, but some black beings were seated on the earth floor in an open circle, and before them was a scatter of objects lit by one window. Jean saw dried beans and cards, a shawl, a fruit, and the bones of a dog brightly painted.

"Shut our door," said a voice.

Jean drew the door in against him, and the shack became more solid and less visible, and the bones glowed, and the white eyes in the faces like ebony, like beautiful alien masks, and like nothing human.

"Sit down with us," someone said. And someone else gave a cruel laugh.

Jean remained in the shut door. They were figments of a new dream.

Finally, a man said from the circle, "M'sieur Dargue is dead. Are you sorry he dead?"

Jean choked back a confused reply. He felt compelled to respond, unbearably excited, could not speak.

"Why you would want him alive?" said the voice.

There was a great attention then. They focused it upon Jean. He did not know how many of them there were, but the eyes fastened on him like claws.

"Alive—so I—" said Jean.

"He not loved, M'sieur Dargue," said the voice. The others purred in the dark. "No one is sorry."

Jean covered his face with one hand. He longed, as though to vomit, to evict the cry: *My father's murder!* It would not come.

"You not sorry," said the voice, soothingly.

The illness flooded from Jean, the words released him. He said hoarsely, "Yes, I came to kill him. Too late."

"Not so. We give him you, for killing."

And the others purred.

They were smiling at him. In every night of a face, a sickle moon.

But Dargue was dead.

"We invite you to come our God-Place," said the first voice. A black hand reached out and took up one of the bones from the ground. The bone moved as if still alive, and animal. "We invite M'sieur Dargue. We fetch him. You be surprised. But we give you M'sieur Dargue, because you want him so."

Jean thought they must have pursued him along Oleander Road on the previous night and read his mind. They were sorcerers, so much was apparent. He had always half believed in sorcery.

But what were they saying? That Dargue was not dead, but in some way their prisoner?

"You pay the price," said the voice.

Jean said, "I haven't any money."

They purred again. The shack reverberated. Jean

thought, Not money. It isn't that. Something they want and I want, but I must pay and then they need not.

He thought, very clearly: What am I doing? Where am I? What is happening to me? And someone else said, *"This is the Religion of the Night."*

Then he was sitting close by them on the earth floor, cooking hot as if above a volcano, with his back to the wall and the tin ceiling above, from which feathers and paper blossoms and bells hung on threads. A mirror floated in space, like a tear, a small lizard clinging to its cracked uneven rim. A black woman was giving him drink out of a calabash gourd. It was rum with something sweet. Jean drank, and thanked the woman, and she laughed and touched his brow with her finger. Her touch was like a star, it burned.

Rain was drilling on the tin roof. They had given him a direction, where he must go tonight, not too late . . .

"No," said Jean.

"Good day."

♦ ♦ ♦

Jean returned to his lodging and dozed feverishly on the bed. He dreamed his Aunt Andromede was standing over him, wringing her hands, saying, "Let me advise you, Jean, you musn't go anywhere with such people." But there were feathers pinned into her tight hair.

The storm flew toward the sea, and the evening descended clear, as stars rose up through it.

He went out and moved toward a market at a crossroads known as Horse Tail. He had already asked the way. He received solemn looks and vague replies, until a wizened black woman had shown him the route, drawing a diagram in the dust. Still, he meant to be late. He did not guess why he was going. They might set on him, though there was surely no motive. He was destitute, he had done nothing to annoy them; except that being alive might be enough. He concluded they meant to play some trick. But he was drawn as if by a magnet. It allowed him to dawdle, but not to resist.

It was dark when he reached the crossroads. There were some carts and awnings, and fires burning on the ground, and candles in gourds strung up. Commerce of a desultory type was in progress, scrawny chickens changing hands, some barter over beans and pots of jelly.

The market ignored Jean, as if he were invisible. Then a man came walking straight between the carts, the refuse, and the market seemed to make way for him. He wore a black robe, black on black, but in his hand was a whip with a white bone handle.

When he reached Jean, there were all at once five or six other men at this man's back.

The man said to Jean, "Come, now. We invite you."

And turning away, he strode off again, toward the forest and the hills. The other men went with him, and pulled as though by a tough cord, Jean walked after them.

♦ ♦ ♦

The God-Place crouched in a somber clearing. Water ran close by, snarled in the roots of an enormous tree, making a weird tearing sound. The roof of the temple was thatched, with an open court beneath, enclosing the sanctum, and full of the night people of Haïssa. As the man with the whip had ascended the forest path among his guard and Jean followed, he heard the subterranean notes of conch shells blowing in the woods above. When the temple came in sight, and they approached it, these shells were blown again, a dubious, threatening greeting.

The man with the whip strode to a boundary of the court, which was marked by some small heaps of meal, petals, and paper. He used the whip's bone handle to point with. "You will stand there. You say nothing. If you fear and run away, you not get what you come for." He did not look at Jean, had never really looked into Jean's face or eyes.

Jean did not protest. He went to the indicated spot at the

perimeter of the court. Five women who had been grouped inside the boundary, near where he must stand, ebbed away, turning their shadow masks from him.

The man with the whip passed into the temple. They had brought a chair and set it by the entry to the inner shrine. The chair had an abnormally high and upright back resembling a coffin. The whip man seated himself, and the crowd in the court deferred to him. Evidently he was their priest, and their magician.

The skull lamps of the calabash gourds burned from the thatch, and here and there glimmered wicks in cups of oil. The light only made one with the darkness. And the smell of the God-Place was intense and disturbing.

A girl in white flaunted over the court. She carried a lighted candle and a jar of clear rum, from which she poured a libation under the central post of the thatch roof. Another white-clad girl came after her, an echo, a smoke-ghost. She poured flour or meal onto the ground in a pattern. A third girl came with a snake's rattle in each hand, and she whirled like a top until her white and her black merged into a vortex, out of which all three girls seemed to vanish away.

Then the three drums of the spirits began, and Jean saw the Dance of the Religion of the Night, a forbidden thing, both prayer and invocation, during which power descends, along the temple's very spine, and rays out among those who call themselves the Night Beasts, the black lynxes of the hills, whose true hills are older yet and whose rites began in cities of stone and bone when white men only whimpered at their cave-mouths, afraid of all things and the dark especially, with some cause.

Jean saw how the people formed into a black serpent of flesh, a body of many parts linked by a communal soul. And they passed about the spine-post of the temple in the ancient, benign, positive right-to right motion known in the Craft of Europe as God's Flowing, and commemorated by artisans in the action of clocks and watches. The steps of the dance were a rapid stamping and tossing, and the ums formed these steps out of the muscle and skeleton of ry dancer, lifting them, setting them down. The names he three drums, which were later told to Jean, were the cat's drum, and the drum of the second, and the ther drum, which roars like a she-bull under the ground, he earthquake birth, the summoner.

As he watched, Jean felt his own body beginning to move with the rhythm of the dance, although, he was rooted to the spot. A crazy exhilaration rose with the sweat and perfume of the God-Place. Naturally, educated and refined as he had been, Jean was instinctively resistant to it. He could not and would not give himself to the surge of power. He stayed outside, his breathing rapid and shallow and his eyes on fire, steeled, aroused, dismayed, in chains.

After a while, out of the dancing serpent, a young woman broke away. She raised her arms and screamed aloud. The dancers gave her room. She was the mare horse, and one would come to ride her.

She was the mare among the Night Beasts and the horseman would possess her, riding in her skin, a god mounting her, and she would lose herself, gaining him.

The woman who was possessed was now in an open space against the central post. Her eyes were like blind windows, yet something flashed behind them. A girl in a pale robe came to the woman, and handed her a black hen. Its terrible fluttering exploded in blood and feathers as the possessed tore off its head and wings with her teeth.

The woman flung the hen down and, drawing a pin from her dress, she thrust it through her arm, once, twice, three, four, five times. Jean beheld the bright point going in and coming out of her, but there was no blood now, no pain. She danced on the carcass of the dead bird, twirling and shouting.

The magician-priest had risen from his coffin-chair. He pointed at the woman, and all at once the bloodbeat of the drumming fell away, leaving behind an extraordinary absence, as though part of the very ground had dropped into space. He spoke in the patois that Jean did not truly understand. It was evidently a welcome.

The possessed ceased her whirling. She stood before the priest, laughing with tiger's teeth. Then she cried out in a deep man's voice; Jean caught the idea that she was now a lord and would be obeyed.

The priest nodded and bowed. Clearly he said: "Lead us."

And then the woman, or whatever she had become, went springing out of the court, and bounded away through the clearing, and the dancers broke and raced after her.

Jean stood still, not knowing what to do, until fingers brushed on his arm and someone said to him, "We go to the graveyard now."

He did not see who spoke, and the hand was gone from him like the flick of a paw.

He turned and half staggered into the rear of the swirling wave. It accepted him, and rolled with him, away across the clearing and up into the matted forest darkness sprinkled with wild stars.

Afterward, that is one month later, Jean conjectured that some drug might have been pressed on him. Though he ate and drank nothing throughout the ceremony of the night, there were certain poisons he had heard the Night Beasts used, and these, rubbed into the skin, worked very swiftly on the blood and brain.

As he ran through the forest, Jean had only the sensation of forward motion, and that his eyes were strangely enlarged, like those of some nocturnal animal. It occurred to him he saw, in glimpses, creatures which normally a man does not easily see—birds upon branches, lizards and frogs, etched in fine silver . . . there were other things, too, of which only the vaguest impression was left—of a huge man, naked but for a cloak, of a species of demon that grew in the trees like leaves . . . of a woman anointing herself in a glade. None of them were real, yet he saw, and acknowledged, each of them, as he ran by.

The graveyard must have been some way up behind

Oleander Road. It was presumably respectable but, to the Beasts of Night, open as a door. They made an invocation at the gate, and again it seemed something went prancing along the wall, but it was gone before Jean could identify it.

His next formed impression—which was abnormally apparent, in fact—was of a woman he took for a priestess standing out before the others at a place where the ground was freshly dug. All around were Christian crosses and ornate monuments on which the lianas fed in a still gray moonlight. There was a headstone, too, naked and unfinished, and here the woman's snakelike shadow fell. She wore white, like the others, but it was a gown that might have come from Jean's city, ivory satin, sashed, and sewn with brilliants, leaving her shoulders bare as smooth black lacquer. She wore a plumed hat also, and a white domino with scintillants stitched about the eyes. He did not know where she had come from. He thought she carried a fan, then he saw it was a bunch of the ugly horse-tail plants. She smiled as she stood over the new grave. Jean could make out no name on the headstone, but there was no need.

The priestess straddled the grave in her satin gown. She frisked the horse-tail in the air and shook her head of plumes. From everywhere there came then the clacking together of rocks and stones.

Jean held his breath, could not catch it, had surrendered. He believed in anything at this moment and, accordingly, liberated night did not fail him.

"Monsieur Dargue!" cried the night, in all its voices, over and over again.

Jean found that he had called out, too.

And the stones clacked.

And something pranced along the wall, and there went the possessed woman whirling with a burning branch in her hands, and a man's face, and the black masks all turned one way and the moon that was like a quartered fruit—

And the earth on the grave shook. It shook and shattered and a piece of wood shot up out of it, and the satin priestess screamed down into the grave: "Come out, come out, come out!" And then half a wooden coffin-lid burst up and stood on end and a colorless white-man's hand came creeping out of the soil like a blind crab.

The priestess stayed as she was. She never moved. The strength that seared from her was hot and palpable as the smell of living bodies and decay.

Then the ground fissured, and Dargue came up out of it.

Instantly the noise of the rocks and the shouting ended in a dense, ringing silence.

Dargue stood in the belljar of it, or what had been Dargue, a sort of man, clad in a nightshirt, and a crucifix on his breast pushed sideways. His nails were torn and dirty where he had used them to thrust off the coffin, a feat of great strength of which, alive, he might have been incapable. His face was a dead man's face. He had lost his good angel, they said, *soul-gone*.

The dead eyes did not look around, the head did not turn, having got up from his bed he did not stir.

*"Ha!"* said the priestess. And she spat a stream of something into his face that glowed; it might only have been the white rum. Then she moved aside.

Some men ran forward. They carried the horse-tails in their hands, and with these they slashed Dargue across the head and body. The spiky plants made wounds in his flesh, but Dargue did not bleed. He did not attempt to protect himself, and when, quite suddenly, he fell to his knees, the gesture evoked neither pity or satisfaction, it was plainly only that the tendons of his legs had relaxed.

Jean stared at what he was witnessing, and now he tried desperately hard to feel something in response. Perhaps he did not even know that this was what he was doing. He was not afraid, no longer exhilarated. If anything he felt very tired, for he had not slept properly nor eaten much, and everything was alien, and therefore somehow all strangeness had abruptly become mundane.

What he tried most to feel was his anger, his hatred of

Dargue. It was there within him, but he could not get hold of it. It had faded to a memory.

The priestess moved up in front of Jean. She looked as though she were laughing at him, her wonderful dreadful teeth glittering. Her hands were gloved as if for the opera, and she was balancing on them, before him, a sword.

She nodded, and the plumes in the hat fluttered, while the sword was motionless.

"What do you want me to do?" said Jean. He used the stupidity he felt as an amulet, but of course it was ineffectual.

"Take the sword," said the black priestess. She put it gently into his hands, which had somehow risen to grasp it.

The Night Beasts waited, and the moon waited and the graveyard, and the island, and Dargue who was dead, he waited, too.

Jean went across the silent ground, toward Dargue, who knelt there, his head sunk on his breast.

In all his least lawful, most incoherent dreams, Jean had never deployed his vengeance in this fashion.

He used both hands and all his strength to swing the sword backward and forward again, ramming it in through the wall of Dargue's chest, through the linen, and through the flesh, which crumbled like biscuit. A trickle of murky stuff oozed out. A rib snapped and jutted from the cavity. The body of Dargue crumpled over and took the sword with it, out of Jean's grip.

Jean stood there like a fool, feeling nothing except a faint disgust. Someone should tell him what to do now.

Shortly someone did come up, and murmured—was it courteously?—that he might go, his portion was finished. Out of the gate and follow the path, and he would soon come to the edges of the town, with the moon to watch over him.

So he stepped off the grave and walked away.

He kept repeating to himself as he went, *"My father's murderer."*

This did not help.

Then, when the graveyard had been left behind and he was on a rambling track through the forest, with the moon glimpsing out like a girl's face among the balconies of the trees, he saw what he had done, that he had cheated death in an odd, insulting manner, and this was why he had been allowed to perform the act with the sword, since death was probably venerated here, and to cheat him was such a bit of cheek it must require payment.

But all Jean wanted, actually, by this stage, was to find his lodging and go to sleep. He no longer cared about anything else. He shook everything off him as he went on, like dust from his coat. And like dust, some of it was already in his system, he had swallowed it, it was a part of him.

When he reached the lodging house he no longer had scruples about waking them up. He knocked and banged on the shutters. When they let him in, he crawled through the house and dropped on the mattress in his clothes, with the dust of night in his belly, mind, and spirit. And without a single dream that he knew of, he slept, like the dead.

III

As it happened—at any rate, as it was told—the story of Jean de St. Jean has here a break or interval. Real life, and its experiences, are seldom completely serial. Yet the space of a year may be recounted quickly, the method indeed of my informant.

Jean's recovery—or lapse—from the hour of his murder of a dead man, seems to have been immediate. His impulse was to ignore what had happened, then boldly to question it. Though he kept his reasons private, by asking casually here and there in knowledgeable, biased circles, for facts concerning Haïssa's religion of the night—that is, among the skeptical white community—Jean learned to behold himself as a victim of drug or fantasy. Perhaps the shock of Dargue's death had unhinged him temporarily, perhaps he had the voyager's malaise, a kind of earth sickness *(mal de terre)* induced by stepping ashore after months on the ocean. Whatever it had been, any slight fears he may have had that some further pursuit might be made of him, or threats or pleas offered, based upon his participation in the ceremony, were allayed by the passage of time. No one approached him to accuse or mock or coerce. He even grew used to the black beings of the island, and came to think of them as inferior men, or sometimes as men, so that they lost for him their appearance of shadows and panthers, lynxes, and night-personified. He was even briefly tempted by their women, but some moral code he had always tried to obey precluded such adventures. He had been brought up on a diet not solely of hate but ironically of an ideal of true love.

The previous votive of working to obtain his passage home he quickly sought and achieved. His city education and person assisted Jean, and he gained the secretary's job formerly mooted. Presently, along with an accumulation of banknotes, he was absorbed into the social context of white Haïssa. Class was held since the Revolution to be immaterial, but was still insidiously observed. However, Jean's manners were of sufficient quality, and his looks of enough attraction, that insidiously observed class did not much hinder him. He rose, and he bloomed, and even as conditions bore the harvest of money to return him across the sea, they drew in about his roots and began to secure him to the island earth.

It must be wondered, in this time, if he wrote at all to his Aunt Andromede and, if so, what he told her. His reports could have, soon enough, been of the nicest news, full of good prospects and nostalgias. How he put it to her that Dargue had perished is conjecture. He could not have made of it the grim joke it was, nor, certainly, even in the most unsolid terms, could he have hinted at the scene in the graveyard. Letters took so long, in any case, going back and forth. It is possible that they were mislaid, or unsent. One senses his aunt did not receive any, but that may be false.

One knows at least she never heard the facts in their naked form.

Presently, along with the rest, Jean became accustomed to the climate. He came to look for the seasonal afternoon rains, the thunder, the moon-drenched nights in which, by then, he would stroll or ride without glancing over his shoulder. He liked the friends he had made. Though assiduously he saved his fare, the act had turned into a sham.

He did not exactly know this until one morning, going to his office along a street above the bay, a carriage slowly passed him. Looking into it inadvertently, he saw a young woman in a dove-colored frock and pearl ear-drops. Her name, Gentilissa Ferrier, he identified from the carriage, which he had seen about before. Monsieur Ferrier was a little known to Jean and had mentioned that his daughter was to come home from one of the other islands, where family connections had for months concealed her. The sight of the girl startled Jean. For some minutes, after the carriage had gone on, he did not know why. Then he recalled the features of a Madonna in a painting he had seen as a boy. The Venus of Haïssa was also a Madonna, both carnal and immaculate, having two aspects, a flower virgin and a black virgin. Jean had in his researches heard the name of this goddess, who is wedded to all men and to none. He did not, naturally, for a second associate her with Gentilissa Ferrier, but by the time he had reached his office, Jean sensed an imminence. His father and mother had fallen in love at sight. In his efforts to re-create them, possibly Jean had yearned to do the same. Now the opportunity was before him. He took it.

Once he had convinced himself of what had happened to him there came about one of those coincidences which, to a person obsessed, indicate the hand of Destiny. Jean found he had been invited to a dinner party at the Ferrier house. This had already happened twice. There had been no reason not to invite him again; he had behaved very charmingly before.

It is curious, maybe, through this sliding frame of a year,

to see Jean now, earlier an incarnation of Hamlet, currently Romeo. But the passion is constant, merely the object has been changed.

With the same headlong zeal that had sent him aboard the ship, that had goaded him along Oleander Road toward the estate of Dargue, in just that way he now prepared himself for his first meeting with the girl Gentilissa. His eyes blazed; he was excited, fiercely determined. He had been disappointed then, by those appalling words: *"He is dead."* But Jean put all that behind him, and could not credit a disappointment now. Gentilissa was there to be won. A year of success proved that he was able to win things. He had a half vision of her in the City on his arm, when his fortune had been made. Or they were driving through the forest roads above Haïssa town in a taper of brief dusk, and she leant her head upon his shoulder.

The Ferrier family was quite wealthy. This pleased Jean only because it meant Gentilissa would have been elegantly reared, though she would not, he understood, be as sophisticated as a girl of his city. What impediment could there be? He had prospects, and it was up to him to make her love him. If only he could do that.

He said a prayer to the Virgin. It was not the Virgin of the two faces, but the albino Madonna in the church. But he had already noted, if he had thought of it, that the shacks of Night Beasts often had their crosses, their icons of Christ. The gods had many names and were everywhere.

♦ ♦ ♦

When he rode up to the house, it had the look he had grown to recognize in the island. He knew it, anyway. Set off the road among large mango trees, ferns and thickets of bamboo, constructed of apparently crumbling sugar, with orchids, and a tame parrot in a cage on the veranda, which called out in the tongue of the City: *"Who goes there?"*

A black servant ran to see to Jean's horse. Jean climbed the steps and went up into the big dining room, lit like the church with candles. Once the sun set, the moths would come in droves to die, and the sun was setting now. The guests were going to see the classical pavilion.

Jean, with his glass of white wine in his hand, was light-headed and anxious. He had not found her yet among the women. He wondered if he had been mistaken about her, if she would look the same.

Below the veranda on the other side, screened by a towering plantain, the kitchen fumed and two black women were poised there to be ignored as Jean had learned to ignore them.

The pavilion stood against a break in the trees, and beyond, far down, lay the sea, with the sun going into it like a bubble into glass.

Jean wandered off a short way. He had seen the sun set before. He was instinctively searching for Gentilissa. And suddenly there she was.

It was perfect. Against a dusky mossy wall, she was sitting on a bench, in her party gown which was white and left bare her throat and shoulders. Her dark hair was done in ringlets, with a rose.

This he observed, and that she was lovely. But he noticed, too, that she cast a shadow, and the shadow was a house woman, who sat with her on the bench. And by the bench there was a plant growing that Jean remembered.

It was true, he had seen it since about the forest tracks and the cemeteries of the town. He had even garnered its title: *la queue de la réne-jument*—the Queen-Mare's Tail. They said it flourished where there had been a death. A graveyard bloom. He had never quite come to like it, or be comfortable in its vicinity, that was the residue of the night he had once spent in the hills.

Now the sight of it struck him a glancing blow, that it should be growing there, against Gentilissa's skirt. And all at once the shadow figure beside her assumed an unnamed identity. For a moment Jean even thought he knew her. But she was only an old black woman, a house servant.

Just then Gentilissa got to her feet, and looking up she saw Jean gazing at her. She must have taken his apprehension for interest, for she lowered her lashes and hid her face behind a little fan she carried, in the coquettish mannerism of young white women of the islands. It was a silly gesture, and it reassured him.

He followed her with his eyes as she went away behind the wall, the black woman slipping after her.

The sun had gone down and night smoldered in the Ferrier garden, and on the veranda the parrot called, "*Qui vive?*" There was nothing to discompose. The family and guests and Jean went in to dinner.

♦ ♦ ♦

Gentilissa Ferrier was beautiful and adorable; she flamed like the candles; she was serene as a nun. Her moods were variable but not hectic. Jean was fascinated. She was all he had surmised. And in addition she had the power of speech, and thoughts, she could play the piano, had a thin sweet voice that sang. When they asked her about books she had read some, and she had a dream of going to the City.

When Jean attended her, she did not seem to mind it. As he turned the pages of her music, once or twice her eyes rested upon him.

When the dinner came to its end, he was sure, and going up to her candidly, with the mantle of the City she dreamed of nonchalantly over his shoulders, he asked if he might have the rose from her hair.

She was prettily flustered. For what could he want it?

"It has been close to you, Mademoiselle Ferrier," said Jean. He was a poet's son. He had the taint if not the gift.

His final sight of her that night was upon the veranda, the whole sugar house caught in a splash of stars. The lamp that twinkled upon her put the stars at her ears and in her eyes to the very last twist of the path. The black woman was her childhood companion, a sort of nurse resembling Juliet's. She dressed neatly and had a bracelet. Jean had been polite to her on the veranda, and the woman bowed. They called her Tibelle.

In the weeks that followed, Jean often found occasion to be passing the Ferrier house. They were never unwelcoming. Monsieur spoke of the City, and of business, Madam was earnest to have cards. Then Gentilissa would come and serve juices in crystal jugs. She would take Jean away to show him birds and butterflies in the garden, and Tibelle would be their chaperon, gliding some distance behind them. And sometimes they would sit in an arbor while Gentilissa coaxed tunes from a mandolin, and Tibelle would sit far off, a black shape still as the iron owl on the gate. The woman had a pipe and now and then would smoke it, and the smoke moved in, rising, but not Tibelle. The jewelry birds darted through the foliage. Jean began to court Gentilissa.

It was pleasant, there was no hurry. Everything acquiesced. Time seemed to stretch forever. If he was impatient, it was only through physical desire. He had not kissed her. These things, this temperance, were inborn. The climate, which could incite, could also calm with its false assurance, "Go Slowly." Lazily, a man and woman drew together. No one denied.

Then one evening, as Tibelle the black volcano sat smoking on the horizon, Gentilissa leaned to Jean and brushed his cheek with her warm lips.

It was as if a barrier fell down. He turned upon her and pulled her to him, but before his hunger found any expression, she moved away.

"No, Jean," said Gentilissa, as sweetly as she sang and out of her nun's face. "You mustn't."

"But why?"

"Because Papa would be horribly angry."

Jean was reckless at last. "But he'll have to be told. I shall ask him for you. You know I will."

"No," said Gentilissa. She looked neither sad nor unnerved. She was entirely at peace.

"You feel nothing for me," said Jean. It was a boastful demand. Despite her look, he was certain by now that she loved him.

"Oh, Jean," she said.

"Then I'll ask him tonight."

"He will refuse you."

Jean hesitated. He had not made his intentions obvious, but neither had they been opaque. Would Gentilissa's father not have sounded some warning previously, if he were vehemently opposed?

"Allow me the attempt," said Jean.

"I can't. How can I? Papa has no objection to my holding court . . . that I should have admirers. But he expects me to marry a man of substance. Already there is someone in view."

"That's barbarous."

"It's how it is done here."

"Nonsense. I—"

"Jean, you will grieve me."

It was so shocking, this development, he could not credit it. He sought to take her hand. Gentilissa would not permit this.

"I love you," he said. "I think you care for me."

"I may not answer."

"Your eyes answer." This was a lie. Her eyes were blank. She said nothing, either. But he had all the evidence of several weeks, when every sigh and tremor and sideways look had concocted meaning. "Gentilissa, in a year or so I might be a rich man. It's been said to me, promised."

"Dearest Jean," said Gentilissa. Her breast rose with delirious softness as she drew in her breath. "I can't go against Papa. He means me to marry a man from another island. There's nothing I can do. I never guessed the strength of your feeling. I thought you amused yourself with me."

Jean swore by God. Gentilissa averted her head. She said, very low, "You must leave me now. We must never see each other again, until after I am married."

Jean sprang to his feet, but already Gentilissa was moving lightly away, like a piece of white cotton down. And summoned uncannily without a cry, the servant woman, Tibelle, was slinking toward them.

In a rage of powerlessness and disbelief, Jean stood in the Ferrier garden until the black woman and the white had disappeared together beyond the mango trees.

♦ ♦ ♦

There is another name for the Religion of the Night among the islands. They term it Nightmare Magic. Once you have been touched by it, there is no getting free. To the devotee that is no problem. To the outsider whom the gods, however obliquely and remotely, have ridden, the religion is fever. It may lie dormant ten years. But it is not to be escaped from, in the end. They tell you, have nothing to do with it. But sometimes wanting is enough to bring it down, like a cloud from the mountain. No sooner had Jean run into the apartment of his aunt with the branch of their hate in blossom, no sooner had he set sail, than he called the devil, and the devil started forth. Before he left the ship, the first night, the entity had shown itself. It was too late. Death brought Jean de St. Jean to the island, and cheated him and bargained with him and claimed him. There is not a boulder or a leaf there without some life in it, or something of death in it. It was not only the forests or the human skin of Haïssa that earned it the adjective "Black."

For a month, Jean dwelled in a condition of misery and fury that was almost lunatic. Initially he did his best to go about his affairs of business and existence otherwise as before. But that was impossible. His heart had been cut out. He was in constant agony and barely alive. Sometimes he would lose himself in awful daydreams, riding to the house and confronting Monsieur Ferrier, bursting in upon her wedding and shooting down the groom. At other, worse times, he visualized his own life stretching to infinity bereft of Gentilissa. It seemed to him his pain would never cease. If he got drunk it might abate for half an hour, only to return with redoubled ferocity. Sober, he was like a man beneath a ton weight, he could hardly raise his head.

He was thought to be ill. He was treated with sympathy, next with concern, ultimately with impatience. This was not the obliging, efficient Jean they knew.

At night he would sit in his rooms and look at his money saved for the homeward voyage. It was like the coinage of oblivion. To go away was out of the question; to remain was not to be endured.

That he also thought of killing himself is conceivable, but it was a symptom rather than an intent.

Then one afternoon there came to his office, where he was sitting in rapt dejection, a letter. He knew at once that it was from her. Tearing it open he read: *I can bear our separation no longer. If you still love me and will dare the consequences, be this evening just after sunset by the statue of the slave. Tibelle will bring you to me.*

The effect upon Jean, after his unhappiness, was galvanic, almost injurious. He shook, went white, laughed aloud once or twice, and generally furthered the prevailing opinion among his colleagues that he was not long to be among them.

The letter he did not let go of, and leaving his post early, rushed to his rooms to prepare himself for this clandestine and romantic assignation. He had not a single qualm, although he did think her a trifle foolish, and very endearing, to trust him so much. Surely she loved him, and through the blessing of that, everything else could be made to come right.

The statue of the slave, a rough and ready work attempted in the classical mode, stood near a crossroad and a market. They were unfamiliar to Jean, although he found the statue easily enough. He had arrived before time, and watched the sun go down behind the towers of a pair of churches, and then the darkness came, and he beheld the fires burning in the market, and the ragged awnings, and the chicken corpses along the carts, and smelled the overripeness of the gourds, and heard the chattering of the black men and women who idled there. An unpleasant memory wakened in Jean. Before he had satisfactorily thrust it off, he saw the woman Tibelle coming across the street. Her hair was tied up in a cream kerchief as always, and on her ebony stick of wrist the bracelet dripped like water. She walked right up to him, and scrutinized his face. *To be sure of me, for her mistress's sake,* Jean thought to himself, but for all that he was not easy with her look.

"Now you come with Tibelle."

"Where?"

"Tibelle take you."

"Where are we going?"

"You come, you see."

Jean shrugged. He no longer felt as he had done, elated, slightly drunk, a little afraid. Now there was something heavy again, something pressing down on him. As he went after the servant woman, his entrails were cold and his heart beat in hard leaden strokes. His father might have told him, these are the sensations of a man en route to the gallows.

Up behind the market the streets rose and then there began to be the wide avenues where the fine old houses had been built, the houses of broken sugar under the poured molasses of the vines.

And then they were on a stretch that could have been Oleander Road, or Mango Tree Ride, or one of those other flowery, fruiting tracks that led into the forest and the hills. Then they came over a stony slope showing the sea in a net of trees, and there was a cemetery before them, a graveyard.

Jean stopped, and in front of him his guide halted and turned to look at him again.

"Where you think she can meet with you," said Tibelle contemptuously, "in the hotel?"

"But here—"

"Here is safe," said Tibelle. "What you got to worry?"

And she went on again, in at the gate with a sort of stumble that might have been an obeisance, and in between the graves.

Jean followed her. There was perhaps no going back. The

night was all around, and the hills of Haïssa. It was too late to fly.

He noticed as he got down the ridged path behind her that things were hanging out on many of the headstones, like curious washing. There were bunches of feathers, and beads, and garlands of paper flowers, with here and there a rosary, a mask on a string with staring eyeless eyes, bones and bells that clinked and rang sometimes as the night breeze twisted at them. There was a feeling of immensity and congestion, everything too close and the night outside vast as all space where hung the bells and bones and stars inaudibly clinking and fluttering in the breath of the gods.

Jean began to cough a little, something that had not happened since he was a child; it was a sign of nerves.

Tibelle said, "Hush, hush, here you are."

And there was a shack or hut before them under a stunted palm, in the middle of the death-place.

Tibelle went aside, as she had been used to before, as if to smoke her pipe, and Jean was left by the hut in the darkness. He knew quite well that all there was to do was to push the door. He knew, and it no longer mattered. The interval of a year had evaporated, its pleasures and agonies with it. Therefore, without hesitation finally, he opened the door and walked into the hut.

He was half surprised. For Gentilissa was sitting there before him, on a small chair, with her hands folded in her lap.

"Jean," she said.

Her eyes were large and luminous. He had always been struck by some quality in them, an effect he had taken for purity or innocence. But it was a sort of vacuity really, he could see as much now, a sort of vacancy, and when she had been with him and seemed to shine, it was because her eyes reflected him: he filled up the emptiness. It had made her attractive, like a flattering mirror.

"Jean?" she said again, now in a questioning tone.

She was wearing black. That was arresting, for Tibelle the

black woman had worn white. Gentilissa in black was changed. Her face was like a moon, a mask.

"Oh, Jean," she said.

And outside, the drums started, as he had heard them countless times from the hills, throbbing and rattling, for some festivity or dance. The little drum and the drum of the second and the mother drum, who roared in the earth.

Gentilissa came to her feet. She stamped lightly and tossed her head and her hair flew out, the heavy ringlets. Her eyes were flat as windowpanes. Then he began to see that something moved behind them.

Gentilissa laughed and gave herself. Her face slackened and became an idiot's. Her eyes rolled. She seemed about to fall. But something caught her and held her. Her head turned on her neck and moved round again to confront him. Behind the mask of her face, another was there, that Jean recalled. It was at the same time black and white, but whether the black lay under the white or the black flushed out upon the white he could not be sure. But in the eyes, there was no mistaking it, the night being, the lord who had come to ride his mare, and to claim the bargain price.

Gentilissa's mouth gaped open. Out of it boomed the note of a deep bass bell. "I *here.* You *know* me," she said, in the voice of a giant man taller than the treetops, older than the island, with the sea for blood and the bones of all the island's dead in a necklace at his throat. "Know *me,*" said Death. And Jean knew him, knew him. Knew *him.*

♦ ♦ ♦

They said he died of a fever in Haïssa Town, having been sick for some while. The island is noted for its seasonal fevers. They said it was a shame he died so young, the same age as his father, indeed, and far from home. You may come across the grave in a shady corner of the Christian Cemetery near Oleander Road. There is no inscription beyond his name, *Jean de St. Jean.* Though sometimes flowers may be left there, by girls in colored scarves, who walk like cats and smile, blackened by the sun to the darkness of night, Nègre girls, who cannot, probably, have known him.

# HE WHISTLES FAR AND WEE

## by Kiel Stuart

Kiel Stuart is a member of the Authors Guild, the Science Fiction Writers of America, and director of the Writers Alliance. Her short fiction and humor has appeared in *Tales of the Witch World I, Magic in Ithkar 3, Pulpsmith, Fantasy Book, The Horror Show, The New York Times, Newsday, Island Women Anthology, Arts and Artists.* She has also written a number of articles and booklets on various subjects. She enjoys challenging herself physically through bodybuilding and power-lifting and is an accomplished artist who has exhibited widely. Kiel lives in Stony Brook, New York.

Brief and not-so-sweet is this short short from a woman whose first submission I returned, saying I didn't take stories from men for this anthology; I realized my mistake when she phoned me. Kiel persisted, and I'm glad she did.

♦ ♦ ♦

*the queer*
*old balloonman whistles*
*far and wee*
—*e.e. cummings*

Eheluena's glorious sun pressed down on her vacationers like a giant's palm, softly squeezing them into the pink sand.

On this most beautiful of the islands, with air like the finest, sweetest honey, where birds like flying jewels filled the air with their music, Balloon Man plied his trade.

Balloon Man smiled his broad polished grin, touching the straw hat on his head and settling it just so. It would not do to look anything less than perfect for the vacationers, coming as they had from their sad gray lands. The manganese-blue sky and sea had done their best, turning out in splendid style, and he could do no less, so Balloon Man took great care in polishing the pearl buttons of his macaw-patterned shirt. Only when he was satisfied with the effect did he turn to the sloping palm tree where he had parked his wares and untied the strings to his six balloons.

He wound the strings together around his scarred palm, for he would not tie them together now, God no! What if some lively young miss or some fine young gentleman wanted a balloon at once, and could not wait while he undid the knot holding them all together in a mess?

He held the balloons away from him at arm's length. They seemed to tremble and seek the lush tropical skies, eager to be off. "My pretty ones are wanting to begin," he laughed. "Very well. We shall walk the beach now."

Balloon Man settled the sisal belt looped through his very long, loose pants. With the hand not holding his balloons (and despite the straw hat), he shaded his eyes, looking up and down the pink length of Magayana Beach.

It was surely a magnificent beach. Beneath the crystal waters lay fish, clinging to the bottom, as lovely as carved amber jewelry, so long as you took care not to step on their spines.

But Balloon Man knew that all things were in balance. No place on this earth was perfect, if you cared to remove the cover and look inside. Some of these people came from places that had earthquakes! Imagine that! Or snow, six months out of the year!

How very sad that would be, not to hear the singing jewels or lie in the warm soft sand. He shook his head, a rich chuckle bobbing the balloons in his hand. "Yes, yes, pretties. It's very sad. But who can be sad possessing a lovely balloon? Come."

Balloon Man did not cry his wares, not like the Fruit Man or Fish Man. No, his whistle was enough. Those who needed a balloon would know.

He moved out from the shelter of the trees, and with his rolling gait and strange high whistle, made the first steps over the line that divided shade and sun.

It was then that his balloons took life.

They were the most beautiful balloons in the world, more beautiful, more ethereal, more delicate than the inside of an abalone shell, lighter than Eheluena's butterflies and more musical than her birds. They were the moon, a pearl, a sphere of precious crystal infused with the very soul of the lovely island. As they trembled along with him, matching the rhythm of his walk, Balloon Man surveyed the people lying on the hot pink sand.

Most sprawled like statues, motionless and dreaming in the arms of the glimmering sand. But children, having been endowed with more energy than the grown-ups, did not pay quite so much attention to the giant's palm blaring yellow in the sky, or to the fact that he stole the vigor out of most living things. The little boy's eyes snapped bright and curious toward him, alive eyes, eyes like luminous stones. The boy started following Balloon Man down the beach, even imitating his singular walk.

Balloon Man smiled, for he could not go to them. They must come to him. He had always, every day, walked the line between the sun and shadow on Magayana Beach. He would hear the vacationers talking, sometimes speaking of the worlds they had left behind, sometimes wondering if they should cancel plans to go on from here to Bimini, to stay instead, another day, another week.

The things they said! Often they would make Balloon Man laugh to himself. Like so, like here. He passed a red-headed woman in a bright gold suit, lying prone, her man at her side.

"This is paradise after Chicago," she said, her voice a lazy blur. The man only grunted, but that grunt spoke volumes of agreement.

From the corner of his eye, Balloon Man saw the little boy circumnavigate her blanket, still following him. The color of the child's hair marked him as the woman's own. Balloon Man tipped his hat to the lady. She did not lift her splendid head from the blanket.

As the distance between the boy and himself narrowed,

Balloon Man stopped, turned, and gave the boy a broad smile.

"Good morning, little Bobby!"

The child chirped "Hello," a bright sound, like the birds watching them from the palms.

"Do you like it here, Bobby?" Balloon Man bent his short frame toward the boy, knowing the answer already.

"It's great! I love the beach! Can't go to the beach in Chicago." The boy's smile was missing a tooth.

Balloon Man winked. "Are you a lad who appreciates a fine balloon?"

The boy hesitated, then answered, "Sure, mister!"

"Then perchance you will like this special one?" Balloon Man separated an irridescent pearl-colored balloon from the pack. It had extraordinary beauty, constantly shifting colors and patterns, almost a life of its own. One could be lost for eternity gazing into its intricate depths.

The boy seemed in awe of the balloon as he took it. Then he tilted his head back to Balloon Man.

"Gosh, how much do I owe you? I've got to get some money from my mom and dad."

Balloon Man chuckled. "Not to worry, Bobby lad. It is Eheluena's gift to you."

The little boy thanked him. He reached out and stroked the treasure that had come from Balloon Man's hand. "Wow," he murmured, his gaze slanting into its depths. He murmured something else, and went on down the beach, heading away from his parents on the blanket, clasping the string of the balloon, intent, happy, peaceful.

Balloon Man licked his lips, carefully rearranging the five balloon strings wrapped around his palm. "Well, my pretty friends, it is a fine start, a fine start," he told them.

Sometimes he imagined that the giant's hand was like a magnifying glass, narrowing and pinpointing the island's energy, funneling it down toward the vacationers, then sucking it up again. Sometimes they would arrive, talking of marital and money troubles, and gradually, as they lay under the lung-collapsing heat, their conversation would move tentatively toward the splendors of their surroundings.

*Ah,* one might say, *the blue sea and the pink sand.*

*Too perfect to be real,* another would reply.

*Wish we had booked an extra week, an extra month,* would say a third. *An extra month here in paradise.* Soon, there would be no talk at all, the giant's palm having ironed them blissfully flat.

Balloon Man continued his walk between the sun and shadow. He glanced back, seeing the mother lift her red head, then raise up on her elbows, calling.

She rose from the blanket, and her man followed. Their walk down the beach turned into a trot, then a run. He heard them call a name, the name tumbling toward the sky as they ran the beach, their heads swiveling this way and that.

Off in the distance his eyes followed the arc of a balloon rising toward the glorious Eheluena heavens.

The man and woman moved down the beach, still running.

As the day wore on, the sun worshipers sank deeper into the hot pink sand. More children followed Balloon Man, and were rewarded for their troubles. More silvery balloons drifted lazily over Magayana Beach. When all his goods were gone, Balloon Man retreated into the shadows.

It had been a busy day, a profitable, perfect day, and he was tired with the effort of good work. Balloon Man stretched, creasing the red fabric of his macaw shirt.

Night would step cautiously in underneath the giant's palm, and rub up against the vacationers, stirring them into retreat. They would mumble and yawn and shuffle through the pink sand back to their hotels, obliterating his footsteps. This was good. This quiet time was what Balloon Man needed. What would the vacationers do if he were to show up without any balloons at all? How could he call himself Balloon Man?

Whistling to himself, Balloon Man shambled back into the shifting green shelter of the trees.

♦ ♦ ♦

Balloon Man smiled as the red-headed woman and her man walked past, hailing him.

"Another perfect day, old man!" The young man smiled his way, wife at his side. "Forget your troubles in the tropics, eh?"

"No worries now! So much nicer than Chicago." Balloon Man chuckled agreement, tilting his hat respectfully. When they passed him, he arranged his six balloons, and stepped out into the sunlight side.

He paused to look into the hollow roundness of one balloon. In the beautiful, iridescent balloon that was no color at all and every color in the rainbow, a ghostly face froze, captive: an expression of half lidded langour, half wakening realization.

Balloon Man nodded into the depths of the balloon, beginning his walk on the beach. The giant's palm glinted in at a steep raking angle, and for a moment he glanced behind him. His face clouded to a temporary frown.

He had been so entranced with the young face in his balloon that he had forgotten The Gait. Now, clear in the glittering pink sand, was the outline of a cloven hoof.

Balloon Man backtracked and carefully scuffed over the footstep, just to be certain nothing would spoil the vacationing people's lovely time. The outline disappeared, blurring and collapsing into soft innuendo. He smiled again. No harm done.

Balloon Man continued shuffling down the pink and beautiful beach, the balloons of Eheluena at his side, whistling his song of secret tropical seduction.

# DIRTY PAIN

## by Lisa Swallow

Lisa Swallow has a degree in systems analysis, and has worked as a technical writer and a freelance nonfiction writer. She takes a strong interest in her children's education, working in the classroom teaching computers, art and writing. She set up the first Santa Cruz chapter of the Young Astronauts Program, and attended the U. S. Space Camp's special session for teachers. Right now she's working on a high-tech fantasy novel set in Silicon Valley. She resides in Santa Cruz, California, with her three children and two cats, and likes to hike, cook, and dance.

This is one of the most graphic stories in this anthology—and one of the most compelling. You won't soon forget it.

♦ ♦ ♦

Not her. He can tell by the way she glances nervously about and hugs her purse that she is no true citizen of the night. She is a social worker, perhaps, or a tourist who has lost her way. For the moment Malcolm retains enough control over his body to let her pass, unharmed.

Malcolm's arm jerks of its own accord. He is shaking now. He dares not open his mouth lest angry, nonsensical sounds leak out, scaring away his . . . his what? Soul mates? Fodder? Prey? He should have taken her, he decides too late. She might not want it, she might not deserve it, but it would have been better than nothing. Better than this.

His consciousness weakens. Tension is growing, pushing, pervading every part of him. At one time he would have taken a knife to himself to cut it out, but that was before he discovered this other solution.

Footsteps. Malcolm sinks deeper into the shadowy recesses of the alley. He sees nothing but the approaching man, backlit by the lights from the street, head cocked to one side, a bottle clenched in his left hand. The orange-red tip of a cigarette dangling between his lips bounces with every off-balance step.

Malcolm links with the other, knowing that it will only draw him further into his personal abyss. He welcomes the grating pain of the stranger's bunion, the suffocating ache of the man's every wheezing breath. He welcomes them, and cringes as they scrape the blackboard of his soul. When it becomes too much, he leaps from the shadows that have sheltered him. With the first slash of the knife he slits the man's larynx, so he cannot cry out.

The pain! Oh, the glorious, searing freedom of it. With each knife thrust, each twist, the man's pain sweeps out in waves that wash over Malcolm, draining the pressure that has built up over the days and nights for weeks on end. The pain cauterizes the death that has been growing inside him.

One wave. Two waves. Three. Malcolm stands, exhaustedly alive, and looks down at the clean red blood that pulses gently from the jagged gash in the man's chest. With a controlled jab to the heart he finishes the victim off, long before the man's shock wears off and sends that other pain, the dirty pain, throbbing after him.

♦ ♦ ♦

For his sixth birthday, Malcolm's brothers decided to initiate him into their club. On the way to their secret fort, they spat, they swore, they told dirty jokes, and they took turns peeing behind Mrs. Applewhite's rose bush.

"Can you see the fort yet?" Samuel asked, stopping them in the shade of the Ace hardware store.

The vacant lot stretched out before them, mottled with tufts of grass, shrubs, tin cans, and yellowed newspaper. He saw no sign of a fort, just a rusted old car, minus the tires, minus the windshield, minus the doors, and the blackberry patch beyond it. Malcolm shook his head.

"That's 'cuz we hid it," Franklin said. "The fort is behind the berries."

Samuel eyed him challengingly. "I still think you're a squirt. But if you find the way in, you're one of us."

"We're gonna get a Coke," Franklin said. "We'll give you ten minutes. On your mark. Get set. Go!"

Malcolm walked along the edge of the thicket, looking for some sort of tunnel. Despite the chill wind, he was getting hot. And thirsty. He grabbed a stick and poked around, pulling the branches aside to search beyond the outermost vines. When that turned up nothing he tried to whack the branches away. Then, exhausted and defeated, he threw the stick down.

How long had it been? Two minutes? Three? Five? He could feel time slipping away.

He grabbed an old cardboard box, a shield, and tried to force his way through. After a few feet the pithy branches would not budge. Worse still, they grabbed the box and caught hold of his clothes. He had to fight his way back to open ground.

He looked up at the bushes towering above him. His throat felt tight. His hands were sweaty. More than anything he wanted to join the club.

Maybe, just maybe, the passageway didn't go through the berries. Maybe it went over them. He backed away from the bushes to get a better view and, sure enough, there was one section where the bushes were not so tall, where they looked matted, broken, and brown.

Malcolm couldn't see his brothers, but he knew they were watching him, timing him, testing him. He looked over his shoulder again and again as he worked to prop one end of the board on the thicket.

The guys had to be coming. He monkey-walked up the plank as fast as he could. He was halfway there when someone grabbed his leg.

"Let me go!" he yelled. He looked down. It was only a

branch, caught on his jeans. He brushed it away, flat palm against sharp thorns . . .

Minutes later his brothers found him sitting cross-legged at the foot of the ramp and staring, amazed, at his right hand. Pearls of blood welled up from each of the many tiny wounds.

"There's two kinds of blood," he told them calmly, not looking up. "There's dirty blood and clean blood. Brownish-red blood washed away the berry juice, and now the pretty red blood is coming out. See?" He held his hand out for inspection.

"You're sick," Samuel said. He stomped up the ramp and out of sight.

"Doesn't it hurt?" Franklin asked, sitting down next to Malcolm so he could watch the clean blood better.

"Not anymore," Malcolm said.

"But it musta hurt a lot."

"I guess so." Malcolm paused. "But only for a minute. Then I felt better." He remembered how he had felt tight, hemmed in, sort of watched. How he'd *had* to get to the fort. But as soon as the thorns pricked him he had relaxed. "Just better."

They let him into the club, but sometimes he visited the berry patch for reasons other than club business. When he felt that nervousness, that almost-ready-to-explode watchfulness, he would sneak off to the berry patch and close his hand around a prickly branch, and the feeling would go away.

Once, though, at his grandmother's house, far away from the berry patch, the feeling threatened to overwhelm him. It only made things worse when Grandma demanded "snuggums," pressing his face into her perfumed sweater.

When no one was looking he dug a paring knife out of the drawer and tried to prick himself, just a little. He rested his left hand on the table and pressed the pointy end of the knife against his palm. Only the blade didn't go in, it just made a dent in his skin. He pressed harder, and it still didn't go in. He pulled the knife high into the air, closed his eyes, and rammed the blade into his hand, through it, into the table—

After the Xylocaine wore off, the wound throbbed. There wasn't just dirty blood and clean blood, Malcolm discovered. There was dirty pain and clean pain, too. Clean pain hurt sharply for an instant and in that instant cleansed the body of that awful fuzziness that had built up. Dirty pain hurt dully for a long time, as his body got back at him for the abuse he had inflicted on it.

♦ ♦ ♦

Malcolm wipes the knife on the dead man's coat and shoves it down into his boot. His hands are bloody. He rinses them with gin left in the bottle that is rolling on the ground. Then he covers the dead man and the bottle with some of the trash that crowds the alley.

He reaches the Eight Ball just as the last patrons stagger out the door. Joey, the bartender, drags one poor sot out by the armpits and leans him against the building. Malcolm squeezes in before Joey locks the door.

"Barbie still here?" Malcolm asks, not wanting to sound too eager.

"Nope. Haven't seen her since two. Sorry."

Sorry? Is Malcolm that obvious? He's only asked for her once or twice before. That's because usually she's still hanging around the bar when he gets there to clean up. Usually she asks Joey for a rum and coke to fortify her on the way home. Then she swivels around on the cracked red bar stool and says something like "Morning, Malky. We got a big mess for you over there, by the jukebox. Some jerk chucked up half a night's drinking and two bowls of pretzels. I cleaned it up best I could, but it's gonna take a pint of Lysol and some down-on-your-knees scrubbing."

Sometimes she gets more personal. "Malky, anybody ever tell you you got the biggest, brownest, puppy-dog eyes around?" When she says things like that she isn't sitting on a bar stool. She's standing next to him, real close, so he can smell her perfume and get a good look at her soft white breasts, hardly hidden at all by the low-cut, almost see-through waitressing uniform. Some bars along this street have strippers or nudie dancers or real sex acts on a platform in the middle of the room. The Eight Ball's only got a couple of pool tables; with Barbie, that's all they need.

Now and then, not very often though, Barbie follows Malcolm into the back room, where they keep the mop and pail and extra ashtrays, and where Barbie sometimes changes her clothes. She helps herself to a mint and offers him one. "God, what a night! My feet are killing me!" She steps out of her high-heeled shoes, unhooks her stockings from her garter belt, and rolls them down, one at a time, real slow. Then she flops down in the misshapen armchair and holds one foot up. "You got such nice strong hands, Malky. I bet you give one hell of a massage. Do you think you could do my feet?" So he takes her foot between his hands and he smooths his thumb along the top of it from the ankle to the toes and she leans her head back and moans. He keeps it up for as long as he can.

For the past two weeks, though, Barbie hasn't been there when Malcolm shows up to clean the bar. He tries not to think about her because he knows that the more he thinks about her the more disappointed he'll be if she isn't there and the faster the pressure will build up inside him. But he likes thinking about taking care of her, about holding her at night. He needs to pretend that if things were different he could maybe have a girlfriend like Barbie. It doesn't hurt, he thinks, to pretend.

◆ ◆ ◆

Young Malcolm knew many ways to feel bad. Sometimes his head felt fuzzy, like it wasn't really attached. Sometimes, when he thought he was being watched, his hands would get sweaty and his throat would get almost too tight to swallow. Sometimes he wanted to hide in a closet, or run away. Always, though, a trip to the berry patch made him feel better.

Once a thing gave him a bad feeling, he avoided it if he

could. He worked hard at avoiding competition and Grandma's "snuggums." And trying to do anything that was harder than it looked, like riding a bike. Being made a fool of in school, he avoided that, too. And dirty pain. Especially dirty pain.

With so many things to avoid, so many things he couldn't or wouldn't do, he had trouble making new friends and keeping old ones. He watched a lot of TV. He looked at a lot of books. He hung around the house, helping his mother with the chores because for the most part they were safe. Still, there was one source of bad feelings, of feeling penned in and watched, that he couldn't escape.

The boys shared a single room. They slept in a triple bunk bed, with Samuel on top, Franklin in the middle, and Malcolm in a trundle bed that he pulled out from under Franklin's bunk at night and pushed back in the morning.

His brothers always fell asleep instantly, leaving Malcolm to listen to each lazy, intrusive breath. *In . . . out . . . pause. In . . . out . . . pause.* Even rolling over so he had his back to them didn't help. Each warm, moist breath slid teasingly across his skin, raising the hairs. And when Franklin slept facing him he had to smell the used air, too. He wanted them to stop. Just for a minute. To let him breathe fresh air, his own air, to let him experience silence for once so he could sleep.

When he'd been younger he would call to his mother at times like these. "What'sa matter, honey? Bad dreams?"

"No. They're breathing too loud."

"Well, just close your eyes and relax. Before you know it it will be morning." Then she'd close the door quietly, leaving him in that room with all that used air.

Malcolm didn't call to his mother anymore. He suffered through each night, gritting his teeth, clenching his fists, moving his right foot around and around in a jerky circle that rustled the sheets and gave him something else to listen to. And he kept a pin—much safer than a knife—stuck in his mattress, just in case.

♦ ♦ ♦

Barbie's two suitcases stand in the middle of his room. It's daytime, and she looks different in tight jeans and a baggy sweater, with probably nothing underneath. A bruise colors her cheek and her hair sticks out in the back, but she is truly beautiful. Malcolm can't stop smiling.

"I didn't know who else to turn to," she says for the third time. She sits on his one chair, her legs squeezed together tightly, her body hunched over. "I should've seen it coming weeks ago. The signs were all there. But I kept hoping that if I ignored 'em they'd just go away. I wanted it to be different this time. I wanted it so bad."

Malcolm doesn't know what she is talking about. He has no idea what she wants him to say.

"That *bastard*!" She sits there for a few minutes, making herself small. He feels something is expected of him so he pulls the hotplate out of the drawer, fills his one pot at the bathroom sink, and puts a spoonful of instant coffee in his only clean cup. Before the water boils she unfolds to stand before him, smiling.

"I wouldn't be here if I didn't like you." She slips her arms around him. "When Joey said you'd been asking about me, it made me feel like . . . like this." She kisses him. She forces her tongue through his lips to his teeth and massages them until he loosens his jaw so she can push through and explore further.

She slides her hand down along his arm and guides his sweaty palm up under her sweater to her breast. She moans deep in the back of her throat when he touches her and pulls her lips away just far enough to mouth, "Oh, Malcolm."

Now she's kissing him lightly, teasingly, on his lips and his cheek and his neck. "You won't regret putting me up," she whispers. "I'll take care of you."

And she does.

Hours later, a sheet pulled off the single bed separates them from the cold linoleum floor. Barbie lies on top of him, her warm body, more squeezable than he'd ever imagined, flattening out against him. "I'm gonna take care of you. I'm a good cook. Did you know that? I can cook just about anything you want. And I will. And I'll wash your clothes and I'll clean the house, and I'll do anything else you want me to do. Anything." She repeats that last word as she inches down his body to give him an idea of what she had in mind.

"But we need a bigger bed," she says later. "And this part of town gives me the creeps. Doesn't that window close all the way?"

He shakes his head.

"Well, maybe we could put some bars up. It's only a small window. It can't cost that much. And can you get a deadbolt lock? The kind that needs a key from the inside, too, so that if someone manages to break a hole in the door they still can't open it. Please?"

◆ ◆ ◆

One night while young Malcolm lay listening to his brothers breathing, to that *in . . . out . . . pause,* the bad feeling grew and grew until it felt as if it was taking up more space inside his body than he was. He jabbed the pin into his thigh and the thing shrank back a bit, but still Malcolm was trapped and lost at the same time.

He climbed out of his bed and slipped under Franklin's covers, carefully, so as not to wake him. He rested his head on Franklin's chest. His own body seemed no longer his own, but there was Franklin's . . . He closed his eyes, and concentrated hard, trying to *be* Franklin. He breathed with Franklin. In . . . out . . . pause. He forced his heart to beat with Franklin's. Tha-lump . . . tha-lump . . . tha-lump.

The next day Malcolm was sitting in the big green armchair reading a Hardy Boys mystery when a pain shot through him, leaving as quickly as it had come. With it went the insulating tension that had cut him off from his own sensations. His body tingled with the absence. His fingers relaxed and the book slipped out of his hands. His legs and toes seemed to float without their burden, his eyes opened wide.

He hadn't dared to move lest he destroy the moment. Then Franklin limped in, crying, supporting his left arm with his right. The arm looked as though it had an extra joint between the elbow and the wrist. A jagged spear of bone poked through the skin on his inner arm, very red, spongy on one side, smooth on the other. Several of his friends accompanied him. One opened the door for him, another carried his battered skateboard, but they all stared at the break in fascination.

"It's just a broken bone," Franklin said on the way home from the hospital two hours later. "No big deal."

"A real good one." Despite the light-headedness caused by the badness being lifted from Malcolm, it began to dawn on him that Franklin's pain and his own release were related.

"Yeah. Everybody'll sign my cast, and I won't have to do PE, and you 'n' Sam'll have to do the dishes without me. For months!"

"Sure," Samuel said, stretching the word as long as it would go. "And it'll itch so bad you have to scream, and Mama will give you a knitting needle, only it won't reach. And before it itches it'll ache and ache and ache."

For once Samuel was right. For days after the bone had been set it throbbed, and for weeks after that it ached. Malcolm felt the pain, the dirty pain, just as clearly as Franklin did. From every room of the house; from the fort in the vacant lot; in school, from the far corner of the boys' bathroom with his cheek pressed against the cold tile, Malcolm felt Franklin's pain.

♦ ♦ ♦

Malcolm has opened himself to Barbie, and she takes it as a personal affront that he will not join her in her excursions to purchase sheets for the new bed, curtains to cover the window bars, or a throw rug for the blistered and cracked gray-black floor.

"I don't want to get up," he says. "I've only had two hours sleep."

"You can sleep in the evening, when I'm at work. I want you awake now."

"Barbie, I'm a night person. That's why I work graveyard."

"But we never see each other. Please come, please." Barbie hangs her head to stare at the floor. "I told my friends about you. I said they'd meet you at lunch."

"I don't want to meet anyone."

Barbie sits next to him on the bed. She reaches out to stroke his hand. "You have such nice hands." She runs her palm along his arms and across his back. "You're so strong." She combs her fingers through his hair and turns his head until she is staring into his eyes. "And you're so mysterious. Sometimes you scare the shit out of me. Did I ever tell you how hot I get, thinking about you, about how you're mine?"

Malcolm rolls over to be closer to her, fully awake now, concentrating on her hands, her voice, her smell. A pressure is building up inside of him, but it is one that he welcomes.

"Think how much hotter I'll get if we go out to lunch. My friends'll look you over, wishing they were the ones going home with you, and I'll know just what they're thinking. Their bodies'll show it all. So I'll watch them watching you, and you'll watch me, and you'll know how it's turning me on, 'cuz you'll see my cheeks get hot and see my nipples get hard, and then you'll get hard, too. And we'll want each other so bad we'll think we're gonna burst, only we won't do anything about it, not just then. We'll get hotter and hotter, until we can't stand it another second then we'll run home and make love until we're too tired to even breathe."

Malcolm pulls her down onto the bed. Later he dresses and follows her out the door, down the hall, and into the light of day.

◆ ◆ ◆

Having exulted in Franklin's clean pain, Malcolm had to suffocate in his dirty pain as well.

He followed him about like a two-faced cheering section. To avoid the dirty pain he talked Franklin out of the more dangerous stunts involving skateboards or dirtbikes. But sometimes, when he needed the clean pain because the bad feelings threatened to overwhelm him, he hounded Franklin, egging him on, daring him to go beyond his abilities. Hurting himself had never been easy; Franklin hurt himself all the time. And Franklin didn't feel pain; not really, not the way Malcolm did.

Then in high school Franklin decided to try out for football. Malcolm asked him not to join the team. "You'll get hurt."

"So? No pain, no gain."

"It's not good for you."

"What's it to you, anyway?"

Malcolm considered all the things he could say. "I hurt when you do," he said at last.

"Look, Malc," Franklin said patiently, "you've been hanging around me for years. You don't do anything yourself, you watch me instead. That isn't right. And thinking you hurt when I hurt, well, that isn't right either. You gotta live your own life, understand? And you gotta let me live mine."

Franklin made the junior varsity team. That season he tore a ligament, sprained his ankle, and bruised and cut just about every square inch of his body. The next year he made varsity. With the rougher playing came knee injuries, broken ribs, a fractured toe.

Malcolm laughed and sang after the games, when Franklin came home battered, taped, splinted, or doped. He withdrew from the world as Franklin healed. He huddled in his closet when Franklin set off enthusiastically to confront yet another team of torturers.

About halfway through the season, Malcolm suggested they go on a fishing trip, just the two of them. He fumbled, on the edge of control, as he gathered up the bait and hooks. On the way to the lake he walked a step or two behind, saying he didn't want to get hit by the pole, but really doing it so that Franklin would not see the jerky way he walked or the tears that he could not hold in check.

"I wasn't kidding. I feel your pain. I really do," he said later, his line in the water, his pole propped up on two sticks.

"Sure," Franklin said. But Malcolm could tell he didn't believe.

"Look," said Malcolm. "I'll turn around, or, no, I'll go way over there by that tree and you take something, anything, and hurt yourself, just a little. I'll holler when I feel it."

"Malc, this is crazy."

"You don't have to hurt yourself a lot. Just a little. Like a pinprick. I can feel all your pain."

"This is dumb."

Malcolm ran to the tree. "Do it!" he shouted. He waited for a long time. "Do it!"

A few minutes later a sharp, teasing pain reached him. "You poked yourself with a fish hook, didn't you."

"Right," Franklin shouted back. "So now I believe you. Come on back."

"How do you know that wasn't just a lucky guess? Do something else." Again he waited, his appetite whetted.

"I caught something!" Franklin shouted. His voice was weak; he had wandered far from their original spot. "It's a big one!"

Malcolm ran to get the net. He grabbed the handle and pulled, but it wouldn't come out of the tackle sack.

"Hurry!"

He scooped up the sack, untangling as he ran. He tossed out the spool of line, the jar of red salmon eggs, the little box of lures. The sack fell to the ground as he approached Franklin while freeing the net of its last obstacle, the knife.

"Come on! I'm gonna lose him!"

The sheath was stuck tight. He unsnapped the guard and slipped the knife out, then he swung the net toward his brother. Knife in left hand, net in right, he covered the distance in two strides and scooped up the dangling fish. His foot hit the rocky shore just as he felt the full weight of the fish. He slipped and the knife flew out of his hand. It landed with a delectable flash of clean, clean pain.

Malcolm stood, oblivious to the water, the fish, or his brother's cries. He responded to an urge, much like the urge to scratch an itch, then to scratch again, just a little to the left. He pulled the knife from his brother's shoulder, moved it over a fraction of an inch, and jabbed it in again. Better, but now it itched a little to the right . . .

♦ ♦ ♦

Malcolm paces the too-small room. "Give me the key!" he says, stopping in front of the bed where Barbie has barricaded herself with the brand-new pillows, blankets, and sheets. She lost her own key the day after the lock was installed and borrowed his to make a copy, but hasn't done it yet. She hoards the key, locking the deadbolt whenever she is home then hiding it in a "safe place" that changes daily.

"You said we'd go out together."

He would like to tell her about the pressure he is feeling. If he could, he would tell her how, like love, it makes him feel full almost to bursting, except that it is a cankerous fullness. Or he would tell her how, like lust, it removes his inhibitions and his fears and instills him with power, except this power is self-centered and blind.

But he is confused. He is so confused that he is here, with her, when he should be out there searching for release. So confused that earlier he hadn't been able to tell which pressure he was feeling and he tried to ease the pressure through her. She will not understand.

"Just give me the key."

"You promised," she says.

His body is fighting him now, it has gone this far. He turns away from her so she will not see his hands shaking and so his hands will not know that release is within their reach.

"At least tell me where you're going."

"I don't know."

"Who with?"

"Nobody. Barbie, please, give me the key!" He turns to face her.

"Now!" His voice doesn't sound like his own, not even to him. "I said, NOW!"

She jumps. "I heard you." But instead of getting the key, she wraps her arms around him and starts kneading the muscles in his back. "You're so tense. I just thought maybe you'd like a massage first."

Malcolm can't answer, it is taking so much out of him to keep from hurting her. Why does she have to be so close?

"What you need," she says, taking hold of his balls, "is a good—"

With the sweep of one arm he knocks her away from him, onto the bed. He has to get out before he loses control completely. The window is only two steps away. He grabs the bars and tries to rip them from their mounting.

"No one can see in," she says meekly. "If you want it rough, that's okay. I won't even scream, as long as you don't leave me."

He turns to her. She's crying.

"Everybody leaves me."

The part of him that would hold her, comfort her, cannot.

He takes a step toward her. He lets his mind reach out and touch hers, experiencing the subversive pain that is Barbie.

"I won't leave you," he says, forcing the words to form. "Not ever."

She keeps to her bargain and doesn't scream, not even at the sight of the knife.

◆ ◆ ◆

Malcolm has never considered himself a murderer. He lives where he does because he believes only two kinds of people would live there, those who deserve to die, and those who want to die.

When the time approaches, his consciousness fades. In his lucid moments he has likened that fading to the ice crystals he has seen growing on windows. They blossom from the edges inward, consuming the open space of glass until he is unable to see out.

◆ ◆ ◆

Barbie is still alive when Malcolm remembers who she is. Somehow she has fallen to the floor, where she lies, contorted, in a pool of blood.

He sinks down, heedless of the sticky warmness, and pulls her head gently, oh so gently, onto his lap. He smooths her hair back into place, then wipes away the blood, mixing it with his own new-fallen tears.

"Why wouldn't you give me the key?" he asks.

"In . . . my . . . shoe." She is wheezing loudly. With each breath a few more drops of blood wash up from her lungs and spill out over her lips. She isn't hurting. He would know if she were. Shock is guarding her from the pain.

"I didn't leave you," he says. He hopes she cares.

"Kill . . . me."

Is it a question? he wonders. A plea? He reaches for the knife, but it slips out of his hand.

Already her pulse is weakening; less blood bubbles up from the deep gash in her abdomen. The red smudges on her cheeks appear darker as the color beneath them fades. It was a statement of fact, he realizes. He could get the key and call for an ambulance from the corner phone, but they would come too late. So he sits with her head cradled in his lap.

"I'll never leave you," he says. He says it over and over, even after the wheezing has stopped.

"I love you," he tells her finally.

Carefully, he slips his legs out from under her. The key is right where she said it would be, in her shoe, her left shoe. He picks it up between two fingers, as though it were some infectious thing, and carries it to the window. He doesn't hesitate an instant before pushing it through the bars and out the crack.

He picks up the knife and washes it, and his hands, so that it will not slip from his grasp the next time he needs it. Then he returns to sit with her in his arms and to wait. The emptiness and remorse he is feeling now is a pain worse than any he has felt before. Some pains are dirtier than others. It will be enough, he knows. The knife is by his side; it won't be long.

# LAST ECHOES

## by Janet Lorimer

Janet Lorimer was born and raised in California, graduating from San Francisco State University with a bachelor's degree and a teaching credential. She taught for four years in upper elementary and intermediate grades, and, in Special Education, working with educationally handicapped children. Her first fiction sale was to *Highlights for Children*. She has sold stories to *Eldritch Tales*, *2 A.M.*, and the *Wasatch Education Systems*. Most of what she writes is geared to children and teenagers, although she enjoys writing at all levels. Four years ago she began freelancing full-time. Janet lives in Hawaii with her husband, daughter (another is away at college on the mainland), and a cat. She is currently working on a dark fantasy novel.

A deceptively simple story with its lyrical nursery rhymes, it reads almost as a rhyme itself, but it is definitely not for children.

◆ ◆ ◆

"Bridge!" Robbie shouted his new word with delight, pointing to the structure under repair. A workman, hearing the child's bright voice, grinned and waved. Robbie waved back, jumping up and down in delight.

Nina smiled. "Like London Bridge," she said. And she sang, "London Bridge is falling down, falling down, falling down . . ."

Ring of hammers, buzz of handsaws—silenced. Just for an instant. Morning filled only with the whispered song of a breeze and the flute-sweet song of birds and the sucking song of the river, lapping against the new stones of the supporting columns. Just for an instant. Sun turned to ice on Nina's bare head. Just for an instant.

And then the building sounds resumed and the day was

hot again. But the ice had penetrated to Nina's heart, and she thought, "Why am I afraid?"

Robbie tugged at her hand, wanting to run along the shore, to chase the little waves and speckled birds that pecked at bugs. They walked down to the water, sand crunching beneath their tennis shoes and Nina thought wearily, "I am always afraid."

She had done three good brave things in her life. She had written a brilliant master's thesis that would have led to a brilliant job, if she'd had the courage to take it instead of opting for marriage. She had given birth to her son, the most beautiful, wonderful child that ever lived. And five days ago she had packed Robbie and herself into the car and driven away from New York, leaving only a terse note for Dan.

*There was a little maid, and she was afraid*
*That her sweetheart would come unto her;*
*So she went to bed, and covered up her head,*
*And fastened the door with a skewer.*

The nursery rhyme leaped unbidden into her head. It was one of many she'd researched for her thesis. Looking back now, she thought that had been one of the best times in her life: researching nursery rhymes, immersing herself in their fascinating history. Linking the rhymes with her own words to form the pattern of the thesis. The brilliant, brilliant thesis that required no courage to write, that was a safe harbor in this frightening century. Why, oh why, had she thought that life after the thesis would be frightening without Dan?

Robbie grew tired of tossing twigs into the river and plopped down on the shore. His plump baby fingers squished wet sand and he gurgled with delight. Nina knelt beside him and began to build a sand castle. There was a moat and a fine bridge with towers flying leaf pennants.

Robbie watched in fascination, then smashed it with his little fist, laughing as the sand bridge collapsed into the pebble-lined moat.

*I'm the king of the castle,*
*Get down you dirty*
*rascal.*

The old rhymes came quickly to her tongue, to entertain Robbie, to comfort her when she was afraid. The old rhymes that came from the old times, the simpler times, the better times.

"You try so hard not to belong to the twentieth century," Dan had chided. "You cling to the past like it was a life preserver. It wasn't perfect, you know. You overlook the horrible events in history."

She had no answer, never had an answer. She knew she did not cope well with the pressures of the twentieth century. She knew Dan despised her for her frailties, for her fear of violence and killing, of snarling traffic, insidious smog and chemical poisons in their food. Knew also that the past was no fairy tale of good overcoming evil. Evil in any century appalled her but especially in her own, the one she had to live in and cope with.

Robbie was growing tired, cranky. Nina looked at her watch and saw it was almost time for lunch. "Come on, Robbie," she said, scrambling to her feet, brushing sand from her hands. He came and leaned against her, whining to be carried. The walk and the fresh air had worn him out. She picked him up, noticing how heavy he was getting. She was small and thin, and Robbie was big for a two-year-old. Built like Dan, big shoulders, broad back.

"Army will play him in guard position," Dan had crowed. "No doubt about it. Oh, what a killer he'll be!"

That had been a week ago and Nina had turned her thin back on her husband and son wrestling and crowing on the living room rug. Turned her back and walked to the window to stare out at the smog-brown sky and cars like ants, fighting for position in the streets below.

*When I was a little boy*
*My mammy kept me in,*
*But now I am a great boy*
*I'm fit to serve the king . . .*

Not my precious son, Nina thought, her heart laden with dread. She realized at that moment that their marriage was decaying stone, and Robbie the only mortar keeping them together. Two days later, she and Robbie were gone, following an erratic course west into the heartland of America.

The name of the town where they'd found refuge was Newhalle. Nina had liked the town from the moment she saw it. The name seemed to strike a chord, but she could not say why. Nursery rhymes popped into her head thicker and faster than ever. The very nature of the town reminded her of those happier days in ivy-clad halls and the sanctuary of the study.

It was a small town in the middle of nowhere, a town that seemed untouched by time. No TV antennas to mar the horizon, no hot black asphalt stinking in the sun, no smokestacks belching into the clean sky. Only sweet green smells of spring. The aromas of newly turned earth in the fields and loaves of newly baked bread, cooling on window sills.

*Come, butter, come,*
*Come, butter come;*
*Peter stands at the gate*
*Waiting for a butter cake,*
*Come, butter, come.*

Nina wondered if housewives in Newhalle said the rhyme as they sat at their churns. It was one of her favorites, an ancient charm thinly disguised as a child's rhyme. She knew, from her research, that this old superstition had survived over the centuries, even into the early part of the twentieth. It had crept into nursery rhyme books like so many others never intended for the nursery. Street cries, bawdy songs, political lampoons. Charms and rituals and old superstitions. Parsley, sage, rosemary and thyme. The stuff of the witch's incantations turned into pretty song.

There was a charming three-story, crowned-with-gingerbread, porch-shaded-with-lilacs hotel. A hand-sewn quilt on the bed and a hand-loomed rug on the floor. The bathtub stood on claw feet and chintz curtains hung at the windows. Nina started to write her married name in the register, thought better of it, thought to use her maiden name, thought better of it. In the end she named herself Elsie Marley.

*Elsie Marley is grown so fine,*
*She won't get up to serve her swine,*
*But lies in bed till eight or nine,*
*And surely she does take her time.*

It had amused her to use the nursery rhyme figure's name in place of her own. Elsie Marley, born and died in eighteenth-century London. Elsie Marley, lusty alewife and bawdy whore, feted for two centuries in a child's song.

Nina carried Robbie up the path. They left behind the river, sucking relentlessly at the last unfinished column. Robbie twisted in her arms to wave to the workmen. A man mortaring stones waved back.

The bridge had been ravaged by a winter storm and a hungry river. By tonight the repairs would be done. Nina sang, "Build it up with gravel and stone, gravel and stone, gravel and stone . . ."

She tried to hurry along the main street because she was growing tired, too. Hungry and tired. Her arms would not bear their burden and she had to put Robbie down, imploring him to walk a little way. He whined, rubbing his eyes, and leaned against her.

*Bye, O my baby,*
*When I was a lady,*
*O then my baby didn't cry;*
*But my baby is weeping*
*For want of good keeping,*
*O I fear my poor baby will die.*

She shivered, wondering why this particular rhyme had washed ashore in her mind. "You are tired," she scolded herself. "You were never good at standing on your own two feet, my girl. But now you must be strong and prove Dan wrong."

The scolding rhyme, purely accidental, gave her strength. She was about to pick Robbie up again when someone pushed past them. Nina looked up and saw the people.

They were walking toward the park, streams of them coming from all directions. Shopkeepers and housewives in aprons. Farmers in overalls and dusty boots. Children darting, dragon-fly bright, through the pools of adults.

Robbie, intrigued, pulled away and scampered into the street, running after the other children. "Robbie," Nina called, but he didn't stop, and she was forced to run after him.

The crowd in the park was growing. Women greeted each other, their laughter carried through the air like the tinkle of wind chimes. Men formed their own groups, male camaraderie underscored by a wide-legged stance and hands thrust deep into hip pockets. And still the children, here, there, everywhere, carefree and careless.

Robbie scampered after them, mimicking their laughter, their posturing, their games. Nina, caught on the outskirts of the crowd, could only watch with amused exasperation as her son tagged after the others, his short little legs pumping to keep up with the older ones.

Abruptly, the crowd grew silent. As if obeying a silent command, the adults moved away from the center of the grassy area and formed a broad ring. The children, oddly sedate, moved to the center. Two of the oldest faced each other and clasped hands. They raised their arms, forming a human bridge, while the others formed a ragged line. To Nina's ears came a familiar snatch of song.

*Broken bridges falling down . . .*

"Those aren't the right words," she thought, bewildered by the crowd's behavior and the absurdity of the game.

*falling down . . .*

She tried to push through the crowd to retrieve her son, but the ring had become a wall, an impenetrable wall of implacable backs.

*falling down . . .*

She side-stepped to another spot and tried to break through, but arms were linked and legs spread to form a strong base. She could not get through, could only watch the game in helpless frustration.

*Broken bridges . . .*

Suddenly the human bridge started to fall, to encircle the "prisoner." It was a little girl with tight braids and a floral-sprigged dress, her socks falling down around her ankles. Nina heard the adults suck in a collective breath. The air was electric with their fearful energy.

*falling down . . .*

The bridge froze in mid-air. The singing stopped. For a split second everyone stared at Robbie. Small, sweet Robbie who stood behind the pigtailed girl, his face wide-eyed innocence. The girl skipped nimbly out from under the half-lowered arms and Robbie stepped obediently into her place. The bridge crashed down, holding him fast.

Nina gasped, startled by what she did not understand. Suddenly the air was alive with a rush of laughter and conversation. As abruptly as the game had begun, it was over. People moved away in the directions from which they'd come, the flow of their conversation ebbing.

". . . a pinch of cinnamon . . ."

". . . an early frost . . ."

The children scattered, reworking their numbers into games of tag and leapfrog. Nina and Robbie stood alone.

"Robbie?" Nina called in a trembling voice. She held out her hand and he came, his face split by a wide grin. He threw himself against her, hugging her, his face buried against her leg. She scooped him up in her arms, holding him tight, and his small arms went lovingly around her neck.

She walked slowly to the hotel, holding Robbie in her arms, like a charm against evil. Why had the people of Newhalle gathered in the park on this fine day? Broken bridges falling down. Why had they left their plows and churns to watch a children's game? Come, butter, come. A sense of impending evil sent the ice deeper into her heart. Parsley, sage, rosemary and thyme.

They had lunch in the dining room of the hotel. A lovely lunch with far too much food for the two of them. It was heavy with fresh churned butter and brown bread, and for dessert a strudel with sweet cream.

The meal was topped off with a pot of hot dark tea, not the tea bag kind that tasted of string and paper. Nina drank a cup of it, then noticed that Robbie was falling asleep in his high chair. It was all the heavy food, she thought, trying to keep her eyes open.

She lifted her son from his high chair and carried him up to their room. She wondered where she and Robbie should go next. They could not stay here forever. There was no place for them in Newhalle. Nina, for all her brilliant thesis, could not stitch a straight seam nor churn a crock of butter.

*Curly locks, Curly locks,*
*Wilt thou be mine?*
*Thou shalt not wash dishes*
*Nor yet feed the*
*swine . . .*

Nina lay Robbie on the wide bed with the hand-sewn quilt. That was why she'd married Dan, so that she might be kept safe, might never be afraid. Marriage had proved a false haven. Broken bridges falling down. She kicked off her shoes and lay down by the sleeping child, and obstinately whispered, "Parsley, sage, rosemary and thyme."

Next to her, the child whimpered in his sleep. She glanced at him, and his beauty all but took her breath away. The fresh air had put apples in his cheeks and the clean sun, butter yellow, had browned the backs of his hands and freckled his nose.

"I can't take him back to the city," Nina thought. "I can't take him back to smog and preservatives and traffic-ridden streets. And Dan's desires to turn him into a linebacker or a soldier."

Suddenly she was afraid to sleep. Afraid to leave her baby unguarded. But sleep would not be denied. Her eyes were heavy, heavy, as if she had been drugged.

*Bye, baby bumpkin,*
*Where's Tony Lumpkin?*
*My lady's on her death-bed,*
*With eating half a*
*pumpkin.*

The rhyme crept into her head as unwanted sleep claimed her. Rocked her gently like the river, lapping at the base of the bridge, singing a lullaby to the stone columns. Broken bridges falling down . . . But those were the wrong words.

She awoke, bewildered by a pounding headache and a

dry, sour-tasting mouth. And the darkness of the room. She reached out to touch Robbie and found . . . nothing. The shaft of ice in her heart splintered.

"Robbie?" Her shrill cry pierced the silence. "Robbie?" She scrambled from the bed, staggered, colliding with furniture on her way to the door.

The hall was dark. The stairs were dark. The dining room, the foyer, the front porch . . . all dark. Out to the street, strength found in the chill wind that hit her face, that whined up and down deserted streets, past empty buildings, their darkened windows blind eyes.

*Boys and girls come out to play,*
*The moon doth shine as bright as day.*
*Leave your supper and leave your sleep,*
*And join your playfellows in the street . . .*

She tore up and down the streets, panic driving her. Near the park she was forced to stop for a moment, to catch her breath. And heard ragged sounds of laughter and song borne on the wind. They came from the direction of the river.

At the top of the path she saw the huge bonfire that had been built on the shore near the newly repaired bridge. The fire threw hot sparks into the dark sky. A handful of figures moved back and forth in front of the flames, black silhouettes wavering in the heat haze. But it was from the top of the bridge that the song came, a sound that sent the splinters of ice coursing through her veins.

"Broken bridges falling down . . ."

The children's sweet voices billowed and eddied. Below, the river sucked at the stone columns. And suddenly she knew why the words were not wrong words, but older words, as old as time.

She ran, stumbling, sliding, down the steep path and across the shore. The river licked hungrily at her ankles, as she moved from one newly mortared column to the next.

"Build it up with gravel and stone . . ."

She found what she dreaded at the third column. The firelight caught the object in bas relief and it seemed to move as light and shadow danced over it. A savage howl of pain and rage gushed from her throat.

"Then we'll set a man to watch . . ."

Words from her brilliant, safe-haven thesis flashed into her mind. *In 1843 in the town of Halle, Germany, a new bridge was to be built. And there was a notion . . .*

. . . staring in shock at the small hand, browned by the butter-yellow sun . . .

. . . *among the people that the bridge would not stand by ordinary means. Even stone would be washed away. So a guardian was required . . .*

. . . the fragile little nails, torn and broken . . .

. . . *and a child was wanted . . .*

. . . as if it had tried desperately to dig its way to freedom.

. . . *to be built into the foundation.*

Not a children's game at all, but the last evil echoes of a long-forgotten ritual, a dark rite to appease the hungry spirit of the river . . .

. . . my fair lady.

# DADDY'S COMING HOME

## by Lynn S. Hightower

Lynn S. Hightower was born in Chattanooga, Tennessee, in 1956 and raised in Tennessee, Georgia, Virginia, and Kentucky. She earned a B.A. in journalism from the University of Kentucky in 1977 and has worked as a commercial copywriter. In the 1986 Writers of the Future Contest she earned an honorable mention, and made the quarter finals in the second and third quarter of the 1987 contest. She works full-time writing fiction. Her first novel, *The Stars As Witness,* was sold to Pageant Books in 1988; This is her first short story sale. She has also since sold to *Final Shadows.* Occasional contributions to her work are made by a cat who has a penchant for the delete key. She admits that she loves Fred Astaire movies, makes chile so good it has passed the Texas in-law test, and really wishes she had a horse.

Lynn's story is an unhurried tale of Southern horror complete with nightsounds and the miasma of a swamp and warm summer eve's languor—just the way I like 'em.

◆ ◆ ◆

It was the letter that brought him finally and reluctantly home. Cort drove slowly down the main drag, passing the Stop-N-Go where he'd gone every afternoon after school for an RC Cola and a Moonpie. He flexed his shoulders and the letter crackled in his shirt pocket.

*Mama's having some kind of trouble,* Rhonda had written. *She keeps saying Daddy's coming home. And she won't go near the river.*

Daddy's coming home. The words stirred the hairs on the back of his neck, and made his skin go cold.

The house was about forty minutes out of town, down a dirt road that was not much more than ruts with weeds in the middle. Trees and tall grasses grew in a tangled mass and crowded the car, scraping against the doors. It was hot out and humid, but Cort rolled down the windows and breathed in the musty, low country smell. He couldn't see the river, but it was there. Gray-green Spanish moss clumped and hung in the trees. It was isolated out where he grew up—land not good for much. Only the down-and-outers lived here, people with nothing to cling to but worthless land or black, ominous religions.

He wondered what Leaha would think. The car bucked and he grimaced. Leaha was six months pregnant and grumpier every day. She wouldn't like these bumps. He was afraid for the baby sometimes, when it was late and he was tired and upset. The further Leaha stayed away from his past, the better—for her and the baby.

A rusted-out '56 Buick (green once, with creamy white upholstery) was barely visible to the right. That was the first landmark. He still had the scar on his elbow from when he'd crashed his bike there. The girls were both tiny then, and they'd all been out together, poking around at the dump. Cort had been showing off on his bike and had turned too sharply. He'd started crying as soon as he saw blood running down his leg. Mama had her arms full with Jenny, and Rhonda was tired and whiny. Daddy had picked Rhonda up in one arm, and Cort in the other. No one had ever seemed as strong as Daddy had that day.

Cort drove another half mile, noting the dump on his left. An orange couch sagged at the top, stuffing visible down the side of one of the cushions. A camper top lay in the weeds next to a clump of mailboxes. He and Leaha had a wood one, sanded and stained, with numbers down the side that he'd carved himself.

Cort pulled onto the lawn of weed and dirt scrub and shut off the engine. The house, or shack, stood on pilings, old mud stains streaking all the way to the front window. Pilings or no, sometimes the water got up to the windows when the river overflowed. Years of junk spilled out from under the house. A cardboard box of trash was on its side, spewing a mess of paper plates, potato peels, Coke cans and ice cream wrappers.

The front porch was screened in—it buckled and sagged just like he remembered. Leaha should never see this place. Cort got out of the car and glanced at his watch. It was after six, still sunny, the heat just beginning to ease. He heard the porch door creak and smack.

And there came Mama.

She hurried down the steps, a peculiar rolling gait accommodating the weight she carried on short, thick legs. Cort took a deep, painful breath, his chest tight and hurting.

"Cort, honey."

She was crying. Her hair, lifeless, brown and dingy, was teased and sprayed, the bangs and sides wet with sweat. She wore blue plaid pedal pushers, the polyester snagged and fraying. Her shirt was dingy white and sleeveless—what they called a shell when he was a boy. Her arms were enormous, pale and dimpled. It was automatic to look for bruises, but there weren't any.

Cort swallowed hard and wiped his eyes with the back of his hand.

"Mama."

She hesitated and he gave her a long, hard hug. She smelled good, like pie and fresh-cut Vidalia onions. He wondered what was for supper.

"You've grown so much, so filled out. Better lookin' than the pictures you sent. Honey, where's Leaha?"

"I told you, Mama, she couldn't come."

"I was just hoping."

"Her doctor said she better not."

Mama's eyes glazed, and she stared over his shoulder like she always did when he lied to her.

"Well"—she led him toward the house—"I knew *you'd* come. I bet one of your sisters wrote and told you."

He clumped up the concrete stairs. "Told me what, Mama?"

She opened the screen door and he followed her across the porch.

"About your daddy, Cort. He's coming home."

Cort studied her face, apprehensive, bewildered. Cousin Pickney and a woman Cort didn't know came through the living room to say hello. He'd talk to Mama later.

A timer dinged from deep in the kitchen.

"The rolls." Mama hurried into the kitchen, glancing over her shoulder. "Ralph called, from down to the Stop-N-Go. Said he saw you was headed home, so I knew to go on and put the rolls in."

"How did he know it was me?"

Mama laughed—a wicked laugh, fat and juicy. Cort remembered it well.

They sat down at the kitchen table. Places were laid with the same faded green Corelle dishes, set on foam-backed plastic place mats. The kitchen was hot, and Cort wiped sweat from his upper lip with his napkin.

Later they sat out on the porch. Mr. and Mrs. Cousin Pickney had eaten two pieces of pie and gone home. Cort could hear bullfrogs in the river. He breathed the rotting, sulfurous smell of decaying vegetation—low country smell. He slapped a mosquito and bent over, squinting at the door. There was a new patch over a jagged tear in the screen.

"Mama, we got to talk."

"You like that beer?"

"Beer's fine."

"Ralph sent that down. Along with a whole box of Moonpies."

Cort smiled briefly. "Mama?"

"Yes, Cort."

"Why did you say Daddy's coming home? You know that can't be."

"Cort, just because he left don't mean he won't come back."

"You know better."

"Cort, I'm going to bed."

All these years and she still wouldn't talk. And he was the same with Leaha.

"You aren't going to bed, Mama. Not till you tell me why you think Daddy's coming home."

She stopped rocking for a minute. Then the chair creaked, swaying back and forth.

"Cort, I was down to the river last month, looking for old Bill here." She nudged the dog with her bare toe and the animal groaned and shifted. "I don't go down there at night, but I heard Bill yelp."

Cort couldn't see her face—it was dark and there wasn't much moon.

"I saw him, honey. Down a ways, in the trees." Her voice was matter of fact.

"That isn't possible. You know that, don't you?"

"Men who leave their families do come back sometimes. Just like sons who leave home and join the army. They come back for their mama's pie."

Cort was silent.

"That wasn't the only time I saw him," she said.

"How could you see if it was night?"

"It was morning the second time. Mist coming off the river . . ."

Cort's spine tingled like it had on patrols near Pleiku. *"Hush."*

"What, Cort?"

He listened hard and wished the damn dog didn't snore. Footsteps, somewhere. Cort stood up slowly, eyes searching, looking for a glimmer, the telltale shift of darkness. Nothing.

"Be right back, Mama."

"Cort, where you going?"

"Be back."

The screen door groaned softly behind him. Tomorrow he'd soap the hinge.

Nothing on the side of the house. He heard a bullfrog raising hell again in the lagoon. Light spilled from the kitchen window into the backyard. Cort saw the woodpile and his knees felt weak. His footsteps were soft as he walked toward it, blood pounding the pulses in his ears.

The ax was still there, blade biting deep into the wood of the chopping block. Raw chips and splinters littered the block and the ground underneath. Someone had chopped wood in the last couple of days. Cort made himself touch the ax's smooth, worn handle. He stood quietly for a long time, taking slow, even breaths.

His eyes narrowed when he heard the soft rustle of weeds brushing against a pants leg. Someone was headed for the porch.

Mama was standing when he got there, biting her fist, making no sound. The man stood in front of the door, his back to Cort. Cort grabbed the man's shoulder and turned him around.

"Hello there." The voice was deep and rough.

"Good God." It was dark, hard to be sure.

"I'm Ron Logan."

*Ron* Logan.

The man smiled, his voice hesitant. "Does Lenore Logan still live here?"

Cort heard his mama catch her breath.

"I'm Cort Logan."

"I thought you might be." The man offered a hand and gave Cort a warm, limp handshake. He looked around uncertainly, confusion in his voice. "I'm your uncle, you know. Your daddy's big brother. Haven't seen you folks since Cort here was a baby. Excuse me for dropping in so late, but once I was here I didn't want to wait another day. Silly of me, isn't it, after all these years?"

Cort took a breath.

"Have you had supper?" Mama said.

"No, ma'am, I didn't get the chance."

"Come on in, let me warm something up."

"I was hoping you'd say that. Will always bragged on your cooking."

Cort followed them into the house, legs rubbery, walking slow. He grazed his hip on the bookshelf. Ron Logan?

Brothers did look alike. But Cort knew those eyes. His daddy's eyes.

There wasn't enough light in the kitchen. Cort stared while Mama warmed ham, beans and rolls. Nobody said much while she poured iced tea, and added a half spoon of sugar and a slice of fresh lemon, just like she used to for his daddy. Ron Logan smiled and took a large swallow.

It could be him. Easily. The man looked older than Cort remembered, changed, but the likeness was close enough. He wore old corduroy work pants, a short-sleeved plaid shirt, and heavy work shoes. There was a down-and-out look about him, careworn. His color was bad, lips bluish. There were lines of fatigue in his face, circles under his eyes.

Mama stood behind Cort, hands icy on his shoulders. He felt sweat trickle down his back.

"Cort here's married now. He and his wife are expecting a baby in October."

Ron Logan smiled at Cort. "Scary, isn't it?"

Cort nodded.

"A grandchild," Mama said.

The man stopped eating and smiled faintly at them both. "Babies." He took a large bite of ham.

Cort watched in awful fascination as the man chewed and swallowed.

"Cort, you hungry?"

"No. Ate already, I'm full."

"Oh." The man smiled and nodded. He quit eating and stared into the corner, eyes unfocused and confused.

"More pie?" Mama asked finally.

Ron Logan patted his stomach, just the way Daddy used to. "Thanks, I've had all I need." He pushed his chair back. "Don't want to impose on you all, and it's late, so I'll be heading out."

"Where are you staying?" Cort asked.

"Oh, I'm camping out. Doing a little fishing." He nodded at Mama and Cort. "Sorry I missed the girls."

Cort followed him out and walked with him down the stairs.

"Can I lend you a flashlight?"

"No thanks. Good night, son."

It was commonplace in this part of the country for an older man to call a younger one son. Cort watched helplessly as the man walked away in the dark. Then he sat on the porch, rocking and thinking, listening to Mama clean up in the kitchen. The light went out. The front door opened and she stuck her head out.

"Night, Cort."

"Mama . . ."

"Not now, honey. Don't stay up too late." The door smacked shut.

He didn't want to sleep. He wanted to stay out front, watching, listening. He wound down after a while, and slipped into a light sleep, the images in his head half dream, half memory.

He was walking down the dirt road, heading home. Fourteen years old, legs long and thin—he threw the baseball up and caught it in his glove as he walked. The glove was worn, the leather soft and flexible. It had been his dad's, and it was the envy of his teammates. They rolled tires on their gloves, slept on them, one kid pounded his with a sledgehammer, but nobody else's had the perfect, pliant feel his glove did—broken in with age, care and countless ball games.

Somewhere, in an objective, knowledgeable part of Cort's mind, he could feel darkness hovering, waiting to pounce on the fourteen-year-old boy. His chest tightened with pity. Something awful was coming. He'd had this dream before.

The boy was tired. He felt the ache of sore muscles in the back of his legs, the bruise on his shin where he'd gotten hit with a ball during practice. Another half mile or so. Coach would have taken him the whole way home, but Cort never liked people to see his house. He thought about supper, trying to push the uneasy feelings away, wondering what Mama had been cooking, wondering if she was all right.

Together the two of them could usually handle Daddy, keep him even-tempered and smooth the way. Daddy took things out on Mama, pounding her arms and sometimes her soft belly. Just thinking about it gave Cort that peculiar, queasy feeling, and he walked faster. This was his first year on the team—the new coach didn't hold a guy's family against him. The practices kept him away a lot.

Cort felt guilty. He needed to be home—to watch the girls, give them piggyback rides, take them outside. He got frantic sometimes, trying to keep them from crying and whining when Dad was in one of his moods. He was scared that Daddy might hit one of the girls—pesky, fragile little girls.

It was almost dark when he got to the house. The smell of decay was coming up from the lagoon, and the bullfrogs had started in. Something splashed and he wondered if it was a gator. Was that one of the girls crying? They ought to be in bed. Cort stopped to listen.

Not the girls. Mama. Crying hard.

He stood very still, left hand drooping with the weight of the baseball glove. The front of the house was dark. Cort walked around back, stiff-legged. The light was on in the kitchen, and mosquitos were thick in the shaft of brightness. Cort looked in the window, and the heat of the evening drained away, leaving him shivery inside.

Blood on the counter, blood on the sink, Mama bent double and crying, cleaning something off the floor. His dad was stumbling out of the kitchen. Leaving? After what he'd done?

Cort's mouth was dry, his tongue thick and heavy. There was a towel tied around his mama's thigh. Daddy must have taken a knife to her this time. The man was dangerous.

Cort didn't think things through or make a plan; his actions were stiff, automatic. The ax blade was sunk in the stump. He wrestled it out and walked around the side of the house. Daddy had come down the steps, and Cort crept up behind him. He raised his arm mightily and heaved the ax into the thick of his father's back. The blade bit deeply into flesh, and blood splattered his shirt. Cort shuddered. His father screamed and turned, his face a study of shock and betrayal.

Why?

The word formed on his father's lips, but the sound never came out.

Cort ran for the woods, into the dank, foggy, low country night. He was stumbling and crying—innocence ended, the nightmare begun.

He woke with a jerk, shuddering, eyes dark and wild. There was no Leaha here to hold him, to rub his neck, and soothe him back to sleep. Cort scratched his arm. He was being eaten alive tonight. He sat quietly, waiting for his breath to steady and slow.

Who was the man who had eaten dinner in the kitchen?

Cort sat in the rocker, creaking back and forth, eyes blank and smudgy with fatigue. The sun came up—too hot, too bright and bringing no answers at all.

That night Cort and his mama had dinner early, neither of them very hungry. They sat on the porch watching the sun flare into orange over the tree line, wondering if they would have a visitor. Cort catalogued repair jobs in a dull, guilty part of his mind, but he was unable to leave his chair. Mama was missing programs on the TV. Dark fell slowly, the light evaporating, taking the edge off the heat. The sky was overcast, the cloud cover bottling the muggy warm air and keeping the temperature in the low eighties. Hot breezes pressed against their lungs and kept sweat popping on the back of their necks.

Cort squashed a mosquito between his fingers, thinking of the dry, musty coolness of the unit air conditioner in the living room. He heard a groan and sat up. The dog sighed and rolled over.

"What you and Leaha going to name the baby?"

"Don't know. We got plenty of time."

"Men always say that."

A soft footstep rustled the dry blades of grass. Cort looked at Mama. He couldn't see her face in the dark, but he felt her fear.

"He's here," Cort said.

"Your daddy's come home."

Cort heard the breathy whisper and felt his balls draw up into small, tense lumps between his legs.

"Daddy's dead," Cort said.

A dark figure came toward the porch, and Cort got up slowly, opening the screen door. The man climbed the stairs, a sheepish smile on his face.

"Evening, folks. I came to see if you had any more of that peach pie left."

Mama stood up and backed to the front door. "Two pieces," she said.

Cort ached with tension. He held the porch door open, waiting for the man to walk through. One more step. Cort circled carefully behind him. He hesitated, then snatched the collar of the man's shirt, yanking it down. The material was soft and worn. The shirt ripped across the shoulder and down the back.

The scar was there, pink and jelly-like, right where Cort had landed the ax. Cort moaned and heard Mama call his name. The man turned and hurried down the steps, pushing his way back through the weeds into the muggy darkness.

*"Dad."* Cort felt sweat run down his face, and he took the stairs in a bone-jarring leap.

He'd gotten his long legs from his daddy. The man moved quickly, and Cort had a hard time, stumbling over bumps and ruts, listening to the tearing of weeds that trumpeted the man's progress.

"Daddy! Wait." He fell, smacking his chin against the ground. His tongue split, and he tasted blood. The palms of his hands stung where he'd tried to break the fall.

He got up, breathing hard. Something was moving in the

woods ahead. Cort followed the noise, straining his eyes in the dark. He ran blindly through the underbrush, tripping and slamming against trees. He stopped, sobbing for breath.

"I got to talk to you, Dad. I got to tell you." There was no answer, no noise now. He'd lost him. He put his face in his hands and cried, shoulders shaking. The saltiness of tears and sweat stung the scratches on his face.

"I got to tell you. I got to tell you." The words were a moan from the smoky depths of guilt. He stood up, cupping his hands to shout. "I love you. I love you, and I'm sorry."

A small light bobbed through the woods. He heard Mama calling. He wiped his face with the back of his hand and shuddered, unable to control the trembling muscles.

"Cort." Mama was panting. She stood and stared at him, flashlight pointed at the ground.

"He's gone," Cort said.

"I know."

"Maybe tomorrow . . ."

"Surely not."

"How do you know? Then he is . . . I thought he . . ."

"Cort. I don't tell you what's going on, because I don't know. But I tell you what I do know. He really did die that night."

"You sure?" Cort gripped her shoulders, too hard, he knew it.

She nodded, teeth chattering. "He bled . . . so much. Bled to death on the porch steps."

Cort let her go and took a step back. "I'm sorry, Mama. I'm sorry."

"Cort, honey, you got nothing to be sorry for. I hid the body in the river. Made slits"—she swallowed"—down his chest and belly, like my daddy used to when he threw dead cows in the river."

Cort shivered. "So the gasses escape."

She nodded. "The body stays down that way. And I got rid of his things, one by one."

"So people'd believe you when you said he'd left."

She shrugged. "He didn't have any insurance, but he still had his army disability. It's what we lived on. Not that it mattered. Nobody looked for him. Nobody missed him."

"But us."

"Yeah. But us. But we were better off without him, Cort, and you know that."

Cort nodded, up and down, up and down. "But, oh, Mama . . . I'm still sorry. I look in the mirror, and I'm not the person I wanted to be. I did a bad thing, my own daddy, and it weighs on me."

"Cort."

He looked up, startled by her tone.

"Look at me, 'cause I got something to tell you." She stared over his shoulder, eyes glazing. "You didn't kill your daddy. You hurt him, but he'd have lived. He was alive when I got there. He was dead when I got through."

Cort's eyes were huge.

"I'm sorry, Cort. It's true."

Cort didn't move.

"I'm sorry, son."

He put his arms around her. "It's okay, Mama. I understand."

He understood very well.

♦ ♦ ♦

Cort slept hard, but he was up when the sun rose. Mama was still asleep. That suited him fine. He was cold this morning, on the inside, where it counted. He blushed, remembering how he'd blundered through the woods last night. There would be no tears this morning. He'd track with his head and not his heart.

The trail wasn't too difficult—his, Daddy's, Mama's. He'd learned to follow Khmer Rouge guerrillas in Cambodia, but he'd never tracked a ghost.

The humidity was thick and his tee shirt stuck to his back. He pushed through spider webs spun during the night and dropped for morning prey. The tracks led down to the river and stopped.

Cort felt a chill brush his spine before he started checking the bases of tree trunks. One was scuffed and rubbed—someone had tied a boat line there. He sighed deeply. The river was deep in the middle, congested with leaves and logs. Probably a gator or two, somewhere.

Cort took off his tennis shoes, tied the laces together, and slung them around his neck. The water was greenish brown and scummy, but it was cool and the shock of it made him shudder. He waded almost halfway across before he had to swim. He kept an eye out, watching the ripples spread and circle to the river bank.

He was breathless when he got across, out of shape. He came up on the other side, sinking almost knee deep in the muddy river bank. His jeans clung to his legs like sealskin, and mud caked his feet and pants legs. He felt a drop of coolness on his neck and his stomach dropped. He reached back, found the leech, and pulled it off. Blood ran down his neck and stained his shirt. He checked his belly and back, but there were no other passengers.

The boat was about fifty yards down the bank—an old rowboat with sky blue paint chipping off. Cort set his jaw, and picked up the trail. A tall man, his daddy.

Cort paused in front of an old sycamore, the grasses beneath matted and scuffed. The bark was freshly shredded, right about eye level. His father had stopped here, to rest, perhaps.

The trail meandered deep into the back country, and Cort kept a careful eye out. He smelled smoke—these people still used cook fires and he wasn't sure he wanted to run into any of them. His daddy's folks had come from over this way. They were a poor and desperate lot—most of them had moved on to better things. His grandmama had told him the people over here followed the dark ways. But that was years ago.

Still, he remembered asking Daddy if he was a Southern Baptist like Mama.

"Not exactly," He'd laughed. "I don't go in much for religion. I avoid the Baptists the same as I avoided my neighbors' little gatherings when I was a kid."

"And what were they?" Cort had asked.

"Wouldn't you like to know."

The tracks led to an old toolshed and Cort peered in through the window. The glass was encrusted with grime, but Cort could see his daddy, sleeping on a stained mattress on the floor. He was on his stomach; bare skin showed through the rip in his shirt. Cort stared. Daddy's eyes were open. A fly crawled across his father's cheek, but he made no move to swat it off.

♦ ♦ ♦

Mama was frying leftover ham when Cort walked into the kitchen. She was cracking eggs, two at a time, in the same pan with the ham. Cort rubbed a dirt-stained hand over his rough, unshaven cheeks.

"'Bout time you got up," Mama said, without turning around.

"I've been up for hours."

She glanced over her shoulder, eyes widening. "You go fishing?"

"I went hunting."

"Get anything?"

Cort straddled a kitchen chair, hunching over the top, chin in hand. "Mama, a ghost doesn't eat ham, rolls and pie. I found Daddy on the other side of the river, so why don't you just tell me what in hell's been going on?"

An egg hit the floor, splattering yolk and shell on Mama's foot. She stepped over it and sat down heavily.

"Hand me that dish towel."

Cort took the cloth off the table and passed it to her. She wiped her hands absently, staring at the mess of egg on the floor. Her eyes were narrow, concentrated, seeing things a long way away.

"Your daddy wasn't dead that night . . . when I found him, and he wasn't going to die unless I took the ax to him myself. I thought about it, I sure did, but I couldn't. I couldn't let things go on, neither. It was affecting you kids in a bad way." Tears welled in her eyes. "You keep that in mind, Cort. I was thinking of you and the girls. So, I told him I was taking him to a doctor. He was hurting a lot and went along with whatever I said. But I took him across the river. I took him to old Hattie."

"Hattie? That toothless old granny with the charms and the voodoo and . . ."

"Yeah. Her. You don't understand, Cort. That lady had powers. And I wound up paying her every last cent we had and owing some still. But she did . . . what I asked her."

"What?"

"Took your daddy off my hands."

"How?"

"A taste . . . a taste of the cucumber. That's how she put it."

"I don't understand."

"It's a drug." Mama hung her head like it was too heavy to hold up. She rested an elbow on the back of her chair, and propped her head on one hand. "A poison. You rub it on the skin and the person gets quiet, docile, no willpower. Stupid, you know, like a . . . zombie."

Cort's jaw fell open.

"Oh, it's not real. I mean, far as I know, there's no real zombies in the sense you're thinking. Not dead people dug back up and brought to life." She pushed a heavy hank of hair out of her eyes. The whites were bloodshot, yellowed. "But don't kid yourself, Cort. Certain things happen and you know it."

He snorted. "So where's he been all this time?"

"With her. With Hattie. Working in her garden and such."

"Slave labor."

Mama bowed her head and nodded.

Cort chewed a lip. "Mama, you remember all those times Daddy, he played ball with me? And slept with Rhonda on his stomach when she had baby asthma and you were down with the flu?"

"I remember, Cort. I remember the good things. And I remember the bad ones."

"So now what? Why come back after all these years? Why say he's Ron Logan?"

"Hattie died a few months ago. I checked and her son was, well, seeing your daddy was looked after. But nobody but Hattie does the drug—her son didn't want nothing to do with that kind of stuff. Hell, he's an old man himself.

"And after a while, it wore off. But after being on it all this time, it affected your daddy's mind. He comes and goes, that's what Hattie's son says. Mostly he just sits a lot, and stares." She took a deep breath. "But he's drawn back home, now. And he's confused, and I guess he thinks he *is* Ron Logan. I don't know."

"You scared of him?"

"Course not." Her hand shook when she said it.

"He chopped the wood, didn't he? And fixed the screen?"

She nodded. "Listen," her voice quavered. "Do you have to leave right away, or can you stay a while?"

"Mama." He heard the thickness in his voice and swallowed back the tears. "Mama, you don't have to be scared no more. He's not going to come back."

Her face went white. "What did you do?"

"Nothing, Mama. Looks like he died in his sleep. Maybe his heart went out—all those years on the drug. I found him, and I buried him. I guess . . . I guess it's for the best. Isn't it? Mama?"

She hid her face in the dish towel and nodded, choking back sobs. He couldn't tell if she was heartbroken or relieved. She probably couldn't tell either.

♦ ♦ ♦

Cort slammed the car door. His stomach was full of the solid satisfaction of an enormous breakfast. By dinner time he'd be home with Leaha. He wanted nothing more than to bury his face in the soft fragrance of her hair.

Mama came down the steps carrying something wrapped in newspaper.

"No, Mama, nothing else. The trunk's full."

She smiled. "Better take a look before you make up your mind."

He unwrapped the paper. The ball glove was soft, like he remembered. He put his hand inside and held it up, inhaling the scent of worn leather and old sweat.

"Where did you find it?"

"In the garage the next . . . the day after. That old ball glove. I couldn't stand to see it thrown away. So I saved it. I thought you might change your mind and want it back."

They both stared at the ground, waiting for the subject to slide away.

"Well." He cleared his throat. "Thank you, Mama. Goodbye."

"'Bye, Cortney." She hugged him, and he heard her whisper that she loved him. "Come see me. Bring my grandchild."

Cort's gaze swept the house and the sagging porch. He'd repaired the holes in the screen, but there was a lifetime of work left before the place would be presentable.

"I will, Mama."

She studied his face. "Cort, you . . . your daddy really was dead, when you found him? Nothing happened?"

Cort smiled sadly. "Nothing happened, Mama."

Her eyes glazed and she stared over his shoulder like she always did when he lied to her. But Mama was safe now. He got in the car and started the engine. She raised a hand and smiled broadly, and a tear slid down her cheek.

She waved until he was out of sight.

The glove bounced beside him on the car seat. Once or twice he reached out and touched it, wondering if his child would have his long legs and eye for the ball. There'd be no shadow in this child's face when his daddy came home. Weeds smacked against the doors as the car bumped down the winding dirt road.

# A TOUCH OF THE OLD LILITH

## by Nina Kiriki Hoffman

Nina Kiriki Hoffman spent her formative years in California, seven informative years in Idaho, and now lives in Eugene, Oregon, near several other assorted "pulp punks." She shares quarters with two cats, one mannequin, and uncounted spectres of the imagination. Her short fiction has appeared in *Amazing Stories, Weird Tales, Alfred Hitchcock's Magazines, Isaac Asimov's Science Fiction Magazine,* and *Pulphouse.* A number of her stories have also appeared in anthologies: *Writers of the Future Vol. 1, Shadows 8, Shadows 9, Greystone Bay, Doom City, Borderlands,* and *Tales By Moonlight.*

We inherit much from our families, but sometimes it might be just too much.

♦ ♦ ♦

Grandma said there was a touch of the old Lilith in all the Meander women, and she flexed her finger, beckoning, to prove it, saying that under the right circumstances the bones of one's finger became the spine of a snake. "Lilith was the first tempter, who took men one step away from God. She offered them the poison of death. Lilith was a Meander, and you's a Meander woman, little Clea. Don't you forget it."

I didn't understand the connection between Lilith and snakes until later, but I didn't forget anything Grandma told me the summer I turned eleven.

That summer comes back to me whenever I smell aromatic pipe tobacco or violet water. Grandma and I spent a lot of time on the porch together in the evenings while waiting for the air to cool enough for us to sleep. She patted violet water on her throat when the sun beat down, saying violets only grew in shadows, so the scent was cool. She smoked fragrant tobacco in a lady's pipe and blew the smoke at me, saying it would help keep off the mosquitos. She sat in the ladderback rocker like a little old toad, her short white hair boiling around her head, her gray eyes bright as thick summer stars. Her fingersnaps particularly pleased me; my mother had slammed all her fingers in a door before I was born, and her knuckles were scarred, their movements restricted.

Grandma was full of strange tales. Two of them in particular she told me over and over—the touch of Old Lilith one, with no explanations, and the bogey one—and I was a long time getting to sleep each night because of them that summer. She came to live with us just after her house burned down and Grandpa died. Daddy griped about that. Mom was the youngest of seven kids. "She has so many children she doesn't know what to do—why pick on us?" said Daddy. But our house had a guest room, so Grandma came to us first.

I asked Grandma about the fire. She said the police asked questions about why she wasn't home at two in the morning—when a neighbor first smelled smoke and saw flames, but too late to save Grandpa. Grandma was out picking flowers. "Phases of the moon," she said, waving a copy of the *Farmer's Almanac* at the police. She had carried it with her the night of the fire. "Got to harvest in the dark of the moon. Poor old Harvey—if only he didn't have that 'rithmatic in his bones—couldn't take the dew chill, otherwise he might have been out with me and alive today."

The last time I saw Grandpa Harvey had been the family Christmas party when I was still ten. His eyes had white shields over them and he couldn't see, and his hands shook. Grandma whispered to me that the shields saved him from seeing all the wickedness in the world; they were called cataracts, which meant waterfalls which meant cleansing and tears. I never understood that either. Mom said Grandpa had been blind since before she was born.

Investigation proved it to have been an electrical fire, bad wiring in the kitchen walls, nobody's fault. Everybody said I was too young to go to a funeral, so they left me with

Lizzy Burns next door when they went off to bury Grandpa. When they got back, Mom's eyes were swollen and the tip of her nose was red, but Grandma looked just as chipper as ever.

That night, when I couldn't sleep, I snuck outside and crept around the side of the house until I was just under Mom's and Daddy's bedroom window. I had had the sense all summer that everybody was protecting me from things without telling me what I was supposed to be afraid of, and I hated not knowing, so I was always seeking out information any way I could. Somehow when I turned eleven in the spring, I figured out the whole world was in cahoots to keep everything quiet, but it was time for me to know. Wasn't I almost a teenager? When I was ten everybody still thought I was a baby, but it was time for that to change now, whether the grownups thought so or not.

Mom and Daddy were talking in the dark. "Poor old Pa," said Mom. "Never hurt a soul."

"Probably a merciful release," said Dad. "I would have done anything to get away from your mother. Maybe even set the fire myself. I might do it yet."

Mom said it was lucky the evidence was so clear, otherwise Grandma made a great suspect, her not shedding a tear over Grandpa or grieving over the loss of the house.

Daddy said, "Will you cry when I'm gone?"

"Peter, you know I will," said Mom, her voice tender.

"Oh, so you're planning to outlive me, are you?"

When I was younger I wished Daddy had a sense of humor like Mom's, but he never did. If he had said that with a smile in his voice, it would have been all right. But he hadn't.

I leaned my chin on my knees and waited for Mom's reply. Around me her carefully tended rose bushes whispered to each other, the flowers spilling a heavy rich scent on the night air. The dark, moist earth chilled me through my thin cotton nightgown and the soles of my feet. After a moment, Mom's voice came again, drifting out the open window of their bedroom.

"We Meander women are long-lived," said Mom in her slow, flat, Scriptures-reading voice.

"You Meander women," Daddy said, his voice sneering. "You sound like your mother. Why do you call yourself Meander? Your maiden name was Stone."

He was off, telling her again how stupid she was.

And when he had finished, run out of voice, she murmured, "Hush." I heard the sheets rustle, and the slide of flesh on flesh, like the sound a snake's belly makes as it crawls across tiles.

I resolved for the fifty-sixth time never, ever, to get married. I wished I hadn't lain awake thinking about the long-fingered bogey that hid under girls' beds and reached up to inject them with zombie juice the instant their breathing slowed in sleep. "When you wake up the next morning, you feel dead," Grandma said. "The bogey whispers the orders for the day and you follow them. You never make another move unless he tells you to. Nobody else notices anything wrong with you, and you can't tell nobody about it." Then she laughed. "I once knew a girl who was bogey-bit and nobody found out till sixteen years later. Nothing to do but kill her, poor thing. They just get too used to being zombies; real life ain't natural to 'em anymore, even if you *could* clean the juice out of their blood. It builds up in the brain."

Between Grandma's stories and Mom's and Dad's fights that summer, I didn't sleep much at all. I was even relieved when I started seventh grade in the fall, though I was at a new school with a lot of older kids at it, when I had gotten used to being in the most senior class. Grandma moved out the week before school started. I thought Daddy must have had something to do with that; he had been nagging Mom about Grandma since the fire. I learned later that Mom wanted Grandma gone just as much as Daddy did. Grandma went to live with my Uncle Kyle, a bachelor who managed an apartment complex—he fixed up a basement for her, and Daddy said that was only appropriate.

With hard work and a lot of reading, I managed to close

up my memories over all Grandma's stories, but they still lay under the floor of my mind, like seeds buried deep and forgotten but full of growth potential, with the right sort of care.

♦ ♦ ♦

When Daddy died two years later, and Grandma came to the funeral, I looked at her in her black clothes and little slivers of summer memory struggled free. She kissed my cheek, and her violet scent brought my eleventh summer back in a rush.

That night as I lay in bed, I bit the heels of my hands, trying to cry for my father. True to her word, my mother had cried for him, but I had not been able to; the funeral seemed to be happening on television, with me a distant watcher. So after I crawled in between the cold sheets and turned out the light, I concentrated on the times Daddy took me to the park down the street and taught me how to catch tadpoles with a pet store fishnet. I remembered him buying me a baseball glove when I was twelve, and playing catch in the yard with me. That eased my mind somewhat; nobody at school played with me much, so it was nice to have someone to come home to—when Daddy was in the mood.

Consciously I reached for what had been my favorite memory of Daddy: when I was nine, he came into the room where I was sitting on the floor, watching some show on television. I couldn't remember the show, I just remembered him sitting on the couch behind me, stroking my hair gently. I leaned against his knee and closed my eyes, feeling his hand on my head, a safe caress. I loved him completely in that moment, but it never happened again.

Though I had cherished these memories of him even while he was alive, they refused to stay with me that night. Instead I relived Grandma's summer at our house, her snapping her index finger at me like a striking snake, her old voice murmuring to me like the buzz of a summer fly on a winter window, the words slipping into my mind before I could shut them out. That night I dreamed, not of my father, but of the bogey under the bed, and I woke with a scream in my throat, lodged there like a bone.

A year later, my mother remarried. His name was Patrick, and he was large and loud and friendly, completely different from my small dark father. Grandma came to the wedding. She wore the same clothes she had worn to my father's funeral, and she shook her head no through the whole ceremony. "Eh, Mother, I saw you objecting," Patrick said at the reception after kissing Grandma's cheek.

"I'm an old woman, boy," she said—or I thought she said; she might have said "bogey." "Old women get shaky."

♦ ♦ ♦

I didn't understand why Danny invited me to the senior prom. Nobody had asked me out on a date during my entire high school career, and I was satisfied with that; whenever anyone came near, I felt somewhere within me the lidless, ever-open eyes of snakes looking out at them, waiting to strike. I let those snakes look out through my eyes, and people always backed away.

I thought Danny must have been dared to do it, but facts were hard to come by later, when he was gone. I only know that when he took my hand and led me out on the floor for the first slow dance, I was more terrified than I ever had been before. His arms around me, his hands at the back of my waist, where I couldn't see them. My own hands out of sight behind his neck, where my fingers might have been flexing any moment, without my volition. I felt intensely aware of everything, the fragile orchid touching my wrist, the heat of Danny through his suit, his hands like solid sunlight warming my back, his smell, a mixture of aftershave and an oily human scent I had never been so close to before. The music we walked on, as though it were a staircase. Fear was so strong in me I felt as if the ground had vanished. My hands shook like Grandpa Harvey's had. I felt sweat trickle down my spine.

They said later it was heart attack. His family had a history. But never so young before.

♦ ♦ ♦

There was a year between high school and college when I ran away. I chased forgetting. When I found it, I came home again.

♦ ♦ ♦

Being the first one to arrive Monday mornings, I got to wheel the cart away from the library drop chute and check in all the returned books. As I pulled due-date cards out of the pockets and replaced them with check-out cards, I noticed a name: Jeffry Chase. He had checked out a whole stack of books on photography.

I remembered I had encountered a stack like this the week before, books on darkroom techniques, with his name on the check-out cards. This week, I found big picture books about the work of Diane Arbus, Eugene Atget, Richard Avedon, Edmund Weston. I paused, opened the books one at a time, looked at an image in each. Here was a man, wife and large-headed baby, all so much closer to the camera than they would be to a person in the normal course of conversation that their imperfections seemed glaring. Here was a street in Paris at the turn of the century, the road surfaced with wet paving stones, the buildings faced with wrinkled and torn posters and, in the misty distance, a bare-branched tree; here, an ultra-slender woman from the sixties with black kohl heavy around her eyes, her hair cut in a pageboy, her clothes short and stark; here, a bell pepper, photographed in black and white, its smooth curves sensuous and startling.

I closed the books slowly and put them on the filing cart, wondering about Jeffry. I tried to picture him in my mind, though I hadn't checked out any of these books for him. Was he a little old man, taking up a new hobby? Trying to connect with a past he remembered but could not picture clearly? Was he a teenager doing a project for high school?

Maybe he had been given a list of books to check out. Maybe he was in college, like I was, doing a photographic internship like my library one.

My supervisor Jenna came in then and got mad at me for forgetting to start the coffee and for sitting over books with my eyes unfocused when there was work to be done.

But later, when a young man came to the desk, his hair curly black and his eyes the color of amethysts, I suspected him of being Jeffry; of course, he also had a stack of large photo books. I thought if I looked as gorgeous as he did, I would probably be interested in photography, too, wanting to preserve my own image in as many ways as possible, and studying which images had survived from the past.

I was the only one at the desk when he came and put down his books and a red backpack. Jenna had taken first lunch, leaving me in charge. I knew that, and still, when he smiled at me, I looked behind me to see if there was someone else who deserved that smile. I went over to the stack of due-date cards and offered him a timid smile in response.

"Hello," he said as I opened his books and took cards out of them. "I'm Jeff Chase, and I've been waiting three weeks for this moment."

"Pardon me?"

"Watching you work, hoping the moment would come when I could speak with you."

I touched my necklace, an amber pendant Grandma had sent me for my sixteenth birthday. I felt an urge to look behind me again, certain this fairy tale prince must be talking to someone else.

"Why?" I said, and would have stepped on my own foot if I had been someone else watching me, to stop me from being so gauche.

"You have a certain beauty—not just in the common run, you know. I was hoping I could talk with you—ask you—I know this must sound like a line—if I could take pictures of you. I'm trying to put together a portfolio."

"Pictures? Of me?" My tone was full of doubt.

He gave me that smile again, his eyes catching light. "So many people say they'll break my camera. It amazes me! Look." He opened the outer pocket on his backpack and took out a snapshot. I looked at a face leaning on a hand, a spill of chestnut hair framing the features. Her pale eyes dreamed, and a smile touched one edge of her wide mouth. She had dark curved brows.

I got an eerie feeling from the picture, the sensation that it was a fossil found locked in a rock, and I wondered why it struck that chord. I turned the picture sideways. No clues.

Suddenly I realized I was looking at myself, a me I never saw in the mirror, where I always focused first on my blemishes, and second on getting the eyeliner on straight. I stared up at the man.

"I took that with my little Pentax three weeks ago. Would you model for me? I can't pay much, but I'll give you proof sheets. Maybe a few prints of the better shots."

I swallowed my first no, and thought a minute. He must have been nuts. Why would anyone look twice at me, especially a man like this? But this picture, maybe there was a me I didn't know how to look for. If we could keep the camera between us, we should be safe. It might be fun. I might see someone I wouldn't recognize who was also a part of me.

"Saturday?" I said.

♦ ♦ ♦

He had some clothes he gave me to wear, a black dress with gold embroidery, a little large on me, and a black velvet cloche hat. He had asked me to bring black tights if I had them, and black high heels. I found some tights in a suitcase in the closet, among clothes I had been thinking about getting rid of but couldn't bear giving away. I brought the tights and my church shoes.

We talked about makeup; I never met a man who knew anything about makeup before. He had some rice powder he said Geisha girls used to pale their complexions. I sat in a chair with a towel over the black and gold dress and closed my eyes as he brushed the powder across my face, another strange caress, light as the touch of a butterfly's wing on my cheek. With expert hands he outlined my eyes in black, touched pale pink on my lips.

He handed me a mirror and again I saw someone I didn't know. My sense of myself as fossil returned, ancient and somehow horrible. My eyes looked clear and bottomless, my mouth silent, my expression remote. I could not smile at myself. In some buried corner of my mind, my grandmother's index finger snapped.

Jeffry took me to the graveyard.

He positioned me between the marble pillars of a Greek-style mausoleum. "The contrast between cold stone and warm flesh," he said, smiling at me. I looked at my pale hand against the white marble and thought he was right: my hand looked translucent, but it had its own beauty against the solid rock, a misty, living reality.

As Jeffry told me to turn and lean, to look toward the sky and think of flying, to glance at the ground and think of autumn, I felt disturbed on some other level. What were we really doing here, with me dressed as a corpse in mourning and posing with lambs and little angels on the graves of long-dead children? I leaned my cheek on a lichen-laced rough-hewn stone, smelling centuries locked in rock, and the acid tang of molding oak leaves. I listened to Jeffry's camera click. If he really wanted to contrast life with death, I should have been wearing red, or green. I felt I had wandered into someone else's dream.

The day was overcast. "Pearl light," Jeffry called it. "A diffuse, indirect light that softens edges." The grass and earth stayed wet with yesterday's rain; I shivered, remembering Grandpa Harvey, burned to death because he couldn't take the dew chill. Jeffry asked me to kneel on a grave beside a tombstone that bore a photographic tile depicting a little dead girl. Her face beamed above the date of her death, fifty years earlier. I touched the tile, wondering about parents marooning their child's image in this death camp. My memory jogged. I wondered if this child had died of bogey-bite.

"Can you get her expression on your face?" Jeffry asked.

"No," I said, standing up. "No."

He studied me for a minute, then nodded. "Let's go get some coffee. I bet you're cold."

In the coffeeshop I went to the women's room and splashed water on my face, hoping I could wash away the stranger Jeffry had photographed. I scrubbed my face with the gritty, pink institutional-scented soap. Then I looked at myself in the mirror. The warm water and the soap brought the blood back to my cheeks, and my lips looked dark pink again, but my eyes still frightened me. The day before, I had believed them blue, but this day they looked steel gray. I stared at myself but felt as if someone else were studying me.

When I got back to the table, Jeffry looked at me. "Coffee's not enough," he said. "Can I take you out to dinner tonight?"

The chill began to seep out of me. "All right," I said. "But this time I get to choose my own clothes."

♦ ♦ ♦

He brought some black-and-white prints with him when he came to pick me up that night. I glanced at them, then put them back inside the envelope, not wanting to think about them. I left them on the table by my front door, and we went out to a place with a wine list, and napkins on top of two layers of tablecloths. Jeffry watched me during the meal. He liked how I looked, in my jewel-red dress, my hair in a chignon. I could sense his intense appreciation. It felt wonderful. It scared me.

I clung tight to my hard-earned forgetting.

We went to his apartment after supper. When he touched me, it was with reverence, and even in the heat that followed, I had the sense that he worshiped me.

♦ ♦ ♦

I went home for Thanksgiving. I wanted Jeffry to come, but his mother wanted him at her house, and it was too soon, he said, to tell his mother about us. "I've never missed a Thanksgiving with Mother," he said. "I don't want her getting suspicious."

Grandma was at Mom's when I got there. "Hello, little Clea," she said to me as she always did, though I was taller than she. She looked exactly the same age as she had when I was eleven, and this time she was wearing colors—a purple and magenta dress, and a straw hat with a large droopy brim and sprays of fake cherries on it.

Patrick greeted me with a big kiss on the cheek and took the pumpkin pie I had bought at Safeway the day before. His bright hair had started to gray, and he was thickening through the middle. He vanished with the pie toward the kitchen. I smelled the rich holiday smell of turkey baking, and wondered why I didn't feel cheerful.

After grace, Patrick carved the turkey and Mom served, silent. I ate a lot of everything, following some instinct I didn't understand—I ate until I felt sick, without really tasting the food. No one talked during the meal, but afterward, when Patrick went in to watch football, Grandma and Mom and I cleared and started cleaning up. I took Jeff's pictures out of my satchel and showed them to Mom and Grandma. "My boyfriend took these," I said. He had tacked prints of me up all over his apartment, so I was getting used to them. "I wanted to bring him, but he couldn't make it."

They were both rock silent as they looked at the black-and-white photographs of my cool perfection among the tombstones. Mom's eyes seemed to grow shallow. Grandma said, "Oh, child. Oh, child." She reached out and took Mom's hand in hers, stroking the scarred knuckles. A tear spilled down her cheek. "I tried to give you everything, little Clea, but I couldn't. So the killing starts."

"What killing, Grandma?" I felt disturbed, as if I knew what she was talking about but didn't want to admit it. An image of Danny's face surfaced in my mind. I drowned it again, a reflex. Grandma had never known about Danny's death.

"Killing you into something other than what you are," she said. "Why can't people leave people alone?"

"Oh, Ma, you know we're put on this earth to be something to somebody," said my mother, pulling her hand away from Grandma and shoving both hands into her apron pockets.

"Don't you do what your Mama done, Clea," Grandma said. "Don't you help him kill you."

"What do you mean?" I asked. My face felt hot now, both with the meal and the tension. I felt sick.

"I'm going for a nap now," said Grandma. She blinked three times and walked out of the kitchen.

"Mom—"

"She's an evil woman," said my mother.

"What?" I asked. I had never heard my mother speak with more conviction.

"She filled my head with tales when I was little. She told us stories every night. Sometimes she told us Bible stories, but she talked as if the people were all relatives. She told you stories that summer, didn't she?"

I remembered. "Yes," I said, feeling again the overpowering dread that kept me lying sleepless in my bed night after night.

"That's why I begged Kyle to take her away. I didn't want her filling you up with all those evil thoughts. I didn't want you to do what I did, and what Jan and Suzle did in their own ways."

I hadn't heard Aunt Suzle's name since I was thirteen. I was looking at a picture book of Mom's family, laughing because my aunt and my mother and my four uncles looked so strange as children. There was another girl in many of the pictures. "That's your Aunt Suzle," Mom had said. "She's dead."

Mom stared at the floor. "Ma told us—oh, Clea, you're

too young to hear this. I don't want you to be scared the way I was."

I looked at the pictures spread out on the kitchen table. In one of them, I stared straight into the camera. Behind me, a stone angel prayed with lowered lids. "Mom, if you don't tell me, I'll make up things worse than any reality," I said.

"I don't know if you could," she said. She stood still a moment, staring through the kitchen table. She sighed. "She told us we were powerful women and if we ever married we'd kill our husbands on our wedding nights. She said we had snakes inside us—in our fingers. And she told all the boys to go out and find wives. Then she laughed. We always knew she was scared of the boys, anyway, once they got taller than her. It was like telling them to go find someone to kill them. She said Lilith was Adam's first wife, but Adam didn't like Lilith because she wanted to be on top. Ma said God was a bully, and Lilith was the only one with integrity. Adam wanted women to serve him, but Lilith walked upright—till he rejected her, then she came back as a snake. She brought death to everyone. And there's a touch of the old Lilith in all Meander women." Her voice came out higher, like a little girl repeating a catechism. Then she began to laugh. "It's so stupid," she gasped, and laughed and laughed. "Hearing it out loud. It's so stupid, Clea!"

I got her a glass of water. She sat on a kitchen chair and laughed her throat raw. After gulping water, she calmed down again. "It was stupid, but it hurt us, because we were children and didn't know any better. Suzle fell in love with a boy when she was sixteen. She was so afraid she'd hurt him, and she loved him so much, she killed herself." Mom stared up at me, her eyes wide, her pupils large and dark. "I found her," she said. "She was lying in the bathtub and she had these wounds on her wrists. She didn't bleed to death, Clea. She poisoned herself. The wounds looked like snakebites."

I sat down, too, feeling sick. "What did Aunt Jan do?"

"Jan became a ballerina. She starves herself, and stays

away from men. Her life for art. I wish you'd known her when she was younger, Clea. She was such a funny girl, a little bit plump, but with a wicked tongue and a wild eye. Then when she got to be fifteen or so, she went through this phase where she had a crush on movie stars. She was crazy about James Dean and Steve McQueen. She plastered her walls with pictures out of movie magazines. But she'd been dancing since she was six. One day I came home and all the pictures had come down, the walls were white in her room, and she didn't eat anything anymore except a couple lettuce leaves and a few spoonfuls of cottage cheese. She's saving mankind by staying away from them."

I remembered the one Christmas my Aunt Jan came out. She was pale and thin, with circles under her eyes, and she couldn't seem to look at me without wincing. "You had a girl," I heard her say to Mom. "It just goes on and on."

"What did you do, Mom?" I asked.

"Oh, I was practical! When I fell in love with Peter, I thought through all Mom's stories and figured out that the only real harm I could do him was with my fingers. I used to play piano, you know." She took her hands out of her apron pockets and stared at them. "Snakes' heads. If I could just rid myself of the snakes' heads. I propped open the coal cellar door with a stick, then put my hands on the doorsill and knocked the stick away. I broke all my fingers. How I screamed! It hurt for months, but I smiled through it all. Peter married me while my hands were still in bandages. No wedding ring." She smiled down at her crippled hands, her face softened with memories.

After a long moment, she glanced at me. "We're only human, after all, Clea. Ma fed us a pack of lies. I wanted to save you from that, and I did the best I could. I'm so glad you've found a boyfriend."

"But Mom—" I looked down at the pictures. Had Jeff photographed some real piece of me I didn't want to believe in? Who was this haunted woman? I picked up a picture of me next to a small pale angel, my pale eyes looking at her, my hand raised to her. My fingers looked curved in a gradual arc that defied human bones.

"Oh, come on. Do you think models in magazines are anything like their pictures? Your boy seems to have a weird sense of beauty, but you aren't what he makes you look like," she said. She gathered all the pictures together, the top one face down so none of them were visible, and put them in my satchel. "Now, come on. We have dishes to do and food to put away. Do you want some turkey to take home?"

♦ ♦ ♦

Jeffry came to my apartment when we both got back from our Thanksgiving vacations.

Grandma had taken me shopping Friday morning, braving the sale crowds at the Plaza. I found myself a little afraid of her, and I wasn't pleased with her gift to me—a silver apple on a chain. But she insisted. "Don't take away an old woman's happiness," she said, tugging on my hair to get me to bend over far enough so she could fasten the pendant around my neck. "I had seven children, and you're the only granddaughter I got, little Clea. Leave me do things for you."

"Am I the last Meander woman?" I asked her.

"No, no," she said. We stood still in the center of the mall corridor between stores, and chattering people streamed past us on both sides, but I could hear her clearly. "There's no end to Meander women. Maybe every woman is a Meander woman."

We got home around noon, and I had a last family lunch with Mom and Patrick and Grandma. Then I drove the two-and-a-half hours back to my apartment. I remembered applying to colleges all over the state, but when I got accepted at the university and decided it was my college of choice, Mom seconded me. "Close enough to visit, but not close enough for me to look over your shoulder all the time," she had said.

I sat in my yard sale armchair, all the lights in the apartment off, my overnight bag on the living room floor in front of me, as daylight faded beyond the gauze curtains. I held my hand closed around the silver apple. It warmed to my flesh.

Presently I heard Jeffry's key in the lock. I wanted to jump up and turn on some lights, maybe put water on for coffee, but I waited. "Clea? You back yet?" he asked, flicking on the entry light. He carried red roses in rustling cellophane; beads of water shone on his hair. I realized I had been hearing the quiet dance of rain on shingles for some time.

"Yes," I said.

"Why so dark? Are you okay? Did something happen at your mother's?"

"I'm just tired."

He turned on the living room lights and came to me, setting the roses in my lap. Stepping back, he looked at me, and I considered my appearance: my chestnut hair spilling over the wide lapels of my long gray coat; my face, undoubtedly pale; the spray of roses as dark as fall apples, with its accompanying haze of white babies' breath and dark green fern, splashing across my lap; and black tights and black Chinese shoes, under a forest-green velvet dress. If he had brought one of his cameras, Jeffry would be focusing now, trying to decide whether to use a flash, and what to bounce it off.

He smiled at me. "Shall I put water on for coffee?"

"Please."

He walked toward the kitchenette, glancing back at me twice. His smile was almost smug. I felt a flick of anger, like a little bruise inside. Did he think because he liked the way I looked that he had created me?

Hadn't he? Didn't we choose this steel gray coat—"the color of your eyes"—together? Hadn't he bought me this green velvet dress at a second-hand shop, and didn't I drag these tights out of an old suitcase because he asked me to?

I lifted the roses, crackling in their cellophane shroud, and sniffed them, but they proved scentless. As I touched the lip-soft petals, I remembered my childhood resolve never to marry.

"Don't you want to put those in water?" Jeffry asked, coming back and sitting on the couch across from me.

I went to the kitchen and retrieved my yard sale vase, a strange twist of blue-and-clear glass as long as my forearm. As I ran water into it I glanced back at Jeffry. "Thank you for the flowers," I said. I turned off the water, unwrapped the roses, and inserted them into the vase.

"They reminded me of you. I was glad to have something nice to think about, after that turkey dinner with my mother."

Holding his roses, I stood and studied him. His gaze seemed fixed on the ceiling. "Rough?" I asked.

"It's the same every year," he said, and pressed his face into his hands. After a moment, he ran his hands through his hair, startling raindrops loose, then stared at his wet hands as if they were bloodstained. "She's done so much for me," he told his hands. "I know she loves me. I don't understand why I feel terrible after I see her. She raised me all by herself, you know, and she paid my way through college, and she loves my photography; she supports my choices. I hate her knowing what I do. I don't want her to like it, because then it isn't mine. I don't want her ever to find out about you. Oh, Clea, I know how that sounds, but I just feel—she would steal you from me, too."

"Hush," I said. I set the vase on the counter behind me and walked to him. He stood up. I buried my face in his shoulder, hugging him. He smelled of wet wool, and male animal, and clean wet human hair, but other odors were trapped in his shirt—cigarette smoke and violet water; instantly Grandma was somewhere in the room with us.

He must have felt my arms tighten. "What?" he whispered.

Paralyzed, I tried to sense my fingers on his back. Were they curved, or straight? If I looked in the mirror, would that fossil self show in my face, full of ancient purpose that had nothing to do with me? I wished all the lights were off. Perhaps then my identity would rest totally in my thoughts.

Jeffry knew me as image, though.

I let go of him, putting my hands behind my back. "Let's go to bed." He would take off the shirt and drape it over a chair, leaving his mother and my grandmother out of it. I could lose all these thoughts and live just under the surface of my skin, and we would climb the mountain together—

"You look so strange tonight," he said, and then the teakettle went off. He went into the kitchenette. "Still want coffee?"

"No—unless you do—"

He took the kettle off the heat and came back out to me. We turned off the living room light and retreated to my bedroom together.

♦ ♦ ♦

I lay awake listening to his deep, even breathing, staring at a narrow slice of street light on the ceiling. Leaf shadows danced across the light, responding to a silent wind. I was blinking, ready to fall asleep, when I saw my own hands rise in the air. Silhouetted against the dim light, I saw my index fingers lash out, fluid movement that looked humanly impossible. I couldn't feel my hands at all; they seemed to belong to someone else.

In that state between dream and waking, I had no feelings about what I witnessed, except a sleepy wonder. Jeffry murmured in his sleep, and my hands, of their own volition, reached toward him.

Waking washed over me like a bucketful of cold water; I was across the room in an instant, the wood floor cold against my bare feet, goosebumps rising along my arms and hackles on the back of my neck.

I went into the bathroom and pulled the chain to turn on the light.

In the blind time before my eyes adjusted, I felt utterly silly and young. I knew I had imagined everything, and it was all Grandma's fault. I closed the toilet lid, put a towel on top, and sat down, studying my hands. They looked very pink and human in the bare-bulb light, and beautiful: I had always loved my slender-fingered hands. It was just a dream; if I had been alone in the house, I would have turned on the radio, gotten out a book, and closeted the fears again, drifting into a quieter sleep.

Like I had been doing so often lately.

I flexed my forefingers. They formed three sides of a bent rectangle. I sighed, and felt tension easing out of my shoulders.

My right forefinger whipped out as though it were as spineless as rope. It struck the side of the sink, leaving a drop of clear, glistening liquid on the white porcelain.

The breath coming from my throat had an edge of voice to it, the shadow of sobs. I thought of Aunt Suzle, entombing herself in bathroom white, mastering her forefingers enough to make them strike her own wrists—was it involuntary, or could one control it? I thought of Grandpa Harvey, whose eyes had been milky and whose mind wandered. Would a touch of venom only half kill? I thought of Grandma whipping her fingers at my four uncles, scaring them all into bachelorhood.

I thought of Jeffry, lying defenseless in my bed. If I went to the living room and finished out the night on the couch, he would surely wonder when he woke alone. And I would not tell him about my strange heritage, though I thought he must know, somehow, considering the contexts he chose to picture me in.

I thought about my favorite bread knife, with its serrated edge. If I just decapitated my fingers—cut off the first knuckle—would that suffice?

I felt cold and sad. I rooted an old cosmetics case out from under the sink, and found two Ace bandages inside, from sprained ankles in my past. I wound the bandages around my fingers, mummywrapping them, leaving only the thumbs free, until I felt constricted and mittened and safe. Then I crept into bed, keeping my back to Jeffry and curling my wrapped hands against my stomach.

"You're cold," he whispered, and he hugged me. His warmth felt comforting. I closed my eyes, and began to drift off to sleep.

Just as the world behind my eyelids began to gyrate in slow, hypnotic loops, I felt the tiny cold prick of a needle. Before my mind stilled, I remembered my grandmother's other favorite story from my eleventh summer.

♦ ♦ ♦

We moved to New York two years later, the gallery demands for Jeff's work were so great. New York has graveyards dating back centuries.

Jeff's most famous picture of me depicts me as Ophelia, floating with eyes closed in shallow water, my hair rayed out about my head, and flowers huddled in the folds of my pale gauze gown. Only I know that within the long slender hands folded on my chest I hold my grandmother's apple.

# FOOTPRINTS IN THE WATER

## by Poppy Z. Brite

Poppy Z. Brite was born in 1967 and spent her first years in New Orleans. She has worked as a short-order cook, an artist's model, and a caretaker for thousands of mice. Her first short stories were all published in *The Horror Show;* she has completed a novel, *The Night Children,* and is working on a new one. Currently she lives in Athens, Georgia. Her interests include animal rights, voodoo and other types of magic, American cars of the 1950s and '60s, music, thrift shop and vintage clothes, black cowboy boots with steel toes, and boys who wear eyeliner.

I don't normally like very short stories, but this one—like the other short short in this volume—demanded my attention, and held it unflinchingly.

◆ ◆ ◆

Dru sat at his desk for hours, hunching his bony shoulders, never bothering to push the childishly fair hair out of his face, staring until he still saw the roundabout in front of his eyes when he blinked. When he closed his eyes, a bright phantom roundabout swam in the pinpricked phosphorescent darkness behind his eyelids. When he opened them, the roundabout was tauntingly solid and still, a needle stuck in a cork, a folded triangle of paper balanced on the tip of a needle. He squinted at it, stared without blinking, visualized the piece of paper beginning to turn as the author of the book on psychic power had said to do. He willed it to turn. He blew on it to see what it looked like turning, then tried to keep it turning by the force of his mind. He vowed he would not close his eyes again until the paper began to turn. He touched it with the tip of his finger and made it turn, pushed it with his mind, forced his will upon it. It sat still, a pale brown creased slip of paper balanced on the tip of a rusty needle. It would turn. It would turn. It had to turn. He knew he could harness every scrap of power that nestled in every corner of his brain if only he could make that roundabout turn. He pushed at it with his mind. He would not close his eyes. His eyelids were stretched open. His eyeballs were dry, burning. If he blinked now, the lids would scrape against his eyes. The roundabout swam and began to dissolve, fading into a field of light that crept in from the edges of his vision. The slip of paper was absolutely still, stirred by no breath, no current. It would never turn. In disgust, Dru squeezed his eyes shut and turned his head away. The needle shot up out of the cork and skimmed past his face, just missing his eye, scratching his cheek deeply enough to make him need three stitches. Bright and vital drops of blood spattered the roundabout, soaked into the tipped-over cork.

Dru was fifteen then. After that, he knew, the earth was his.

♦ ♦ ♦

Nineveh. Pacing through the crop of stones, the only pale thing in a black night. Nineveh always dresses in white now, white silk jacket, white shoes with soft white soles, hair of the palest silver-blond falling like wings of light along his pale, pale cheeks and forehead. He moves through the yard. A brittle slice of moon gives off a cold light, fluorescently harsh, in which Nineveh nearly disappears. He cannot live in harsh light. Harsh light is for the electric white ceilings of morgues. The stones glitter and he moves among them, paler than they are and less sharp-edged. The moonlight paints the stones, runs off them and soaks the ground; at the base of each stone is its black reflection. The mirror image of a gravestone. But there can be no more mirror images. All is lost. Your mirror image only dazzles and sinks as you stare into his eyes, his eyes obscured by black water. The moon is not Nineveh's twin.

He stops and stands over a stone, his eyes hidden under a wing of silvery hair, but perhaps glittering, painted by the moon. His feet are hidden in the black pool at the base of the stone. The shadow melts over his ankles. He stands there until the moon, no longer hard-edged, fades into a delicate yellow-pink sky that becomes whitely hot by midday. The sun bleaches the grass and the stones. It cannot burn Nineveh's pale, pale skin: his cheeks never show a tinge of rose; his lips are translucent. The sunlight, hot as white metal, burns a sheet of fire into the gravestone of his twin brother.

♦ ♦ ♦

The house of Frixtons, Dru's mother and father, began to be plagued. Records, books, random desirable things appeared on Dru's bed, things he had seen in shops but hadn't been able to stretch his pocket money to buy. His parents made him return them to the shops, but they kept coming back. Water and a slightly thicker, clear substance drooled from the ceiling, but the plaster was always found to be dry to the touch. Often the walls shook with invisible raps, and objects—antique chairs, marble eggs, small Chinese statues—flew about like heavy wingless birds. When Dru told the disturbances to stop, they ceased, but would begin again within a few hours.

Dru still sat hunched at his desk over the roundabout, his hair hanging in his eyes, a long, slender tail of a braid snaking halfway down his back. Sometimes he pulled the braid up over his shoulder and sucked absently at it, staring at the roundabout, staring, willing. He still could not make it turn. He could slam doors without looking at them; he could make an empty glass fill up with water; he could make a small truck roll up a hill and stop, but that tiny, creased piece of paper stayed still. Now and then a breath of air stirred it, and his heart leaped. He turned sixteen, seventeen. His fair hair darkened two shades.

Dru was interviewed, tested in laboratories. He bent spoons, emerged from empty locked rooms. They put a paper-and-cork roundabout in front of him, but he could not make it go around. He produced living snakes out of the air; they were albino, and their eyes were always red. Two books were published, a scholarly journal study, and a glossy paperback with a mystic eye on the front. Both featured the name Dru Frixton prominently on their covers. When Dru was eighteen, he caused a mouse's neck to be broken by an invisible blow. After the mouse had been examined and pronounced dead, Dru restored it to life.

Headlines glared off the newspapers. Nineveh's pale hand rested on the glossy cover of the paperback. His finger sought the address of the publisher, whereby this boy might be found, and hovered indecisively: he could not write the letter.

Nineveh's twin brother Dylan had been dead three years.

♦ ♦ ♦

Dylan is laughing. The inside of his mouth is dark pink and his eyes are wet and happy. He was never as pale as Nineveh, never as colorless; now he seems a warm and joyous blaze of color, with his bright hair, with his pink laughing mouth. He shakes his head and his mouth opens wider, and he beats his hands on his knees helplessly as he used to do when he couldn't stop laughing, back when he and Nineveh were children. Now he is laughing at himself for laughing so much, and his laughter is breathy and jagged. He must ache from so much laughing. His hand is in the air, messing Nineveh's hair, entwined there. He teases Nineveh for being so neat, so pale, and a smile touches Nineveh's lips. Nineveh's only smiles are for Dylan. They are floating together in water, water as warm and thick as the sea they must have shared before they were born. Dylan's mouth is closed now; open, closed on Nineveh's, wet. And

and the water is black. Black under an electric white sky. Dylan is being sucked into a glittering black vortex of water. His mouth is open, gulping for air, and Nineveh wants to shout not to do that, not to swallow the water, that the black water is bitter, bilious, poisonous. Nineveh cannot hang on to his brother's hand. Dylan is pulling away, screaming for Nineveh to let go, not to get sucked in with him. He is screaming for Nineveh to save himself. His voice is choked, gulping. Dylan is strangling on the black water. It is seeping into his lungs, covering his head. And with the last semiconscious effort he can make, he pushes Nineveh away from the vortex, wills him with smooth, strong strokes toward the white shore far in the distance. When Nineveh has made it halfway there, Dylan's face floats up in the water beside him, still under the water, under the glossy black film, and Dylan's eyes are open and full of water and his mouth is open, gaping, letting the water fill him—

♦ ♦ ♦

Nineveh surfaces from the dream screaming, floundering in the white sea of his bed. The sheets twine over his mouth and he spits them out; they are dry. He reaches for Dylan's hand, tries to touch Dylan's face before he remembers that the dream is real. Drowned. Drowned on holiday, far out in the water where no one could see them, not parents, not even God. Nineveh's idea to swim out there with Dylan. Drowned. All Nineveh's smiles, drowned. His love gone into the black water.

Nineveh's trailing hand touches the cover of the glossy paperback on the floor, next to the bed. His fingers pause over it for a moment; then he strokes it gently and takes it into bed with him, flipping through the pages again.

♦ ♦ ♦

Dru has taken to wearing black eyeliner when he and Nineveh meet. They sit in the coffeeshop, ignoring the afternoon outside. Dru's fingers pull the braid over his shoulder and twist it, play with it. Several times he brings it to his lips and takes it away again. He is dressed in black. Nineveh, luminescently pale in the coffeeshop gloom, stirs sugar into his tea.

Three years, says Dru.

Nineveh is quiet.

Transfer of energy into matter, says Dru. Infusion of the life force into inanimate matter. Transport of an entity from place to place through another dimension. Restoration.

Nineveh will not meet his eyes.

Dru becomes ashamed of his cheap mediumistic babble. He makes Nineveh's tea cup slide away, dance on its rim around the edges of the table, and return to rest primly between Nineveh's outstretched hands on the tabletop. Not a drop of tea is spilled.

Nineveh smiles. His lips are very pale. Glory, he says.

♦ ♦ ♦

It is a night of drooling rain and sluggish, dim flashes of lightning. Dru is in Nineveh's house, in the bed where Dylan once slept. The sheets are white and cold. On the couch, Nineveh pretends to sleep.

Dru is concentrating, willing, pushing his mind. The tip of his braid is in his mouth; he sucks fiercely without being aware of it. Behind Dru's eyelids, the field of stones spreads. The stones glisten with moonlight filtered through clouds and the wetness of the viscous rain. A stirring. A rupturing. Dru gasps; his black-rimmed eyes fly open. *Glory wasn't worth the price.*

Minutes later, the mud outside the front door sucks with footsteps. Nineveh darts to answer a knock at the door.

Dru huddles under the cold sheet, trying to disappear into the sea of white. The smell is not what he had expected. No corruption, no gray-green fluid rot. A dark, wet smell, this, a smell of earthworms, of soggy leaves disintegrating and falling away under the ground.

I could have loved bones, says Nineveh's voice.

Independent of his brain, Dru's fingers twist the sheet away from his face. Two shapes are in the doorway. No shadows-and-bars framework of bones. A mass far softer and darker. A black smiling mouth with black gums. Somehow he had expected the eyes to be red, like those of the snakes he materialized. But they are dark, softly, deeply dark, far darker than they could be if there were anything in the sockets. The shape shifts in the doorway. Nineveh is holding its hand.

You are glorious, says Nineveh to Dru.

So you are, says another voice, a wet, gulping parody of Nineveh's. The shapes move toward the bed.

How can you harm me? asks Dru. His voice quavers. The tip of his braid slips out of his mouth and streaks his cheek with spit.

Harm you? says the gulping voice. I love you. You gave me back my life.

And mine, says Nineveh.

Two figures slip into the bed, one so pale it seems to fade into the sheets, one dark and seeping. Their hands are touching Dru. His skin is streaked with darkness. On his lips is the taste of rot, soft and dark and sweet. He realizes that he is being kissed.

Dylan's mouth is open now. Open, wet.